CHAINS OF STARS

CHAINS OF STARS
The Astrology of Power Exchange

Raven Kaldera

Alfred Press
Hubbardston, Massachusetts

Alfred Press
12 Simond Hill Road
Hubbardston, MA 01452

Chains of Stars:
The Astrology of Power Exchange
© 2020 Raven Kaldera
ISBN 978-0-9905441-5-9

All rights reserved.
No part of this book may be reproduced in any form or by any means without the permission of the author.

Printed in cooperation with
Lulu Enterprises, Inc.
860 Aviation Parkway, Suite 300
Morrisville, NC 27560

*Dedicated to all the power dynamic couples we've counseled
and befriended over the years
who allowed us to study their charts*

*and as always,
to my darling slaveboy Joshua,
whose existence in my life
is proof that the Gods love me
and want me to be happy.*

Contents

Introduction: Power Exchange and Astrology 1

Me, You, and Us
Interpreting Natal Charts 11
Houses of Power.. 14
Interpreting Synastry Charts.. 33
Interpreting the Composite Chart 35

Power, Discipline, and Sacrifice
Pluto: Passion and Control 42
Saturn: Authority and Discipline... 106
Neptune: Surrender and Sacrifice.. 183

The Other Planets
Uranus: Conformity and Community 248
Mercury: Communication and Transparency..................... 251
Venus and Mars: Attraction and Motivation 254
The Moon: Breaking the Mold.. 258
Jupiter: In Santa's Lap 263
The Ascendant: Sculpting the Mask 266
The Asteroids: Going Deeper.. 272

Epilogue: Mastering the Relationship... 282
Recommended Books 283
About the Author... 285

Introduction: Power Exchange and Astrology

I first got my hands on an astrology book when I was nine years old. This was the 1970s, and my mother picked up one of those pop Sun Sign books of the sort one gets from the grocery store paperback section (or used to at that time; I was a precocious reader and while my parents shopped, I was inevitably standing in the paperback section and reading something). I devoured it eagerly, clocking traits of my various family members and friends. I started asking people their birthdays so that I could read up on them. (Even then, I was fascinated with figuring out how people ticked, how their personalities worked … and how to be one step ahead of them.) I remember asking my mother why, if I and my best friend of the time had the same Sun sign, we were such different people? She didn't know at the time, of course, and shrugged it off as just the foolishness of pop astrology books.

It would be years later before I learned about the glory of the entire chart, with planets and houses and angles and asteroids and so many extra points. It was like a treasure chest of the art of explaining people, and that was even before I tackled its predictive potential. Friends who picked up books more serious than pop paperbacks and became intimidated by the array of numbers, symbols, and jargon donated their copies to me, my library grew, and so did my knowledge base. Sometimes my studies were difficult, though, as when one older astrology manual told me that some of my more challenging aspects meant that I was at risk of becoming a violent terrorist.

Probably the hardest incident was when I ventured into relationship astrology for the first time in my twenties after getting married. A friend who was as enthusiastic as me — and had more money to spend on books, not having a toddler to feed on a meager income — lent me a well-written new book that detailed not only the secrets of chart comparison, but also of making a composite chart. This, as we'll detail later in the book, is a chart of the relationship itself, and how the two people involved are drawn to interact with each other. If only I'd read that book before I'd gotten married the first time, perhaps my life would have been a little different … or perhaps not, as I'm not immune to the mistake of ignoring advice and continuing on my blithe and blind way anyhow. While my then-spouse was a good person, our composite chart looked like no one I'd ever willingly hang out with … and I realized to my dismay that I was being forced into that pattern by a life I hadn't chosen. It weakened my resistance to the idea of an amicable divorce, and eventually we both concluded that this was the right ending for both of us. The next time I married, I did a full astrological workup on my prospective spouse, including comparison and composite charts, and deemed the marriage Acceptable. (We have an egalitarian relationship that has lasted 28 years to date.)

But let's backtrack for a moment. My first astrological scrutiny of power dynamic relationships happened when I was still in my late teens, and slowly learning how to interpret charts. I had three pairs of grandparents, because my father's parents had divorced when he was two years old and had separate families. To me, this simply meant that I got more presents at birthdays and holidays, and had more grandparents to visit for cookies, toys, and attention. We didn't even think of them as "step-grandparents"; they were all in the same slots as far as my sister and I were concerned. My mother's parents had an amazingly egalitarian working partnership, especially so for their 1950s era, which I tried to emulate in the first few relationships of my own.

On the other hand, both my paternal grandparent-pairs had what I would now call an unspoken power dynamic. There were no slave contracts, no protocols, not even any kind of an open acknowledgement. There was simply one dominant personality who clearly ruled the roost, and one follower who clearly adored them, was grateful for their guidance, and seemed quite healthy and happy — and not codependent at all — to be the one who took orders and cheerfully obeyed. My step-grandmother was a regal and slightly imperious Leo lady with a large red bouffant who decorated her house in impeccable white and gold, and my loquacious Gemini grandfather gallantly leaped to provide for every whim of his Queen. My step-grandfather was an ex-military Navy CPO who ran his home like a boot camp, and my slightly ditzy grandmother seemed perfectly content to be a traditional housewife and fall into line raising their five sons. During the period of that first pop astrology book, when I was babbling about it to all and sundry, my paternal grandmother happened to be visiting. I told her that she was a Pisces and that Grandpa Mac was an Aries, and then I read off the keywords for those signs — Pisces was "I believe" and Aries was "I am". "That's right," she said sagely. "I believe that he am."

My parents, on the other hand, didn't have a power dynamic so much as a power struggle between two dominant and rather unstable personalities, and I heard some snide comments about the spines of my father's birth parents, or lack thereof. It was not lost on me that the two who would eventually be the submissive parties had married, fought, and divorced, quickly remarrying dominant partners. Even then, I was able to understand (perhaps better than my parents) the idea that some people were just "that way", and some people weren't, and the best thing for everyone was just to pick the person who wanted the other half of your ideal situation. (For me, the hard part would be facing down what I really wanted.) As a teen, I scrutinized my grandparents' charts to figure out why they were made happy by these different options. I hadn't absorbed enough information to see the pattern yet, and I had only two pairs of charts, with my egalitarian maternal grandparents as a "control", but the fascination remained with me.

When my slaveboy Joshua first applied to me, somewhere in the first couple of months — during our "test phase" to see if both pairing and power dynamic would work out — I did the same full astrological workup that I'd done for every partner since I'd learned how. Unlike my wife who was disinterested in hearing me natter on about the results ("That's nice, dear..."), Joshua's eyebrows shot up and he wanted to hear everything I'd figured out—about him, and about us. Before I even got to "us", while I was still talking about what I saw in his chart, I noticed that he was sitting very still with a bit of a frown on his face. I inquired as to whether he was all right. He shifted, frowned some more, and then said—proving that, indeed, he was a Scorpio Sun—"I wasn't ready for you to know that about me yet."

Years later, our power dynamic relationship slowly solidified into an Owner/property situation and I had complete authority (and responsibility) for everything about him. I often resorted to astrology to figure out why he might be doing something, or how he was likely to feel about something ... or why the heck I was acting so out-of-character in this moment with him. We went to conferences and gatherings, joined MAsT (Masters And slaves Together, an international support group for people in voluntary power dynamics), wrote a bunch of books, and sometimes ended up being the senior couple in the room and counseling people who were having trouble with their alternative relationship style. Sometimes I was able to get a look at their charts, and some points began to congeal in my mind. I didn't see any specific placements or aspects that they all had in common (including with us), and I still haven't found any; the magical "master point" or "slave point" seems not to exist. However, I did find patterns around what sort of person-in-charge or person-who-follows-orders they actually were, what came easily to them, and what was a grinding struggle.

Eventually I began to do more research, and started offering couples astrology analyses for people in this demographic, possibly going where no astrologer had gone before. (If there are others, I'd love to talk to them.) Those analyses were the inspiration for this book.

My guess is that this book will be read by three different sorts of people. First, it will be read by the small minority of folks who are practicing a power dynamic relationship (or would like to be), and actually happen to be reasonably well versed in astrology. For you, I probably won't have to explain introductory anything, and you can all go on ahead to the technical stuff. Second, it will be picked up by power dynamic folks whose knowledge of astrology is on the same level as my nine-year-old self poring over the pop Sun Sign book. I'm going to have to warn you folks that this book is somewhat more advanced than that, and while I've tried to make it as accessible as I can, there will be a certain amount of jargon, and you'll need to study those intimidating spirographs that astrologers assure you is actually a map of your soul. You might want to take this book to an astrologer friend to translate, if it gets too thick. On the other hand, it may be easier than you expected, and maybe this will inspire you to learn something about this huge field of knowledge.

Third, it may actually catch the eye of astrologers who have barely any idea what modern consensual negotiated power dynamic relationships look like, and may also have some rather negative ideas about them. You're probably already tensing after having read some of the terms in the previous part of the introduction. For you, I suggest picking up the book *Dear Raven and Joshua: Questions and Answers About Power Dynamic Relationships* (available at Alfred Press; www.alfredpress.com) and read it while you're reading this. I won't tell you to wait to read this until you've absorbed that book, because I know how curious astrologers can be. (I also recommend this to astrology-oriented people who are interested in power exchange, but not sure how it actually works.) Suffice it to say that these modern custom-built, unequal-by-design relationships are not about repeating old cultural patterns or forcing anyone into a situation that isn't healthy for them. They are about choice, and structure, and honor, and very often love.

Because there are so many names for the different roles in these demographics, fluctuating from area to are, coast to coast, and continent to continent, I'm sometimes going to use the terms "dominant" and "submissive" for roles based on personal qualities, "M-type" and "s-type" for umbrella terms for roles, "Master" and "slave" for full-time power dynamics where one person has a considerable degree of authority over the other, and "Owner" and "property" for power dynamics where one person has authority over everything, or nearly so. I use the term "Master" as a gender-neutral term, largely because I know a number of female Masters who prefer it to "Mistress", and I've not yet met one single male M-type who preferred "Mistress". (Mostly I'll be using "M-type" and "s-type", though.) If your term of choice is not mentioned, feel free to mentally edit it in. Ditto if you don't like my definitions. I'm sure you're smart enough to mentally insert the word you prefer, but it's impossible to for me please everyone.

This book covers three basic areas:
1) The natal charts of people drawn to either side of a power dynamic and how they will be instinctively moved to enact that dynamic.
2) The comparison charts of two people in a power dynamic relationship and how they mesh or clash.
3) The composite chart of two people in a power dynamic, and what it tells about how things will go.

We won't, however, be covering everything about natal charts, or comparison charts, or composite charts. That would take fifty volumes, and plenty of good books on those subjects already exist. (A few of my favorites are listed at the end of this book.) I will be concentrating on the areas that are most relevant to power exchange relationships. The other parts of the chart are relevant to a whole lot of other things in life, and I encourage the beginners to dive in and find out more about yourselves in other books and websites.

The three most important planets in power exchange are Pluto (power and control), Saturn (authority and discipline), and Neptune (surrender and sacrifice). For these three planets, because they are so important to this work, I've written them out cookbook-style (which is a term used by astrologers to describe lists of traits whose entries plod through every planet or sign or house or aspect) for the signs and houses, and for natal, synastry, and composite charts. For the other planets, I kept the chapters more theoretical (if I'd done them cookbook-style, the book would be a thousand pages long!) and discussed the generalities of what they might indicate in an unequal relationship.

Please understand that everyone, and every couple, is different; each chart has at least a hundred major variables, or more if you get esoteric. Some attributes may not apply to you, not because they don't apply to most people with that placement or aspect, but because you may have other things going on in your chart that counteract it, and I can't predict those from this distance. Take what's useful, and use it to have a better relationship. If I can do that with even one point of information, I'll have done my job.

RAVEN KALDERA
MARCH 2020

Note to readers: I've tried to make this as simple as I can given the complexity of the information. If, while reading through this book, you despair of figuring it all out in relation to yourself and your loved one(s), and you don't know where to look for astrologers who understand power exchange, I am available to put together astrological chart analyses, comparisons, and composites with or without power exchange commentary throughout. Please check my hub website at http://www.ravenkaldera.org to contact me.

Me, You, and Us

Interpreting Natal Charts

If you've ever tried to decipher an astrological chart, you'll see that there are twelve sections (the houses, each one indicating a separate area of life) and ten planets (which includes the Sun and Moon, even though they are not astronomically planets) with various lines between them that represent the relationship of one planet to another. "Challenging" aspects (squares and oppositions) are internal arguments, with one part of the Self struggling with another. "Enhancing" or "harmonious" aspects (trines and sextiles) are places where the parts of your Self are in harmony, and can work together easily without much effort. Conjunctions — meaning planets right next to each other — can go either way, or be both challenging *and* harmonious.

You're usually also supposed to take the four "angles" of the chart (the lines at the left, right, top, and bottom) into account, especially (for relationship considerations) the Ascendant (the left-hand point) which is your outward "look" and actions, and the Descendant (the right-hand point) which is what you're looking for in someone else's outward "look" and actions. Some astrologers (myself included) also add in asteroids, usually the five biggest ones — Chiron, Pallas, Juno, Ceres, and Vesta — and two opposing mathematical points called the North and South Nodes, which have to do with karmic goals for this life and from past lives.

Obviously, a good chart reading can tell a potential partner a good deal about the personality of their object of desire, and these lists of personality traits can be found in innumerable books, as well as all over the Internet. What we don't find are lists that tell you whether someone would be good at the dominant or submissive role in a relationship — or, more to the point, whether they would be good at being that with *you*. After all, these relationships require a higher-than-average level of initial compatibility, and someone who is an excellent Master or slave is still only an excellent Master or slave for specific people.

Some Sun Sign books try to claim that certain signs will always be the dominant party, and others always the submissive party. I think that's nonsense, personally, as limiting as the idea that dominance and submission are wired to races or genders or types of genitals. It just isn't true. By these examples, my Sun sign Scorpio slaveboy ought to be a dominant, because Scorpio is one of the signs that is constantly touted as being extremely dominant. That's an inaccuracy that misinterprets Scorpio's drive for intensity. Scorpio simply doesn't want to bother with anything unless they can go all the way. It's the sign of all-or-nothing, no dicking around with moderation. Thus, I have a Scorpio-Sun man who wants intensely to be the submissive partner, and dammit, he's going to take that as far as it can go and become all-out *property*. Because that's the true nature of the sign.

It's also about adding up the many variables in the chart, which can override the basic nature of the Sun; thus, my friend the Aries submissive with the quiet, service-oriented Virgo rising covering it up. So don't assume until you've tallied.

When looking at a natal chart for potential power exchange, it's less useful to look for "tendencies for power exchange" and more practical to look for "How does this person handle … ?" A slave with Mercury (the communication planet) in wandering Aquarius or vague Pisces is going to have a hard time with highly structured and complicated verbal protocols, but further elements in the chart might make them excellent at other submissive challenges. The Master with that Mercury may have a rough time forcing themselves to give detailed, explicit instructions, but they might have dozens of other redeeming dominant qualities. Neither is necessarily a bad Master or slave.

However, while there isn't a list of chart points that make one a True Master or Slave, there are a number of points that can make someone desire an unequal relationship. These mostly consist of major aspects between either Pluto or Neptune to the Sun, Moon, Venus, or Mars. Possession of one or more of these aspects doesn't mean that they will express that desire by finding a healthy D/s or M/s partnership, though. They might repress those feelings because they believe them to be unhealthy, or wrong, or at least unwanted by potential partners—as I certainly did. They might find subtle, manipulative ways to gain power (or make their partners take power) in egalitarian partnerships—I'll admit that I sometimes slipped and caught myself doing just that, in the days before I had a slave and a place to put those urges. They may get involved with people who treat them badly as a substitute for healthy submission. They might get into an actual negotiated power dynamic and handle it poorly and dishonestly. They may also just find love in a romantic egalitarian relationship and successfully work around those tendencies. Urges and predispositions are no more than that; real skill has to be learned and worked for. (In addition, I've seen plenty of happy power exchange charts without those aspects, so they aren't necessary or always present for those drawn to these lifestyles.)

As we go through the planets, houses, and aspects, we'll start with looking at how each one affects a specific important part of power exchange—discipline, control, sacrifice, communication, and so forth—for both sides of the slash. Then we'll move on to its effect on relationship charts.

Houses of Power

When I first began to research the charts of people in power exchange and interview them about their desires and relationships, it quickly became clear that certain "houses" in the natal chart had a distinctive effect on how each person manifested their dominance or submission and preferred to organize their relationship. For the beginners, the natal chart is divided into twelve "pie slices", into which all the areas of life are sorted. The sign that is on the first cusp of each house has a strong effect on how one pursues the areas of life covered by that house, and any planets which may fall into that house also have an effect. While every house has an impact on every person's life depending on what they are doing, the important houses for power exchange relationships turned out to be the second, sixth, and tenth houses.

These houses are all traditionally ruled by earth signs, though the sign on your particular cusp might be any of the twelve available. The second house rules possessions—your money, your objects, and your values—and thus rules whether and how a dominant partner wants to own and possess a submissive partner, or whether and how a submissive partner wants to be owned and possessed.

Aries on the 2nd House/M: Aries is a fiery and impulsive sign, and having Aries here can make the M-type impatient to move straight into having the s-type locked in without waiting and working long enough to fully gain their trust. It's important for the M-type with this placement to go slow and respect their trust timeframe, even if it makes you grit your teeth. Aries also tends to react with anger when denied things they've had their heart set on, and if the s-type is not interested in being possessed, these M-types may become resentful. Once they have the s-type, however, the next problem is that they tend to take the situation for granted, rather than continually working on maintaining that trust. Building regular check-ins into the relationship will be crucial.

Aries on the 2nd House/s: It's not just M-types who sometimes want to go too fast. S-types with this second-house placement want to rush in and leap off the cliff while the romantic and/or sexual feelings are high, possibly without checking to see whether the M-type in question has proved themselves trustworthy. Aries on the second house often has a rather carelessly generous attitude toward possessions, and for an s-type, that can mean giving themselves too quickly and without forethought. It can also indicate someone who quickly becomes tired of it, and wants out when it becomes inconvenient. They need to go slow, do their due diligence, and not push your M-type to go further down that path than they may be comfortable with.

Taurus on the 2nd House/M: Taurus is an incredibly possessive sign, and having it on the second-house cusp means that these M-types like their possessions to be where they left them, and not to have wandered off on their own. They are usually willing to be patient and wait for the s-type to give themselves, but once the deal is struck, they settle back in their new rut and don't want to let, go, no matter what happens. Whether this feels safe and secure or claustrophobic to the s-type will depend on their own chart, and the quality of the relationship. On the positive side, this Taurus placement is usually willing to do the patient work of maintaining the ownership bond, if it is pointed out to them that it needs to happen.

Taurus on the 2nd House/s: Taurus is a sign that understands possession, and possessiveness, probably better than any other. The problem with Taurus here is not getting the s-type to adapt to being possessed—they are probably fine with that, once any other more freedom-loving or fearful parts of the chart have been dealt with. The problem is that they may return the favor, wanting to possess their M-type, in some way, as much as their M-type possesses them. Whether this is acceptable or a quality to be furiously removed will depend on the M-type they're dealing with. They may have a fair amount of trouble being willing to hand over their physical possessions as well, including money. Taurus loves touch, and the best way to make them feel owned is to give them constant—and possibly objectifying—random touch, showing that their body is the M-type's object to casually play with.

Gemini on the 2nd House/M: With Gemini on this cusp, whether the M-type will even want to bother claiming and possessing an s-type will depend on how interesting they are. Mostly they may want the s-type to be fairly self-sufficient, if on call for when they are bored and want the s-type's company. They may only be interested in possessing the parts of the s-type, or the s-type's life, that interest them, and can be quite fine with the s-type having plenty of freedom if it means less responsibility for them. If it does come to full possession, they will write up lots of plans for how it will be done, but they need to remember that many plans fail in the face of reality, and flexibility is key.

Gemini on the 2nd House/s: The s-type with Gemini here may well be initially turned off by the idea that they could be possessed, and they are highly likely to want to build in limits to hedge their bets. The ones I've met who fell into ownership did so almost without noticing, after a great deal of loud talk about how it wasn't what they wanted. However, this will not be achieved quickly as the M-type will have to earn their way past the nervous anxiety. (Another sort of s-type with this placement writes up grand plans about how it will go, and then chickens out when it becomes difficult.) They have a horror of being found boring, or finding themselves in a boring situation, so the M-type must keep things interesting. On the positive side, they are usually quite willing to talk at length about their experiences of being possessed, so communication is rarely a problem.

Cancer on the 2nd House/M: Cancer is a sign that clings to things out of insecurity, which can be a problem if you're supposed to be the person in charge. It's all right to use an s-type as a comfort tool, so long as the M-type is careful that none of their restrictive rules are created out of a fear of the s-type leaving. It's better to unclench the crab-claws and let the s-type stay because they desire it, which will show the M-type their own worth far better than clinging or hedging them in.

Cancer on the 2nd House/s: Having the clingy, security-oriented sign of Cancer here can create someone who wants to be owned and completely possessed because they want to feel secure and never be abandoned. The problem, of course, is that just because someone takes possession of them doesn't mean that abandonment won't ever happen; if nothing else, the M-type may die someday. In addition, people with Cancer on this cusp can rush too fast into giving themselves away in the desire for security, and then feel trapped afterwards if the situation is not what they expected. They need to find their own inner security and go into the relationship for cleaner reasons.

Leo on the 2nd House/M: Having Leo here can indicate an M-type who wants to possess someone because they think of themself as nobility, a special class of person in some way, and they are always a little unhappy when people don't see that. Owning someone, or at least owning part of their lives, can feel like they're actually getting some of the respect and adulation and luxury that they secretly feel they deserve. So long as they can laugh at that in themself, and they manage to stay humble in the face of all that "power crack", this can be a harmless indulgence.

Leo on the 2nd House/s: If the s-type with this placement is going to be owned and possessed, they want someone who will see them as a royal luxury item, a special gift not given to just anyone. If the M-type is not suitably impressed with the s-type's willingness to give themself, or doesn't communicate that they see the s-type as a high-class luxury item, something in this s-type will droop. This will be the case even if they have trouble thinking of themself that way — on some level, the M-type believing this will help them believe in it themself.

Virgo on the 2nd House/M: The M-type with Virgo on this cusp wants a possession who is also a useful tool. They're not very interested in investing themselves fully in ornamental s-types who won't do the laundry or change the oil in the car — that might be fun for a relationship with limited authority and responsibility, but the more responsibility they invest in the relationship, the more usefulness and productivity they want out of their opposite number. They're willing to work hard on maintaining the relationship — in fact, they expect to have to do that.

Virgo on the 2nd House/s: In Virgo, which longs to be useful, if this s-type is going to be someone's possession, they want to be their useful tool rather than their ornament or pampered pet — preferably a multi-tool will a lot of skills that they can point at problems to make them go away. In preparation for this, these s-types might think about learning as many useful practical skills as they can get under their belts, so as to add to their "market value" and ensure a M-type who wants a very useful thing.

Libra on the 2nd House/M: Libra is ruled by Venus, and unlike the M-type with Virgo here, they're actually very interested in owning an attractive human property. While aesthetics are going to be on their list, physical looks matter less in the end than graciousness and pleasant companionship. They like the idea of owning a geisha, of whatever gender. Libra is also the sign of fairness, and they're concerned with making sure that the exchange is fair — that being possessed by them has enough benefits to the human possession to make it worth their while.

Libra on the 2nd House/s: Traditionally, it's said that people with Libra here — the sign of marriage — have a tendency to value themselves on whether they have a relationship, and what sort it is. In the case of this M-type, they can find value in being in a fair, honorable power exchange ... and this can move without much difficulty into seeing a good deal of their value as something to be possessed. Libra is ruled by Venus, the planet of love and beauty, and Libra values aesthetics, and their beauty and grace may be seen as something to be possessed — and perhaps bargained for. Since Libra is also fairness, they're all right with bargaining it away as long as the tradeoff seems fair to them, and they are seen as valuable.

Scorpio on the 2nd House/M: The M-type with Scorpio on this cusp is going to feel extremely possessive about their s-type, and may have trouble refraining from taking possession of their entire being very quickly. Try to go slow and let the s-type move at their comfort level, rather than pressuring them to give up more than they are ready for. The trouble is further exacerbated by these M-types enjoying a bit of struggle on the s-type's part, but with the assumption that it's just to make things exciting, and eventually they'll give in and be captured. Honesty on both parts is important here—don't assume anything until it's discussed, and respect boundaries even if you wish things were otherwise.

Scorpio on the 2nd House/s: Scorpio, like its opposite sign Taurus, is extremely possessive. However, Scorpio is a water sign, and thus emotionally motivated; having this placement shows that these s-types want the thrill of being claimed. Sometimes that may include some initial fighting to show that they're not a pushover, even while they wish the M-type would just fling them down and force the issue. They may also feel the need to act up and challenge that possession, just to make sure that the chains are all still there, or to get that thrill again. The only problem will be that they might also be transferring some of that possession-urge to your dominant partner as well ("…that's *my* M-type!") and whether or not that works out will depend entirely on that partner and whether they find it endearing or annoying.

Sagittarius on the 2nd House/M: Sagittarius is the sign least interested in being weighed down by possessions, and tends to generously scatter them or give them away on the journey, so the M-type with Sagittarius on this cusp may not be all that interested in completely possessing their s-type, including all those areas of responsibility and effort. They are likely to be fine with the s-type having a lot of freedom, and may actually be taken aback if the s-type is disappointed in this gift. If they do take possession of all parts of the s-type and their life, they may think of the s-type's other obligations as "sharing" their property, in a generous and casual way.

Sagittarius on the 2nd House/s: Having the freedom-loving sign of Sagittarius on this house cusp can make an s-type extremely wary of any relationship that puts too many restrictions on their freedom. Trust is a big deal anywhere Sagittarius is found in the chart, and this s-type wants to be trusted to go out, do their thing without interference, and come back to the M-type. They are happy to be owned in the way that rural people used to own dogs—they would do their job and then wander in the woods until it was time to get dinner, sleep by the fire most nights and go out hunting on others.

Capricorn on the 2nd House/M: In Capricorn, a sign which is very concerned with both practicality and public status, it's important to that their s-type is a useful, practical tool rather than merely a decoration. On the other hand, it's also important to them on some level to be *seen* as having someone who obeys them, thus making them a more important person. It's all right for them to indulge this as long as they're careful about the venue — keep it for spaces where people understand power dynamic relationships, rather than egalitarian spaces where ordering your partner around will get them the opposite of a positive, respected reputation.

Capricorn on the 2nd House/s: The s-type with Capricorn on this cusp, if they desire to be owned and possessed, also wants to feel like they were bought and paid for, and that their cost was not cheap. That doesn't have to be acted out in actual money; it can be a contract drawn up that assures them how much time, effort, resources, trust, and — most of all — respect will be owed to them by the M-type in exchange for their surrender. These s-types, like those with Virgo on the cusp, also want to be seen as useful, but they also want to be seen as important to the life of their M-type.

Aquarius on the 2nd House/M: Aquarius here indicates that these M-types have a spontaneous attitude toward possessing — they take possession as they are moved to, and don't bother to "own" anything that bores them. They are fine with leaving an s-type freedom, so long as areas connected to the parts of the s-type's life they care about are firmly in hand. They may be good at feeling like they "own" someone even if the s-type doesn't live with them and is only seen once a year.

Aquarius on the 2nd House/s: This sign is almost as freedom-loving and chains-rejecting as Sagittarius, so it will be a rare s-type with this cusp sign who will agree to be fully possessed. Mostly, possessiveness makes them antsy, and they want plenty of room to follow their desires. They may be attracted by a new reframing of the concept, however — especially if ownership, in this new model, does not include micromanagement and allows them to have their own interests, so long as nothing interferes with their basic duties.

Pisces on the 2nd House/M: With the vague and watery sign of Pisces on this cusp, the first issue these M-types have is overestimating their ability to comfortably take on the amount of responsibility that possessing another adult will require. To keep from overextending themself and disappointing their s-type, it's best for them to start slowly and give over only one area at a time, and make sure they can handle that before moving on. They need to prevent themselves from getting lost in a fantasy of what possessing someone will be like; this can be aided by talking to experienced people first.

Pisces on the 2nd House/s: Pisces is the sign of the dreamer, and here on the house of possession, the s-type will have lots of wonderful dreams about how it would be, without necessarily understanding the sometimes-challenging reality. They shouldn't give away more than they're sure of, and they should be prepared to take it back if they overestimated what would be comfortable to give away. They may also hate conflict around the issue, and must be careful not to hide feelings of being repressed until they explode, or drift off when the M-type isn't looking.

The next important place to look is the sixth house. Traditionally, this house ruled one's health, diet and food, mentorship, and all the scut-work jobs in the world, from the maintenance you do to keep yourself and your world in order to the labor you do for others that does not necessarily contribute to a great career, but helps to keep you alive. It's also the house of service, however, which is a very important part of most power dynamic relationships. A strong sixth house—one with multiple heavenly bodies in it, especially strong ones like the Sun or Moon—usually indicates someone for whom service is very important, regardless of whether they are on the giving or receiving end. The sign on the cusp of the sixth house will give important clues as to people's attitudes toward service.

Aries on the 6th House/M: Fiery, fast-moving Aries on this cusp can indicate a preference for reactive service—telling the s-type what to do in the moment as they feel like it, rather than planning out a lot of services for them to do regularly or over time. These M-types may have a problem with steady consistency, though, including remembering to follow up and check to make sure something is done, and giving feedback about it, unless it annoys them in the moment.

Aries on the 6th House/s: With Aries here, these s-types are very enthusiastic about doing things for their M-type, but their attention span can be short, and repetitive or dull labor gets old very fast for them. They're not interested in details and tend to rush through things, so they may want to let someone more detail-oriented check things over for them. Mindfulness exercises probably make them want to scream, but are worth it to help them learn to take their time with service activities.

Taurus on the 6th House/M: An M-type with earthy, sensual Taurus on this cusp wants sensuality and touch—a body to grab on demand, and maybe some good cooking. Whatever crazy things they do with their lives, they're going to want steady, consistent, practical service, focused on their own physical comfort. Once they settle into a service routine with the s-type, they won't like to change it.

Taurus on the 6th House/s: S-types with Taurus on this cusp want to get into a settled routine of service as quickly as possible, where they know exactly what they will be doing every day, in every situation, and it won't change much at all. They will have trouble with M-types whose lives and service needs change from day to day, perhaps due to a fluctuating lifestyle. They can adapt to it with difficulty, but the more "anchor" chores they have—services that will need to get done regularly no matter what—the easier it will be for them.

Gemini on the 6th House/M: One of the best services an s-type with a sixth-house-Gemini M-type can perform is keeping them company and talking to them, preferably with stimulating non-stop conversation. It might help to read up on subjects they might find interesting. These M-types jump from task to task at a rapid rate, because long-term work bores them, and the s-type will be expected to keep up.

Gemini on the 6th House/s: S-types with fast-moving Gemini on this cusp will get bored easily with long, tedious tasks, and might do better with short tasks that keep them interested. They make good companions, and can easily see "being interesting for the M-type" as a service. Unless other points in the chart interfere, they're pretty good at multitasking and may enjoy the challenge.

Cancer on the 6th House/M: As Cancer is the most domestic of the signs, the M-type with this placement will want all the domestic services to go well, first and foremost. Keeping a pleasant and comfortable home for them is paramount. Giving emotional comfort is another useful activity that the s-type can render, if they can learn to think of it as an on-demand service.

Cancer on the 6th House/s: While the s-type with Cancer here can be assigned to other tasks, they will feel uncomfortable if they are sent to proofread a manuscript while the M-type's home is in disarray. Domestic chores make them feel like they are really doing something that makes a difference, regardless of their gender. They enjoy getting gestures of physical affection as an act of praise.

Leo on the 6th House/M: The M-type with Leo on the sixth house definitely wants to inhabit the role of Master of Servants. They adore services rendered to them in a dramatic and/or romantic way—the s-type kneeling to bring them the drink, the fancy garnishes on the salad, all the little flourishes that say, "This is a luxury service." They enjoy having their preferences taken into account without having to ask, and while they can be lavish with praise, they often forget to do it. A respectful prompting from the s-type can be one of the services offered.

Leo on the 6th House/s: This is not an s-type for whom invisible service will come easily, nor does it make them feel good about serving. They need approval and a fair amount of positive feedback; they will accept negative feedback better if the M-type leads with the positive, if only to point out that how hard they are trying has been noted. If the M-type has a difficult time remembering to compliment them for their work, they can be trained to come ask for approval when they feel the need. They will enjoy dramatic and lavish services, especially if they are "cast" as being a luxury service for the "noble" M-type.

Virgo on the 6th House/M: Virgo rules the sixth house, so the M-type will want someone heavily service-oriented and will be quite particular about the quality of services that are rendered. They may drive a more romantically-oriented s-type crazy with their insistence of hard work and precise attention to details, however. Getting the work done is very important to them, and they will likely drive themselves just as hard as the productivity expectations they place on their s-type.

Virgo on the 6th House/s: Virgo is very comfortable in the sixth house, and this s-type is extremely service-oriented, pays attention to details, and has a strong work ethic. They want to be useful, and will not be happy when forced to be merely decorative. This is a good placement for an s-type who is also a personal assistant, personal care attendant, or unpaid employee in the M-type's small business, in addition to or even instead of more personal roles.

Libra on the 6th House/M: A cooperative s-type can be a wonderful palliative for a hatred of scut-work, because they can so often make short work of it, which is a wonderful thing for someone with somewhat languid Libra on this cusp. Venus-ruled Libra is also very taken with aesthetics, and the grace with which an s-type serves is important to them. They enjoy those little touches—the nicely plated food, the attractive outfit, the graceful bow—and they're willing to take the time to polish someone's service in order to get that.

Libra on the 6th House/s: People with Libra on this cusp do best when they have a balance between work and social life, and s-types are no different. While service is all well and good, they will want an equal amount of time getting interpersonal attention from their M-type. Spending all day cleaning the house followed by an hour of sex-play, after which everyone falls over exhausted, will not fulfill them. Their favorite service is that of being a charming companion.

Scorpio on the 6th House/M: Scorpio on this cusp can indicate an obsession with one's work, and in this case the M-type with this placement may become obsessed with perfect service, if they're not careful to keep an objective eye. Unlike the folks with Virgo on this cusp, however, since this is an emotional water sign, they may feel hurt or betrayed when the s-type disobeys or makes egregious mistakes. They should take a breath and calm down, and remember that in most cases it's not personal.

Scorpio on the 6th House/s: The s-type with this placement can be obsessive about their service, and as this is an emotional water sign, they may take it very personally when they fail in any way, even if their standards are higher than those of the M-type. A wise M-type will make it clear that the M-type's standards are the ones that count, will divert them from self-castigation to problem-solving, and will make sure that they neither push themselves too hard nor give up in frustration.

Sagittarius on the 6th House/M: M-types with wild, fiery Sagittarius on this cusp are not people who does the same old thing the same old way all the time. In fact, they're continually changing up theirr routines, perhaps to the dismay of s-types who would like things to be the same forever. They like service in form of a sidekick to their Adventurer, a travel companion on their physical or mental journeys. Part of the service their s-type can render is being a professional good sport with their spur-of-the-moment ideas.

Sagittarius on the 6th House/s: The s-type with Sagittarius here wants to be of service for idealistic reasons, but often stumbles when the reality of hard, tedious work sets in. They hate routines and chafe at being made to do activities they hate, on a regular basis. It's best to vary the service and change it up frequently, or help them find different ways to do the same service. They will need plenty of time to be social, and if the M-type loads them down with too much work, they may simply take their social time anyway and damn the torpedoes.

Capricorn on the 6th House/M: Capricorn here can make the M-type a rather brutal taskmaster, especially when they're stressed or coming close to their own limits. If they're going to be assigning someone scut-work and evaluating their performance for speed and precision, they will need to be careful not to run them into the ground. They probably drive themselves hard, and may drive an s-type just as hard ... but they should be careful to take the s-type's health, mood, sleep and energy levels into account.

Capricorn on the 6th House/s: While Capricorn here gives a good work ethic and a strong desire for practical service—useful for an s-type—Capricorn likes being an Authority, and these s-types may have to watch out for arguments about whether their way is the "right" way to do something, as opposed to the M-type who may have different opinions about how to do something, and may want their opinions to take priority. If these s-types tend to push themselves too hard, they should ask their M-type to mandate down time when they're staggering, even if the dishes aren't done.

Aquarius on the 6th House/M: The M-type with Aquarius here will want the first order of service to be assisting them with their various weird projects—"Pull the switch now, Igor!"—and the second order to be providing them with such items as food, coffee, and clean clothing so that they can keep working without worrying about it. Their work ethic is variable, depending on what has captured their eye in the moment (so the s-type will get a fair amount of time to pursue their own projects) and they may love the idea of high-tech services.

Aquarius on the 6th House/s: An s-type with Aquarius here has the most rebellious and nonconforming sign of the lot on this cusp. They're not going to be happy with dull, ordinary service; they want to find new and different ways to do it, and they're especially happy if there is cool new technology involved. It may be a struggle for them when they want to improve and perfect their service and the M-type wants them to do it exactly the same way as before.

Pisces on the 6th House/M: With Pisces on this cusp, the M-type may like more "soft" services such as snuggling and being kept company. They may not care so much about chores anyway, although a highly service-oriented s-type may look around their house in dismay and ask plaintively to be allowed to clean things up. They get tired of work easily and the s-type may end up finishing a lot of the jobs they start.

Pisces on the 6th House/s: In Pisces, the sign of sacrifice, the s-type with this placement enjoys serving and has a good feel for it, although they do need to be careful not to martyr themself. They also have to be careful not to lose themself in a fantasy about serving and then be disappointed when the reality of grubby chores (to be done when the M-type isn't even around!) comes upon them. Services that visibly help the M-type or clearly show them getting pleasure are more fulfilling to this s-type than ones done for long-term gain with no short-term payoff.

The next important house for power exchange is the tenth house, which traditionally rules one's career and public life. It is also the house of authority, as it is traditionally the Saturn house. In the Saturn chapter we discuss how Saturn affects one's ideas about authority, and being under authority. The tenth house is similar, and the sign on the cusp of this house simply affects how we respond to being in or being under authority.

Aries on the 10th House/M: In Aries, the sign of the Warrior, this M-type feels on some level that courage is the main qualification for being worthy of being followed. They're certainly right that it's important, but they need to remember that courage is not fearlessness, and sometimes the bravest thing of all is to admit that you're scared shitless, but you intend to do the thing anyway, as soon as you get your bearings and breathe past the fear. They should try not to get caught up in the idea that one must never show fear around one's s-type — the right s-type will admire them for being afraid and doing it anyway, more than for simply putting on a fearless mask.

Aries on the 10th House/s: This s-type wants an M-type who is braver than they are. In exchange for giving up authority, they want to be protected from the frightening problems in their life, and may be disappointed by an M-type who funks out when things get scary. They expect quick decisions, and they expect to do a little struggling and be fought down.

Taurus on the 10th House/M: The M-type with Taurus here is very patient with s-types, and is willing to repeatedly explain orders. They don't like to make decisions quickly, so more impatient s-types may get frustrated while waiting for them to finish making plans. They base their authority on the fact that they have Common Sense, and that they are practical and down-to earth.

Taurus on the 10th House/s: With Taurus on this cusp, the s-type wants an M-type who is stable, sensible, and straightforward. They need to take their time with tasks and would rather do a thorough job than a fast one. They would rather have everything spelled out exactly than to have to think on their feet and make quick decisions without the M-type present.

Gemini on the 10th House/M: Gemini likes to think of themselves as smart and quick, and on some level M-types with this placement will feel like this is the basis for their authority. They do a lot of talking about how things are going to go, but unless there are more practical aspects in the rest of the chart, they may have trouble getting around to implementing their own rules. They may go back and forth between lots of attention and focus on the power dynamic, and ignoring the job when other shiny situations come up.

Gemini on the 10th House/s: The s-type with Gemini on this house cusp wants a dominant partner who can outthink them, and who is willing to do a lot of talking about the dynamic. Lack of communication will damage their respect in the M-type's authority. They may be slippery, trying to find loopholes and get out of chores just to challenge themselves and see if it is possible.

Cancer on the 10th House/M: The M-type with Cancer on this cusp may be very parental in their authority style, and they want to be obeyed for the same reasons that a child obeys a parent. They may be a little defensive about their authority and may take disobedience or even questioning very personally. They need to remember that s-types should be able to ask anything about an order and get a clear and patient answer.

Cancer on the 10th House/s: In Cancer, the sign of the Mother, this s-type expects to be nurtured and taken care of in exchange for giving up authority. It's impossible for them not to mentally model a power dynamic on a parent/child dynamic in some way, even when they're well aware that both partners are consenting adults. As such, it's very emotional for them—this is a Water sign—and they tend to retreat into their shell when they think they're not loved.

Leo on the 10th House/M: With Leo on this house cusp, this M-type secretly likes to be thought of as a feudal lord and have peasants obeying them because of their innate rank. Either that, or they want to be a rock star, and their s-type should be their biggest fan. They like showy authority, with all the fancy trappings according to what they consider powerful-looking.

Leo on the 10th House/s: The s-type with Leo on this cusp wants to be appreciated—and possibly even adored—in exchange for giving up authority. They love it when their M-type takes visible pleasure in having such a wonderful s-type in their lives, and in return they will go all out with showy acts of submission.

Virgo on the 10th House/M: With Virgo on this cusp, the M-type may well have a service-oriented career themselves, or at least one that deals heavily with details. They may feel that the dynamic is one of mutual service to each other and to the relationship; they simply render their service from the top down. They may hold themselves up as a role model for the s-type's service, and expect to be obeyed on that quality.

Virgo on the 10th House/s: The s-type with Virgo here is going to want an organized M-type who cares about details—even if only to point them out so that the s-type can take care of them—and can perhaps help the s-type to be more organized. They want to see an M-type who Works, not one who does the minimum in their life and then sits around playing video games, perhaps using the s-type to be lazy. They prefer a hard-working role model.

Libra on the 10th House/M: The M-type with Libra on this cusp tends to charm people into accepting their authority with a warm smile and a gracious tone. They will enjoy working together with their s-type on various projects—Libra is couple-oriented, and even if they're very much in charge, they will want a team situation. They like to look good and seem polite while giving orders, and will not be happy with an s-type who thinks that dominance means a roaring brute.

Libra on the 10th House/s: Libra is concerned with attractiveness and harmony, and the s-type with this placement is going to want an authority figure who is courteous and can give orders graciously. They are also going to want one who wants them around to do things as a couple, as opposed to someone who will mostly leave them to their own business and whatever chores need to be done. They may want a role model for fairness; if the M-type is perceived as constantly unfair, they may rebel.

Scorpio on the 10th House/M: In Scorpio, the sign of intensity, this placement indicates that being in authority is a very emotionally intense area for these M-types. It is also a place where they tend to go All or Nothing—they want to control totally when they're in authority, or they see it as not worth the trouble and want to walk away. It's not something they can be casual about.

Scorpio on the 10th House/s: S-types with Scorpio on this cusp often base their scale of worthy authority on the moral takedown. They want a dominant partner who understands the darker side of human nature, including their own darknesses, but is unwaveringly ethical in how they handle it—preferably more ethical about it than the s-type, so that the M-type can be a role model.

Sagittarius on the 10th House/M: Wherever one has Sagittarius in one's chart, there one has the urge to overcommit and take on too many projects. M-types with this placement base their authority on their learning and knowledge—how much information they have not just about power exchange, but about many subjects. They may be a trifle inconsistent when it comes to checking on the s-type's work and giving feedback.

Sagittarius on the 10th House/s: The s-type with Sagittarius on this cusp will respect their dominant partner a lot more if they have a wide range of knowledge and expertise in a number of provable areas of life. They are drawn to the idea of a teacher who can guide them in ways to make their lives better, and they work well in master/apprentice situations.

Capricorn on the 10th House/M: This is traditionally the house associated with Saturn, and Capricorn is Saturn's own sign, so the M-type with Capricorn on this cusp does have a tendency to feel that their authority should be based on the fact that they have declared themselves the authority, or other people have done so. It's important for them to learn that trust needs to be continually earned; these are relationships where one salutes the person and their integrity, not the office and its importance.

Capricorn on the 10th House/s: S-types with Capricorn on this cusp tend to be impressed with status, especially if it is acknowledged by others, but sometimes even if it is self-proclaimed in an imposing enough way. They want an authority figure who is good at achieving practical goals in the world, and who can help them achieve their own goals.

Aquarius on the 10th House/M: With Aquarius here, to a certain extent this M-type sees authority as something earned by being brilliant, and ideally socially radical as well. They'd agree with Thomas Jefferson, who said, "There is a natural aristocracy among men. The grounds of this are virtue and talent." With Uranus ruling this house, they want to use that authority to make change in other people's lives, which probably means that they'd start with their s-type. Intimacy in authority-based relationships may not come easily to them.

Aquarius on the 10th House/s: These s-types want their M-types to be far-seeing, brilliant planners who inspire their followers with their grand plans. Freedom means a lot to them, and they may balk at a "traditional" authority relationship. They may not immediately expect intimacy in an authority-based relationship.

Pisces on the 10th House/M: The sign of Sacrifice on this cusp may push an M-type to believe that it is their job to sacrifice for their followers, or else to rescue them. They may attempt to hide their true selves behind a mask that is more "traditionally" dominant at first, but when they settle into their authenticity, they will be kind and compassionate managers who prioritize the well-being of their charges.

Pisces on the 10th House/s: Pisces on this cusp makes the s-type extremely vulnerable to someone with a dominant manner; they may need to learn to set firm but kind boundaries with dominant-acting people who haven't yet earned their trust. They may also assume that there will be no recourse, and should learn to negotiate from a place of good self-worth.

Interpreting Synastry Charts

After we look at how the individual tends to handle various situations, we look at how they interact with each other. A "synastry" chart (also called a "comparison" chart) is simply a matter of laying one chart on top of another, lining up the signs, and drawing aspects from the planets of one to the planets of another. Where challenging and enhancing aspects indicate arguments or cooperation between parts of the self, in a synastry chart they indicate arguments or cooperation between two people. (I find that drawing them on clear plastic page protectors can help with a visual view of these interactions.)

It's important to remember that every one of these aspects has two ends. The two planets affect both parties with equal intensity, regardless of who's been placed in charge. (A child's planets can affect a parent's chart, and their life, just as much as the parent affects the child.) It's just that opposite sides of the power exchange slash may react very differently to being poked by a contacting planet. For example, my slaveboy and I have both our Saturns in a close-degree major angle to each other. My Saturn challenges him by laying on disciplines of thought and behavior that aren't always easy for him ... but his Saturn challenges me in return, pushing me to become more organized so that I can better utilize his time and effort, and my own. Through this mutual motivation, we both grow as Master and slave, and as people.

Another important piece of the synastry puzzle is noting where one person's planets fall in the other person's chart. This is because other people's planets "light up" and stimulate that house, and thus that area of your life. A partner who transposes three planets into your seventh House of Marriage is going to get you at least thinking seriously about commitment, even if it was just supposed to be casual. A partner who puts a major planet into your tenth House of Career will kindle new ambitions by simply being in your life, even if they never mention your job. Someone who transposes planets into your eleventh House of Friendship can make you feel like you've been chums forever.

Of course, the nature of the "lighting up" is dependent on the nature of the planet in question. No matter what the chart of the new person you met today, they've got a Sun that's lighting up some part of your chart with happiness, a Moon that's hitting you somewhere and threatening to make you feel emotional, a Mercury that will inspire you to talk about something in that house, a Jupiter that will cheer you up, and a Saturn that will push you to be more disciplined and possibly make you feel as if they disapprove of you. It's just a question of *where* those triggers will fall.

As we pass through the planets, houses, and aspects, we'll first note how some synastry aspects can enhance your power exchange while others create problems. Then we'll discuss what planetary transpositions do the same.

Interpreting the Composite Chart

The concept of a composite chart is actually fairly simple, although in this age of computer programs almost no one does it by hand any more. Simply take both people's Suns, check the degrees, and do the math to find the exact midpoint between them. That's the composite Sun. This is repeated with all the planets in order to create a chart of midpoints. The math to find the composite Ascendant and the houses is much trickier, and I suggest that you find an online computer program—of which there are several—which will take both partners' time, date, and place of birth and give you a composite chart. (If one person does not have this information and can't get hold of it for some reason, see a professional astrologer for help.)

Then you've got a chart of midpoints, which is triggered only when those two people are interacting. It's as if the relationship was a person, and this was their natal chart. When the two of you are together, you naturally tend to pull toward acting like that chart, perhaps as much as or even more than your own. It's why people sometimes exclaim about how they don't know themselves when they're with Person X; they act out of character and shock themselves with unusual behaviors. If someone has a particularly difficult natal chart, and the composite chart with their partner happens to be particularly blessed, they may crave being around that person all the time because it's so much easier to be with their partner than to just be themselves, alone. While many psychologists would recognize that behavior, not many would know that it has a solid descriptor in astrology.

Husband-and-wife astrology team Steven and Jodie Forrest wrote the first really accessible book on composite charts, entitled *Skymates*. In that book, they proposed a new categorization of composite charts, based on their own observations of, I assume, crunching the data from a whole lot of relationships. They noted that composite charts tended to fall into three categories, which they named Culture Shock, Feudal System, and Democracy. A Democracy chart shared roughly equal points between the two individual charts—for example, the composite Sun being in A's

Sun sign and B's Sun house placement, and so forth. It was considered the easiest and most healthy. A Culture Shock chart was dramatically different from the charts of both parties individually, and often forced both of them into behaviors that were out of character — stretching their personal boundaries, perhaps, but also requiring a good deal of alone time (or time with others) where they could relax and be themselves.

Feudal System charts were the hardest; in this case the composite chart resembled one person's chart more closely and the other person's not much at all. The Forrests have noted that not only does such a composite force one person into an unfamiliar mold while allowing the other person to still mostly be themselves, it also seems to stack fate (at least regarding incidents that affect the relationship) in the favor of the person "on top". That first composite chart that I did during my first marriage was a Feudal System chart, and I was not on the top of it. Writ large across that chart was why my spouse thought everything was fine while I was dying inside.

The first thought that some readers will have at this point might be, "Well, those words do indicate a power inequality, don't they? Wouldn't it be OK if the Master had the top side of a Feudal System relationship?"

I'm ambivalent about answering that wholly positively. Yes, it's a power inequality, and perhaps it would be easier to handle in that case, but it would still put a tough burden on the s-type, who would be pushed to become a very different person. I know slaves who've done that and are glad they did it, but it would also require the M-type to be very aware of the difficulty in what they were asking, and frequently check on the s-type's well-being and sense of self.

The Forrests don't toss out all Feudal System relationships as doomed. They simply admonish that the Person On Top has to "…not abuse that power. If you're the sovereign in such a couple, strive to become that conscious! Make every effort to consider your mate's point of view … Such compromise creates positive outcomes: trust, openness, willing commitment and participation. Sovereigns can be benevolent when they recognize where their bread is buttered."

To be that conscious as a Master is a wonderful thing regardless of chart configurations, but when a Master is on top in a Feudal System chart, it's not just a nice option for the future when the Master gets over their issues and evolves. It's necessary from the get-go, or the situation may collapse.

As challenging as that is for an M-type, imagine what it's like to be the s-type and be on top in this situation! It would probably take three times as much care and mindfulness, and the M-type would have to be very committed to self-improvement, very good at setting boundaries, and not driven mostly by their ego. It's still possible, and it might be an amazing growth situation for both parties, but it wouldn't feel easy or simple at all.

The composite chart's planets, houses and angles also need to be taken into consideration. I've heard D/s and M/s couples say things like, "The slave serves the Master, and both Master and slave serve the relationship (or household)." The composite chart is a map of the personality, if you will, of what they're both serving, and it affects how they react to each other. For example, sometimes each member of a couple will end up "embodying" two ends of a composite chart aspect—and if that's a square or opposition, it can mean an argument or a standoff, at least until everything is sorted out. On the other hand, sometimes composite aspects that are difficult for egalitarian couples are easier for people in power exchange, so there are some consolations.

Here I have to give kudos to astrologer Robert Hand, because right at the point where I was astrologically vetting my new slaveboy, someone gave me a copy of Hand's book *Planets In Composite*, which had a long list of planetary aspects in the composite chart. Joshua was the new thing in my life at the moment, and after he got over his initial spooked feeling and put it down as just another way that I could master him, he was quite interested in hearing what the book had to say. As I read off the relevant relationship traits, we both noticed one sort of phrase that popped up again and again in various forms. It was a warning from the author that this or that aspect could "…lead to one person trying to gain power over the other one" or "one person sacrificing for the other one".

After several of these warnings, Joshua asked whether this sort of thing was just scattered regularly throughout the book, and I started thumbing through it. No, most entries didn't mention that. It just seemed that we had won the lottery for most of the ones that did. I continued to read, but on the next iteration of "…they will have to be careful not to get into an unequal relationship…" we both burst out, almost in unison, with "But what if we like it that way?"

We laughed and finished up, but Hand's book did make me think about how some relationships just inspire a romantic inequality (willing or ambivalent) even if the people in question weren't exactly searching for that. I'd talked to a lot of D/s and M/s couples who set out looking for a power exchange, and also a small but substantial minority who said things like "He just brings that out in me," or "I wanted to marry her, and that meant being a subordinate, and I did it because it just felt right when I was with her." These folks all stressed that they didn't feel like they were naturally dominant or submissive, but it felt natural to be that way with their partner, and only their partner. While Joshua and I were both actively deciding to be master and slave, I can see how a concentration of aspects that tempted tendencies toward inequality, combined with an overall compatibility, might create such a situation.

Again, tendencies don't create destiny—and in anyone's life (and chart) there are probably quite a few tendencies that it's in their best interest to resist with all their might—but there is a qualitative difference in our relationships as to what feelings are and are not appropriate. We still need all the basic relationship skills, and we may need a higher level of such qualities as honesty, good communication, patience, self-discipline, mindfulness, and self-awareness, than an egalitarian partnership, but we often find a healthy place for feelings and desires that would be damaging elsewhere. It's part of the beauty of a power dynamic, which has often been described in terms of people with internal monsters finding compatible monsters to love, and helping each other to realize that they actually aren't monsters at all ... because sometimes it takes someone else's gaze to show you your own beauty.

As we pass through the planets, signs, and houses, we'll be pointing out the composite features that are most relevant to power exchange, and those that may create difficulties for you.

Power, Discipline, and Sacrifice

Pluto: Passion and Control

You may be surprised that we're not starting with the Sun and working outward. Instead, we're starting from the outer perimeter with Pluto, the planet of intensity, extremes, transformation ... and power. Where Pluto lies in your chart, there you are extremely sensitive to power, and you may react angrily when you feel those things being taken away from you. The Pluto position in your chart—sign, house, and planets aspecting it—shows the places where you really like having control ... or you want someone else to control you.

Control, in a relationship, is a tricky thing even to talk about. On the one hand, we have literally millions of examples where one person attempting to control another went horribly wrong. On the other hand, we have the power dynamic demographic, where informal surveys routinely list control as one of the two major motivations for people on both sides of the slash (the other being service). There are other, rarer motivations, of course, and you also find the occasional voluntary servant who is entirely service-oriented and is not at all interested in control, but joy in taking or rendering up control is such a common motivation among D/s and M/s people that we can't ignore it. Some M/s couples have actually suggested that control ought to be a sixth love language that most people don't have, shared by only a token few. Certainly, in high-control M/s relationships, it can be called a love language unto itself.

Control is not the same thing as *authority*. When you give someone authority over an area of your life, you give them decision-making power. When you give someone control over an area of your life, you give them decision-*taking* power. Of course, this assumes that they will effectively be able to take it, meaning that you (in this case, the s-type) are confident enough in the M-type's effect on your will and their ability to extract obedience even in uncomfortable situations that you feel it's realistic to turn over control. A great deal of problems arise, of course, when a starry-eyed s-type (perhaps mistaking being in love for being enslaved) verbally writes control checks to the M-type that their emotions, when taken aback by an unpleasant order, can't cash. Another source of problems may be when M-types push too hard and too fast to get control of areas that mean a lot to them (perhaps because of Pluto-ruled feelings of all-or-nothing), and the s-type isn't wholly ready to go there.

The result, of course, is usually a sudden and unexpected blowup. While Mars is the anger that springs up when we're immediately wronged, Pluto is the simmering rage that hides for a long time and then explodes, usually with a desire to destroy what caused it. Playing with control isn't just playing with fire ... it's playing with nuclear weapons. That's a truth we all need to remember, even as we carefully create our relationship containment programs.

Pluto may indicate control desires, of course, but those desires don't necessarily line up nicely with Master/slave porn ideas. An s-type with Pluto in, say, the sixth house of service might feel incredibly intensely about servitude, but they might also feel incredibly intensely about how it ought to be done, to the point of not being able to bend to the M-type's preferences. An s-type with Pluto in Cancer (the sign of the parent-child relationship) might desperately want to be a little girl or boy of a parental dominant, or anything to do with their childhood might be so intense that they don't trust anyone to get near it, and have to set boundaries around that. An M-type with Pluto in Virgo (the sign of chores and details) might keep despotic control over their s-type's highly detailed chore list, but might not be able to trust anyone to help with secretarial tasks, even if the s-type is objectively better and it and would make an excellent personal assistant. How we respond to these urges has a lot to do with how we were raised, our trust issues, and our general emotional openness.

So how do we tell what's a control desire that works with the give-and take of a power dynamic relationship, and what's a desire to keep control of something ourselves? By communicating it, of course. Talk over each point between you, and be painfully honest about them. Pluto also rules the kind of rip-your-skin-off transparent honesty that doesn't care about saving face or keeping your image intact. This shows us that Pluto is also in charge of transparency, a very important part of power dynamic health.

While there is general agreement that a slave must be mentally and emotionally transparent to the Master or they won't be able to do their job properly, there's a lot of debate as to whether the Master should be transparent to the slave as well. My slaveboy and I compromise on that: I am transparent about anything to do with him, our relationship, the household we live in, or anything else that I believe might affect him (which actually covers most things in my life). All else I can tell him is not his concern, if I choose to, although I tend to tell him most of that anyway, because he is my most trusted confidant.

On a higher level, of course, Pluto is about a lot more than just where we guard or outsource our power. It is the planet of transformation and regeneration, which is why Pluto transits tend to be violently purifying (read: "burn it all down and start over"), and Pluto doesn't like it when you hold on to something too tightly until it stagnates. This means that the Pluto areas in your life (and your relationship) may go through transformations over time, and that's all right. Much as Saturn would like things to crystallize forever, Pluto will never let that happen.

Let's look at Pluto through the signs, houses, and aspects, and see where our power desires might lie. Note: I am skipping Pluto in Aries, Taurus, Gemini, Aquarius, and Pisces. This is because no one with these Pluto signs is alive today, and we have no living examples of personality, so we can only theorize. If I'm still alive when the Pluto in Aquarius generation comes of age, I'll do a second edition for them. But it can wait until I have more information.

Pluto Through The Signs

Pluto in Cancer/M

The Pluto in Cancer generation, among American gay men, were the ones who we think of as first starting communities in the leather bars. Having the planet of Power in the sign of Family explains why it felt so important to them to create pseudo-familial bonds (sparking the inspirational genesis for later "leather families") to replace the lack of positive nurturing in their conservative early lives, but built around extreme sexual desires and/or power exchange. Pluto in Cancer feels very intensely about Family and Home and the structure thereof; a dominant person with this placement may want their power structure to resemble a family or tribe, with them as the matriarch or patriarch. Since Cancer tends to prefer subtle sideways movement to direct, straight-ahead confrontation, they may try to use more subtle methods of control. The danger is in them trying to manipulate others without letting the manipulation be aboveboard and on the table; they need to take a deep breath and tell themselves that their authority can survive directness, even if it feels like manipulation will be emotionally easier for them in the short-term.

Pluto in Cancer/s

This placement can indicate a strong desire to find a new Mom or Dad, to replace imperfect parenting with a new chosen authority figure who won't repeat the mistakes of the originals. While they may not be openly looking for ageplay, something in them is seeking at least some of the "ideal parent" in an M-type. The danger is that they are also more likely to carry "parent baggage" around authority — not that people with other placements aren't going to have any of that due to their own inner charts — but here there is a strong emphasis on "earning the right to parent me", and the M-type will be scrutinized for their skills, patience, and possibly "lineage" — from whom did they learn to do this? It's done, possibly unconsciously, with the same "feel" of checking a potential partner's "breeding" or home life.

Pluto in Cancer in a Composite Chart

The composite Cancer Pluto indicates a couple who want to create a tightly controlled little world of their own, where no outside influences can penetrate and upset the fantasy of Perfect Home. Of course, what each person brings in with them — especially those memories of their own parents, and their baggage around that—may turn out to be unwelcome but nonevictable housemates, at least until both parties deal with them. The relationship gets stronger when both parties can get past blaming the other person for their own emotional issues. The power exchange is probably strongly built around either a parent/child relationship or a 1950s-style marriage.

Pluto in Leo/M

Pluto in Leo created what was sarcastically referred to as the "Me Generation", because self-expression is intensely important to these people, although they may "express" in many different ways. Leo here gives people an intense focus on themselves, sometimes to the detriment of others. This can become an obsession with self-improvement in its best form, however. Above all, though, the Pluto in Leo person wants to be told "You are special!" This generation came up with the idea of being "born" a slave or Master by innate personality (which makes you "special"), and with the idea of awards and titles for those roles. For the Leo Pluto M-type, it's important that the relationship makes them feel special; they may not appreciate an s-type who will render service or submission to anyone remotely dominant, and may want those actions to remain "special" for them, unless they can play the part of Royalty who lends their servant as an act of regal generosity to get kudos from their peers. Worship, from outright spiritual adoration to just sincere admiration ("I'm your biggest fan!") warms their hearts. They are either very theatrical in their gestures of mastery, or they would be if they weren't inhibited by inner-planet repressive obstacles, and they dream about it.

Pluto in Leo/s

Even on the s-type side, Leo Plutos want to be seen as special, if only to their M-types (but ideally to a whole community). They tend to prefer a romantic single-focus relationship ("I am your desirable, valuable property, and the only one who can give you this gift of submission with a whole heart") rather than being a depersonalized, interchangeable slave. They respond strongly to acts of pretend-uncontrolled lust from the M-type if they can convince themselves that it proves their uniqueness and desirability, and unless there are more inhibiting aspects in the personal planets, they are quite willing to be theatrical in their gestures of slavery. In fact, the more dramatic the gesture of submission, the better they like it. Their M-types may find that "You're already great at this, but you could be even better!" will have startlingly positive results. It's also very important for them to be able to show off their talents and be complimented for them.

Pluto in Leo in a Composite Chart

The power dynamic has to find room for a mutual admiration society, without both partners competing for the spotlight of attention. Both parties need to make the effort to ensure that the M-type is not starved of worship, nor the s-type of compliments. Both parties may respond well to a structure reminiscent of King/Queen and Consort, where the s-type is also acknowledged to be royalty, just of a lower rank. The couple may have a desire for public acknowledgement of their power dynamic; just make sure this is resolved in an appropriate venue. Strut your stuff at the right club or group rather than walking through the grocery store with a scantily-clad s-type on a leash, tempting as that may be. Since power for both parties lies in self-expression, they need to take the time to research different archetypes of power exchange and create the structure that is unique to them, and then they can talk about it in public.

Pluto in Virgo/M

Virgo is the sign that is associated with health, hygiene, all the laborious scut-work chores of maintaining a household and a good life. It's probable that having power over these areas in the s-type's life is very important to this M-type. Virgo loves details, and while some dominants with Virgo Plutos can be micromanaging (making long and detailed lists of chores and protocols), others simply find it satisfying to use the s-type to make sure that all the details are taken care of. Virgo is the sign of Work, and they are willing to work hard to earn and keep their power, rather than just assuming it will be given to them. "I was a good

Master *today*, and I can only hope to continue to earn that tomorrow," is a very Pluto in Virgo way to look at it.

On the negative side, Virgo is prone to criticism, and having the planet of power there can mean that they use criticism as a weapon to display their power, with incisive and sometimes vicious results. Be careful with this weapon—don't use it in anger or defensiveness, and take care to soften it when using it as a scalpel in everyday events. Virgo is also a reticent sign, and these M-types may find it difficult to be open about everything with their s-type; they may feel more powerful if they can hold their privacy in at least a few areas.

Pluto in Virgo/s

People with Pluto in the sign of details love taking control of the details of a situation. Since details are often the job of the s-type—while the M-type gets to deal with the bigger picture—it can be very satisfying if the M-type trusts them to take care of the details according to the M-type's stated wishes, without micromanaging them. Virgo is also the sign of the quest for perfection, and they're happy to throw themselves into that quest—it's a very intense experience for them. Just remember that perfection is impossible, but excellence is achievable. The M-type needs to be sure that the s-type is not setting their standards unrealistically high.

On the negative side, Pluto in Virgo means that they may use criticism as a weapon when they're frightened or angry at their M-type, or just overly irritated and stressed. Verbal protocols that allow them to bring up any subject, but only in kind, loving, and respectful ways can help with this propensity. Virgo is a reserved sign and values its privacy, so they may have trouble opening up fully to their M-type. They can think of it as just one more thing to work at, and repeat to themselves a mantra about how it is *right and proper* that they reveal themselves.

Pluto in Virgo in a Composite Chart

The composite Pluto shows where your biggest point of power struggle will be—and in Virgo, it will be over the niggling little details of the household—budgeting, remembering to pick up another bottle of shampoo, debating whose job it is to do the dishes or deal with the ugly trash can. It can also lead to power struggles over both partners' physical health; both should try not to use their own or their partner's health as a club to beat them into giving them their own way. On the positive side, when they come to an accord over something like health or maintenance processes, they'll have a wonderful intensity to tap into, and it could become a pleasant mutual obsession.

They may both feel the urge to use lots of rules and protocols to build a cage of control around the s-type, with a lot of details as to what should be done correctly at any time. While that can be a lovely, graceful thing, make sure not to bring on the rules and protocols too fast. Habits take a while to settle in, and take even longer if they are difficult. The usual rule of thumb is not to introduce a new rule or protocol until at least two weeks have gone by since the last one, and if the s-type hasn't got it quite right, wait longer until they do. Pluto here wants to strive for perfection, and perfection isn't possible, so be careful about holding unreasonable standards.

Pluto in Libra/M

In Libra, which is ruled by Venus, the M-type may be very invested in the aesthetic "look" of their s-type—their clothing, hair, perhaps even the way they move. Making them attractive to the M-type's personal standards—whatever those may be—is important to their control needs, and they may never quite feel that they "own" an s-type if they can't alter their aesthetic style. Since Libra also rules marriage in general, dominant Pluto in Libra wants control over commitments—no "until we get tired of each other" agreements. The sooner the s-type is locked in for life, the better.

Since Libra likes things peaceful, calm, and harmonious, using the s-type to control their environment can be a big draw. However, the biggest pitfall of this placement is that Libra's dislike of confrontation and ugly disharmony can discourage the s-type from having a place where they can express their uglier emotions, or bring up unpleasant problems. Pluto here may tempt the M-type to use their power over the s-type's expression to insulate themselves from the thoughts and feelings of the s-type which they dislike or which makes them uncomfortable, and that's the road to an explosion, or a sudden departure. They should make sure that there are times and places where the s-type can express their difficult aspects to the M-type, and see the M-type accepting the worst parts of them with equanimity, and this will foster trust. When it comes to honesty, they need to be careful not to fall into situations where they withhold important information out of unwillingness to endure their s-type's reaction.

Pluto in Libra/s

With Pluto in Venus-ruled Libra, the s-type may be very invested in their dominant controlling their aesthetic "look" — their clothing, hair, perhaps even the way they move. Having the M-type make the s-type attractive to their personal standards — whatever those may be — is important to these s-types' need to feel controlled, and they may never quite feel that they are "owned" if they can't bring themselves to let the M-type alter their aesthetic style. Since Pluto can be just as frustratingly explosive in the opposite direction, no matter how much they consciously or unconsciously want it, they may fall into inner rebellion when it's time to give it over. Since Libra also rules marriage in general, submissive Pluto in Libra wants a commitment, and ideally a socially validated one.

As we've said, Libra likes things peaceful, calm, and harmonious, so using the dominant to control their environment and shield them from outside disharmony can be a big draw. However, the biggest pitfall of this placement is that Libra's dislike of confrontation can make these s-types hesitant to show their less attractive feelings and struggles. They may try to use the rules of the power dynamic to insulate themselves from thoughts and feelings of theirs which they dislike and prefer to believe they don't actually have, but that's not a sustainable situation and sooner or later it will melt down. One of the best rules a dominant can make for them is that they have to let the M-type know when they're having ugly thoughts, even if those thoughts are about the M-type.

Pluto in Libra in a Composite Chart

The composite Pluto is where your greatest power struggles will be concentrated, and in Libra this is the clash between justice and harmony. It's a Libra truth that while both are valuable, sometimes the need for peace stifles fairness, and sometimes justice stirs up conflict. With Pluto here, both partners may go back and forth, one calling for fairness and the other trying to calm things down and create harmony yet again. Libra is also the sign of argument, and they may both find themselves compulsively embracing the opposite perspectives in their arguments on principle, whether or not they necessarily wholly believe in them.

From a power exchange perspective, this Pluto placement is likely to have more arguments about what limits and boundaries are fair than other placements, and possibly more guilt on the part of one or both if desired activities seem too selfish, or unbalanced in some way. The aesthetics of the relationship may take on great importance—how the s-type looks, moves, or presents themselves, and whether the M-type is physically convincing in their role. Focus on what works and not what doesn't "look" like the romantic porn models in your respective heads, and concentrate on the beauty that is already present.

Pluto in Scorpio/M

For the millennial generation, Pluto is in its own sign of Scorpio. This Pluto placement wants power for the sake of being able to experience emotionally intense situations that they wouldn't be able to have otherwise, and they also love getting the chance to dig into someone's head and uncover all their secrets. While we advocate the s-type's transparency anyway just to make these relationships function, it will be a serious draw for the dominant with Pluto in Scorpio. The problem is when they either push too hard and too fast, before trust has been earned—or they want it to be entirely one-way and present an opaque front to the s-type, because impenetrability means power to them.

It's worth it for them to at least be willing to be transparent about their thoughts and feelings about the s-type, the relationship, and any pending situation that is likely to affect either of those. They should save the impenetrable black boxes for personal hobbies, and let the s-type know clearly where the edges are. It's also worth it for them to do the work of earning trust before demanding the emotionally intense gestures of their dreams. Remember also that building trust is an ongoing process, not something you do once and then can knock about at your leisure.

Like Pluto in Cancer. this placement may also be tempted to use subtle manipulation, but their motivation is less about the disharmony of confrontation and more about enjoying the power in underhanded sneakiness. However, it is worth it to keep the authority aboveboard, or at least let the s-type know that this kind of manipulation is on the table, or it can be crazy-making for them.

Pluto in Scorpio/s

It must be said: s-types with this placement like the takedown. They like viscerally feeling the M-type's power, and they may (consciously or unconsciously) test boundaries for the joy of feeling slapped down again. Another Pluto placement might be horrified, but the Scorpio Pluto s-type feels secure when they know that the boundary will be held with implacable commitment that they cannot manipulate—and manipulation is definitely something they will try, because it's their deepest experience of power. It may be best for the M-type to refrain from joining them on that playing field, to emphasize that manipulation is dishonorable, and expect both parties to hold to a policy of honesty-till-it-hurts.

If Pluto is afflicted, this s-type may also secretly want an M-type who can put the brakes on them when their intensity dial has gone over the top and their emotions are out of control; it would behoove them to be honest about that, and about the fact that they may well fight the M-type's attempts with everything they have—at least the first several times—but that they need the M-type not to give up on it too easily. If the M-type is at sea with this, enlisting a therapist to help with tools and tricks may be useful. It's also important for the M-type with this sort of situation to be honest if it's above their pay grade to offer.

This placement has more difficulty than other Pluto placements in opening up and offering transparency, but after their discomfort wears off, they will respect an M-type who determinedly continues to delve into their psyche until all is revealed. They will also respect one who can be a step ahead of them, so it's worth it to study psychology, and to watch them closely. Being under surveillance makes them tingle.

Pluto in Scorpio in the Composite Chart

Scorpio is Pluto's own sign, and it wants to bring everything that is hidden into the light—which requires digging into it with abandon, even when it's scary—and the composite Pluto in this sign means that there will be a high value placed on exploring the dark places of the subconscious. The two of you will be each other's supportive partners in this work, perhaps goading each other to go further and further into the scarier areas of your lives, and face those fears together. You encourage each other in emotional courage. You may also use a lot of the imagery of death and destruction in your relationship, even if only in stylized form.

It's important to remember, however, that you are not each other's therapists, even if you do push each other to deeper understanding and exploration of taboos. The two of you are by definition not going to be objective enough with each other, and paid perspective may be useful as an outside voice, especially if either of you are dealing with trauma or other psychological difficulties. As with the above entries, make the extra effort to keep everything aboveboard and not resort to manipulative ways of gaining power. Pluto in Scorpio can get very good at radical honesty but only if they feel extremely safe; work on making the relationship an emotionally safe space for both parties, no matter what that takes.

Pluto in Sagittarius/M

As we speak, the first batch of Pluto in Sagittarius people are coming into adulthood, and some may well be exploring power exchange. At its best, this is a placement of strong ethics and honesty; at its worst, it is about impulsivity and inconsiderate fanaticism. The M-type with this placement needs to be willing to take it slow, and not enthusiastically push the s-type further than they are ready to go. Just because you are ready to run doesn't mean that enough trust is built up for the s-type to follow. Breathe and give it time.

Power over such areas as religion, education, and morals will have to be carefully discussed; just being an M-type does not guarantee that you are always Right, and this placement shares with Saturn in Sagittarius an intense urge to be seen as Right, not just The One In Charge. Be prepared to prove your morals, and remember that honesty about your flaws should be seen as strong, not weak. M-types with this placement may want full transparency on demand without having to do the work of teasing it out, and their impatience can lead to even more clamming up on the part of the s-type. More positively, they are generally willing to reinvent the relationship as many times as it takes.

As this generation comes into its own, conversations about polyamory and general nonmonogamy in power exchange will become more common, because freedom is power to this Pluto placement. As the M-type, you may feel more powerful when you have more sexual freedom than your s-type, and this needs to be negotiated. Also, since trust is so important to this placement, it's important for the s-type to earn your trust, just as much as you need to earn theirs.

Pluto in Sagittarius/s

Even in someone who feels that they are very much an s-type, there's going to be a certain amount of rebellion with this Pluto placement. It's not done for Scorpio reasons—to test the dominant partner's power and resolve—it's done almost instinctively, as freedom and power are bound up for them. It's crucial that they should give over areas of freedom as they are moved to do so, rather than the M-type demanding or expecting them. This may seem interminably slow to some M-types, but it's important to understand how precious every crumb of freedom relinquished is to them. Show appreciation for each one, and thank them for having that kind of trust in you. Trust is important to all s-types, but it is hugely important to this placement's natives, who want to be able to trust so badly that they may give it away impulsively before they are ready, which leads to more of the aforementioned rebellion. It may be useful to expect and accept their overenthusiasm, place no blame, and simply back up to, "OK, what would make you trust me enough for that? Time? Track record? A specific action?" and work from there.

Sagittarian Pluto s-types may see an M-type's power and worthiness in how often they are Right, and they may hold them to standards impossible for a fallible human being to achieve. Since they have a keen nose for dishonesty, brushing off or covering up mistakes will be less useful than just acknowledging them. Have an honest conversation not just about their errors, but about the s-type's impractical standards.

Pluto in Sagittarius in the Composite Chart

With Pluto here, the subjects you have the most power struggles over will be trust, honesty, and religious faith. On the positive side, the two of you can encourage each other's faith into a state of ecstasy, and you have the potential to develop deep trust in each other through the sharing of Plutonian darknesses. Since a power dynamic rides on trust, work hard at gaining and keeping the levels of trust in this relationship. Remember that anything that builds trust in the relationship is money in the bank, and anything that damages trust is shooting yourselves in the foot. You both tend to get over disappointments with reasonable speed and not sulk about it, even if that's not your personal style. You prefer radical honesty between you — you'd both rather know and be hurt than not know and be comfortable — and you help each other to find the strength to endure the most painful truths. The negative side of Pluto in the sign of religion, however, is fanaticism, so be careful that you don't encourage that in each other as well. A relationship structure with a strong emphasis on teacher/student (or guru/chela) may work well for the two of you.

Pluto in Capricorn/M

The Pluto in Capricorn generation are just children right now, so we haven't had a chance to see what they will look like. However, Capricorn is all about ambition and efficiency, and Pluto here means that climbing to the mountaintop in the face of all odds, and organizing the trip beautifully, is going to feel very crucial to these folks. An M-type with this placement is likely going to feel very strongly about M/s as a *working* partnership rather than a merely romantic or recreational relationship. Capricorn's keyword is "I use", and "How can I use this s-type to further my own goals and ambitions?" will be the question hovering in the back of this M-type's mind.

In this placement, intense Pluto is ruled by law-enforcing Saturn, and discipline becomes a driving force. In some cases, due to the fact that Saturn is also the planet of obstacles, it's the only way for the native to get these obsessive goals met. A strong focus will be placed on discipline for both M-type and s-type, and they may have to be careful not to place so much emphasis on rules, formality, and protocols that the joy is squeezed out of the relationship. On the positive side, the urge to *get things done* may drive the M-type to do some amazing things with the created machine that is their structured relationship.

Pluto in Capricorn/s

While we can't be sure until we see this generation in action, astrological rules suggest that Pluto in Capricorn, for an s-type, will create an intense need to feel useful and not just decorative. They will have a strong love of protocols and disciplines, and may idealize a dominant who is more distant and formal rather than casual. Being part of the M-type's ambitions and goals may feel very valuable to them, but they might also want to surrender power to someone else so that the M-type can direct and push their own frustrated ambitions and help them to rise in their world. The couple may need to work out whose ambitions take priority, and under what circumstances, and how to handle conflict between them. Because Capricorn is the sign of the Father, the s-type may respond strongly to a "father-like" demeanor or relationship structure, whether kind Daddy or strict patriarch, regardless of the gender of the M-type.

Pluto in Capricorn in the Composite Chart

The couple will be intensely drawn to enacting rules, disciplines, and protocols, even if they are not generally drawn to this approach as a whole. A punishment context, or at least a situation where one or both parties are challenged to hard work, may be extremely attractive to them. However, the punishment dynamic will be less about making any kind of improvement in the s-type's behavior and more about just letting the s-type feel the M-type's power on a regular, formal, structured basis. As long as both parties are clear about this and are not trying to justify it for other reasons, and as long as neither party has trauma issues that this will exacerbate, it could work out well.

Having some kind of outward ambition and goals will feed you; don't waste all the energy of your relationship in domestic game-playing. A relationship structure based on a business model, such as CEO/COO or captain/lieutenant may work well for you.

PLUTO IN THE HOUSES

Pluto in the 1st House/M

Any planet in the first house leaks out through your outer self, no matter how hard you try to hide it. This can be an asset for an M-type—it's no effort to come across as intimidating—or a problem, since an s-type who doesn't know you well can assume that you are angrier about something than you actually are. A shy s-type, or one with low self-esteem or who has been damaged by bullying, may have trouble speaking up and being transparent for the Plutonian demeanor—complete with piercing gaze and intimidating body language—of the M-type they are confronting. If the M-type is loud with their Plutonian outbursts (which will depend on the sign of the Pluto in question) it can be even more daunting. For a more fragile s-type at the beginning of a relationship, the M-type may have to learn to speak gently and dial back the overwhelming mien.

Since the first house rules appearances, M-types with this Pluto placement may feel robbed of their power if they cannot have control over the outward appearance of their s-type—clothing, hair, body size, and perhaps the way that the s-type carries themselves and interacts with others, especially when they are in public together. Using the s-type as an accessory for their own presentation (which is probably either intimidating or unusually striking in some way) feels very powerful to them. They may phrase it as "not bringing shame on the house" or perhaps denigrate the s-type's original style, but honestly it's just that this is a serious power-trigger for them, and being aware of one's power-triggers is a useful thing for a dominant person.

Pluto in the 1st House/s

An s-type with a first-house Pluto—the sign of intensity right out there where everyone can see it—has a bit of a handicap when it comes to expressing submission. People tend to accuse you of being ferocious or combative, whether or not you mean to be—it's the intense Pluto energy leaking out. This can mean that even a strong M-type may be taken aback by your attitude, thinking perhaps that your feelings about something are more intense than they actually are. This can cause some M-types to just back down, thinking, "If they feel this strongly about the issue, it isn't worth pushing," or trigger other M-types to jump on you in rage, attempting to forcibly throw down the perceived threat to their authority and obliterate the perceived rebellion, which can surprise and hurt you when you weren't trying to be rebellious. You may be accused of not being a "real" submissive, or of constantly trying to grab control, when it's just that Pluto here "leaks" your most intense emotions out in public, even when you desperately want to play it cool; your M-type needs to understand this. Also, this placement is notorious for wanting extreme styles of dress and body decoration that cause intense reactions in others — no looking plain and modest for you! — and that has to be OK with the M-type, or you have to be willing to go with their favorite extreme style.

Pluto in the 1st House in the Composite Chart

As a couple, you are striking and stand out. This may be due to extreme differences in age or body size between you, or that your dynamic is unusual in the communities you move in, or just that you choose to dress in an unusual and striking way. Since any planet in the first house "leaks" through at least a little no matter how hard you try to dial it back, your power dynamic is clearly visible to others, although you can soften that for occasions when it's not appropriate by channeling the energy into an affectionately benign leader and a cheerful, contented follower.

A first-house Pluto tends to make people suspicious and they constantly scrutinize others for potential ulterior motives. This is no different in the composite; be careful not to mutually incite each other to paranoia, to the point where you hide from everyone in a little fearful world of your own mutual making. The more high-control your power dynamic is, the more seductive this option looks, because fewer people will understand you. In spite of this, try to keep a toehold in some kind of community, because with the intense emotions swirling around your little world, it's important to have some perspective.

Internally, Pluto here will make the relationship into your therapist, in the sense that you will learn a lot about yourselves by dealing with each other ... and much of it will be about the parts of yourselves that you don't want to look at, because they aren't very flattering. Pluto here will transform you both, if you let it. It may be painful, but you'll grow into better people because of it.

Pluto in the 2nd House/M

The second house is the house of your physical resources (your things) and your values. With this placement, the M-type really gets off on thinking of their s-type as their "thing", their possession, but they are also a valued possession the M-type would defend with bared teeth and snarling. They probably already have a lot of possessive feelings around the inanimate objects they own, and it's easy for them to transfer those feelings of "My thing!" to a willing person. They see the s-type as a resource to be used, not just an ornament to hang on the wall. It's also very important to them to have a say in the s-type's values; they may be upset if both partners differ strongly on that, even if it is only differences in areas outside of the relationship, and they may keep hammering at the s-type to change and learn to love what they love.

They may find it either sexually exciting or emotionally comforting (or both) to play at objectifying their s-type, turning them into anything from furniture to pillow to stuffie to cupholder. Some s-types love that and find it satisfying to their submissive urges; for others, it triggers bad things from their past, so the M-type must make sure to find out up front if this is something the s-type can learn to enjoy. On the other hand, woe betide the s-type who breaks one of their inanimate possessions — sparks will fly and mountains will be made out of molehills. They should keep reminding themselves that their live property is more valuable than any of their inert property.

Pluto in the 2nd House/s

S-types with Pluto in the house of possessions and values really love the idea of being someone's most valued possession. It's easy for them to link their own worth to whether they are valued by their partner, and that makes them vulnerable. They need to do their due diligence and not give themselves to someone who isn't willing to make them a prized possession, or thinks that their "thing" status is degrading. Remember that there are many "objects" in the world that people would kill for, risk themselves to steal, defend with their lives, and deeply cherish. That's what this s-type wants to be.

They may find it either sexually exciting or emotionally comforting (or both) to be treated as an actual object, expected to be still and stay in the position they're put in while being used or manipulated without apparent regard for their agency. However, they won't feel safe enough to relax into this fantasy unless they are sure that they have value in the M-type's eyes, and are not just a disposable item.

Pluto in the 2nd House in the Composite Chart

Money, finances, and resources will be the biggest points of argument and power struggle. Pluto in the house of possessions may mean that the M-type wants to possess more of the s-type than the s-type finds comfortable. It can also mean that the s-type strongly resists having their possessions under the ownership of the M-type—they want to keep their things, and become rebellious when that is threatened. Don't try to make that transfer if there are good real-world reasons to keep finances independent; find other physical objects that can be given to the M-type and "allowed for use" by the s-type—for example, all clothing, all food, etc. Since this house has a strong wire into both your self-esteems, the s-type may feel bad about themselves because they can't give up more to the M-type, and the M-type may feel bad about wanting so much and having trouble letting go of those desires. Mutual compassion can help alleviate these private pains.

The two of you may idealize the idea of an Owner/property relationship; just remember that this is a great deal of work and responsibility for the M-type and a great deal of surrender on the part of the s-type. (Neptune placements should be considered before making this sort of transition.) Talk to long-term O/p couples about the reality of their lives before jumping in. It might be better to start with an "owner/pet" sort of relationship first, to see how viable it is.

Pluto in the 3rd House/M

The third house rules the mind and communication, including speaking and writing. With Pluto here, the M-type wishes that they had magic powers of mind control. They are certainly tempted to change the way their s-type thinks, and may be drawn to voice protocols, or even correct their written spelling and writing style. They also want the right to define what important words mean, and would prefer that the s-type adapt to their meaning, regardless of how the s-type has been defining those words. (Usually "words of power", like love, trust, commitment, obedience, etc.) They might also be drawn to learning "command voice", often used in the military and in corporate situations; this is learning the skill of voice tone control to grab attention and add to the audience's willingness to instantly obey.

Written material may form a large part of their "slave training"; however, they should make sure that their s-type can handle large amounts of reading. Having access to their email is a power trigger for them, as is controlling their Internet access and where they are allowed to post. These M-types probably love using the s-type's cell phone as a virtual leash.

Pluto in the 3rd House/s

These s-types love hearing a dominant tone of voice, be it a sharp, firm command or a velvety caressing tone. It makes them weak in the knees, and they have to be careful not to be "rolled" by people who've learned those tricks but haven't earned their trust. On the other hand, angry tones or yelling may actually have the opposite effect, making them dig in their heels and rebel, triggering Pluto's wrath. What they're looking for is confidence, not out-of-control yelling.

They may spend a lot of time reading about power exchange, which puts them in danger of getting caught up in too much fiction and fantasy. Voice protocols hit them where they live; they may love them or hate them, but even if they hate them, you can bet that part of their dislike is how useful those techniques are for changing their heads, whether they like it or not. The same goes for affirmations and mantras; hearing themselves speak the words aloud does something to their heads, so they need to be careful what they agree to. They may fantasize about hypnosis or brainwashing, even if they're frightened of it.

Pluto in the 3rd House in the Composite Chart

The third house Pluto placement means that this relationship will have a profound effect on the way that both partners think, and the ways that you speak publicly in the world. (It may also reverberate out through their words and affect the way that others think.) They will spend a lot of time talking about deeper feelings and ideas that affect the way they function together. They may also have a higher-than-usual rate of miscommunications, or situations where both people understand what was said, but don't like the way in which it was stated, and they can have epic power struggles over whose vocabulary is appropriate.

Pluto here does mean that the M-type has more power than usual to change the way that the s-type thinks, and that's pretty serious. The M-type needs to move very carefully with this and check in frequently. If they get arrogant and play God, they may crash and burn, especially if they are playing with tools like hypnosis or other forms of thought control. This is another situation where transparency on both sides of the slash is probably a good thing.

Pluto in the 4th House/M

This is the house of home and family, and with this placement, keeping control over the home space is crucial. That includes its atmosphere, and an s-type needs to be cognizant of that. If the s-type is in charge of doing chores or keeping your homespace clean and neat, these M-types may be fairly demanding about what constitutes "clean" or "neat", and what methods should be used to get them to that state. It may be useful for the s-type if they can explain that they need a high level of control in their home in order to feel safe. They'll probably also want to own the home, and may be more territorial about the kitchen than many M-type stereotypes.

Since the fourth house is also ethnic heritage, they may demand that their s-types integrate themselves into that heritage, possibly at the expense of their own. This may include religion — not for its faith, but for its cultural and social value — or just doing the little home customs the way that their parents did. These M-types should talk this through before insisting that only their tribal customs will enter their house.

Pluto in the house of family often indicates a childhood where the parenting wasn't all that healthy and the child did not get the nurturing they needed. This can be a problem for an M-type whose wounds have made them shut down, or be unable to take full power because of fear of rejection. One of the best things they can do for themselves is to figure out ways that their s-types can express support that makes them feel loved and safe, and which don't set off any personal triggers. They can remind themselves that they are in control of it, they can change their expression of it whenever they want, and start and stop it at will. This can help them on a life quest to learn healthy interdependence and independence.

Pluto in the 4th House/s

Pluto in the house of home and family, as mentioned above, often indicates a painful childhood where these s-types didn't get their nurturing needs met. This can create a lot of problems and vulnerabilities for anyone, but an s-type may yield to the temptation to give themself to M-types who replay those childhood patterns (perhaps by being emotionally unavailable or too critical), or they may desire a relationship where they can live in the childhood utopia they didn't get. The problem with this is that Pluto won't stand for it long (being as the point is to get yourself to a healthier place with it) and no parental dominant is ever quite good enough. This doesn't mean that you can't have a parent/child relationship with your dominant; it just means that it needs to be carefully negotiated and extremely mindful, and it also needs to be a tool that helps you to heal those childhood wounds rather than becoming a way to avoid them, because resorting to the latter crutch will cause it all to go sideways.

Household chores are a very intense issue for them, and they may either use them as a way to avoid your issues when they're feeling bad, or rebel against them. Either way is problematic. A good mantra for them would be, "This is a kinder home than the one I grew up in, and it deserves to be clean and beautiful."

They may get off on play that involves their cultural heritage in some way, whether respectfully or disrespectfully, and they may have an intense love/hate relationship with play that consciously and deliberately repeats your family patterns. Just make sure that it remains "play", and doesn't leak into day-to-day life in a way that causes projections of that early pain.

Pluto in the 4th House in a Composite Chart

Be prepared for your power exchange to unearth a wealth of old issues from the past for both partners. It's not uncommon for power exchange to bring up childhood baggage, because our first experience of human interaction is in a power dynamic, and a particularly unequal one at that. Either partner may find themselves triggered, and possibly both at once. If they want to make this relationship work, doing separate therapy work to deal with childhood issues may be necessary; in fact, it's probably why the Universe brought them together in the first place. They should be careful about keeping secrets from each other and turning the home into a place of enforced, dangerous quiet.

Living together will seem crucially important, but they may find that they have fewer arguments when they live apart and have their own home space. It's certain that there will be arguments over how the house looks and how the household chores are done, if only silent ones happening in the s-type's mind. The M-type may want the privilege of invading the s-type's room on demand; the s-type may feel a need to keep a calm, private space with a closed door for longer than the M-type is comfortable with. On the positive side, you will see each other as family, and be doggedly loyal for that reason.

Pluto in the 5th House/M

This is the house of romance, and people with Pluto here don't have light, playful affairs. They fall hard and become obsessed. As the M-type with this placement, it's crucial to them that their partner is as romantically obsessed with them as they are with the partner (or even more so). They see gestures of control (or submission to control) as romantic, and may choreograph the way the s-type is allowed to show them love and affection. This obsessiveness doesn't guarantee monogamy, though, and since they don't do casual, it's best for them to be up front about how they intend to manage their love life, and perhaps gain some skills and wisdom about effectively handling those areas.

This is also the house of children, and these M-types tend to be controlling with them, too—possibly even with ones that aren't theirs but come in with the s-type. Children aren't consenting property, though, so they need to unclench their fists on stepchildren and focus it on their willing s-type instead. For their own children, they need to be consciously aware of the difference between disciplining a child who will grow up and out of their reach, and a consenting adult.

Since this is also the house of creativity, they may want to control their s-type's creative work. This can be great if the s-type is looking for a coach to encourage them, and the M-type knows enough about it to be effective, or it can crush the s-type's creative urges. As the house of fun and playfulness, they may want to control how the s-type has fun, which is also something to be cautious and communicative about. Finally, as this is the house of gambling, the M-type may not feel like they "own" the s-type unless they can risk them in some way; be very, very careful with this one. Trust is a beautiful gift and risking that is counterproductive.

Pluto in the 5th House/s

With Pluto in the house of fun and risk-taking, it's possible that these s-types have already deliberately taken some risks in the area of recreational activities (which can be anything from ski jumps to drugs to promiscuous sex) for the sake of the thrill, or in search of deeper and more intense emotional experiences. However, if the s-type is looking to put themselves under the control of a (hopefully trustworthy) M-type, those risk-taking behaviors may no longer be on the table. Unless they choose an M-type who likes to take the same risks and can supervise the s-type through them, the s-type may have to submit to the M-type's judgment on whether they should be taking these risks at all. The s-type may actually desire, on some level, the M-type who will take control of that and tell them where they're allowed to have risky fun; just make sure to find an M-type with good judgment who can set limits on potentially self-destructive behaviors while still being sensitive to the s-type's need for creative projects and "special interests" to obsess on. If they can channel the partying urge into something more productive and lasting, all the better.

This is the house of romance and falling in love, and also of children, and it may feel very important to these s-types that the M-type can get a handle on where the s-type is allowed to give their heart (especially if they are polyamorous), and has a say in how children are raised. The latter issue, though, may take some power struggles to settle, and it's all right to keep that out of the power dynamic until those are worked out, especially if the M-type is a stepparent who has not dealt with children before. This is also the world of creativity, and the s-type may feel that they are more productive with someone to push them through creative projects, or encourage them to branch out into new areas.

Pluto in the 5th House in the Composite Chart

In the mutual house of romantic passion, this placement can create amazing, fiery romantic passion complete with declarations of possessiveness and foreverness (of the sort that lasts until you are dead and buried) or jealous, obsessive, clingy passion (of the sort that ends in restraining orders). It's likely that your relationship will have some of both; be aware of the tendency to go overboard and ride the line between exciting love and exciting rage.

This is the house of risks, so when you risk together, you do it on a huge, explosive scale. It's also the house of creativity, and Pluto here gives you both a penchant for darker and more dangerous "arts". If you do BDSM, you may revel in edgeplay; if you don't, you'll find other risk-taking activities to engage in together. Just be vigilant for Bad Idea Bear and his various friends, and don't become adrenaline junkies.

Traditionally Pluto in the fifth house was a bad indication for children, as it predicted endless angry power struggles with them; in a power dynamic, there may be disagreements over whether the s-type's parenting decisions can be overridden by the M-type at their whim, especially if the children are not the M-type's biological or legal offspring. Remember that children are sensitive to power dynamics and can use them to play one parent off the other; make sure that you have a united front emotionally, or they'll know.

Pluto in the 6th House/M

This is a dominant for whom service is a Big Deal. It may well be their love language, and they hold s-types to a high standard because they feel so intensely about it. Anticipatory service can be very important to them; either they eat it up with a spoon and demand more, or they've been burned by s-types who couldn't pull it off and they pretend that it's impossible to get, while still secretly desiring it. Keep in mind that anticipatory service takes time to learn, and possibly requires some training in problem-solving. With this placement, the M-types will want an s-type who is heavily service-oriented, or they may be continually disappointed (or try to force them into a service role that does not resonate for them). Chores and household maintenance are hugely important to them, and they want them done in a very specific way. An s-type who can't manage this may be seen as inadequate.

This is the house of health, and these M-types probably have either serious health issues or serious ideas about health, or both. Taking control of the s-type's medical care and health disciplines is emotionally important to them, especially if they think the s-type could be doing better at it. Power struggles may erupt over their own health issues, with them not wanting to be told what to do by doctors and their partners being honestly frightened for their continued health. Remember that being someone's s-type is a vulnerable situation, and the spectre of their dominant partner becoming ill due to personal neglect is deeply disturbing. On the other hand, they may also have a (possibly extreme) health and/or diet regimen that works for them, and which they want to foist onto their s-type, for whom it may or may not be right. Get outside advice and perspective before going ahead with this plan.

Pluto in the 6th House/s

Service is hugely important to these s-types. Being told that they are useful or resourceful is a huge compliment; seeing their M-type's life be made visibly easier or more pleasant by the services they offer makes them feel better about themselves. While single, they may go back and forth between giving away service to people who may well take advantage of them because they identify as "the helpful helper", and rejecting people for not being worthy of their service. This is an example of the intense Plutonian all-or-nothing; they have high standards for their own service (which may sometimes include a standard of sacrificial generosity) and high standards for leaders who help themselves to it (which can make the s-type rebel if the leader can't live up to those standards). The right M-type for them will set those boundaries so they don't have to swing back and forth. However, the intensity with which they hold their standards of service might mean that they find it difficult to accept the M-type's standards, which can cause arguments.

Since this is the house of health, it's not uncommon for s-types with this placement to want their M-type to create a health regime for them, and hold them to it in the face of their own waffling. Conversely, they may overreact when an M-type pokes a toe into having authority over medical decisions, until that M-type has proved themselves worthy. The s-type will probably scrutinize the M-type for how they handle their own health, as part of determining that worthiness.

The sixth house, like the twelfth, is also associated to a certain extent with monasticism, or at least the spiritual aspect of service, and s-types with this placement may respond devoutly to the concept of spiritualizing their path of service.

Pluto in the 6th house in the Composite Chart

This is traditionally a classic indicator for a boss/employee relationship where two people work together at a job (regardless of whether they are in a personal relationship or not). Astrology books warn that if this happens, one person may end up with all the power. For our purposes, this indicates that both partners may see the M/s as a job as well as a personal relationship, and/or that they may actually work together as boss and employee.

This is the house of scut-work and maintenance, and power struggles — or at least very intense feelings — may erupt over how ordinary chores are to be done (housework, cooking, changing the oil in the car, etc.) and what the "proper" way to do them might be. Little details around how they are done (and how competently they are done) may become huge Plutonian issues, and may come to reflect the relationship commitment itself. The M-type may need to take extra care to explain chore procedures in detail, perhaps writing them down in a manual that the s-type can refer to. The s-type needs to learn and focus on the M-type's priorities around chores, even if they don't agree with them. On the positive side, this placement gives a strong need to Get Things Done, and it makes both partners very productive together. However, they need to put time aside for personal interaction and not focus only on work, or they will end up reverting to boss/employee in truth.

As the house of health, they may come to power struggles over whether the M-type has authority over the s-type's medical care and decisions. This is also the house of mentors, and this placement may give a sense of mentor/mentee to the relationship.

Pluto in the 7th House/M

This is the House of Marriage — or more specifically, the house of one-on-one partnerships. Pluto here means that the M-type wants a companion, and preferably a spouse, whom they can control. This includes control over both relationship decisions (such as monogamy vs. polyamory, and/or whether they will get legally married) and how they will come across as a couple together.

On a higher level, astrology traditionally sees this placement as a karmic deal that for this lifetime, one agrees to allow one's greatest transformative experiences to come through one's partners. One of the stereotypes of fictional Master/slave relationships is that the M-type transforms the s-type, but the reverse doesn't happen; the M-type remains personally untouched and that is visibly part of their power. The M-type with this placement has to throw out that limited and inaccurate idea, because having an s-type in their life will be an intense and powerfully transformative experience for them. It will change them, no question, but they've still got their masterly will, and they can decide whether those changes will be for the better or for worse. They need to ask themself whether they will allow the experience of having someone at their beck and call to make them lazy, or complacent, or selfish, or unwilling to do hard internal work on themself — or whether they will allow it to transform themself into someone who is more honorable, competent, and compassionate?

This placement is notorious for being suspicious and controlling relationships. Under it all, this is because they know, instinctively, the intense power that any close relationship has to change them, and they see that as vulnerability. It's important for an M-type with this placement to see being moved to change by the presence of a willing subordinate as a tool that can be deliberately used for personal transformation, if they're conscious and aware. Otherwise, there will never be enough control to satisfy their insecurities. Once they've moved past that fear, they can relax into leadership that is clean of those ulterior motives, and be better able to take the s-type's reality into consideration.

Pluto in the 7th House/s

As noted above, having Pluto in the seventh house of marriage means that these individuals will be transformed by the close partnerships in their life. In fact, they've probably already been transformed by some of them, possibly not in a good way. The s-type with this placement yearns for a power dynamic as the most intense possible relationship, and simultaneously rebels against it, because they know that partnerships get deeply under their skin.

Relationship structure is a hugely sensitive area for these people, and they may not be able to submit in other areas of their life unless they get a lifetime guarantee from the M-type that the basic structure of the relationship (especially such contexts as monogamy vs. polyamory, or how the partnership looks to the outside world) is set in stone and will not change. This can become a definite problem if the M-type finds, twenty years down the road, that they are seriously interested in changing the deal.

S-types with this placement may also suffer from jealousy and resentment even if their M-type is monogamous, if they perceive that nonsexual play-partners or even platonic friends are given titles or privileges that they perceive as being the sole right of the primary life partner. This can be as trivial as who the M-type is seen with regularly in their recreational life. On the other hand, having this placement means that once the M-type is under their skin, the M-type has a more effective ability to change them — and their minds. They need to do their due diligence and make sure that any potential partner has a world view that is at least as healthy as their own, and ideally more so, because no matter how hard they fight, they are very much at risk of absorbing it.

Pluto in the 7th House in a Composite Chart

These two people came together, whether they know it or not, to transform each other through their relationship. This will be an extremely intense relationship; they will either strongly bond or blow up. Traditionally, astrologers gave this placement two possible outcomes: either they will work very hard together to evolve and transform enough to make things work, or the relationship will have so many power struggles that it will tear itself apart. Since just instituting a power dynamic does not mean that there will never be power struggles, especially in the early days, having this placement means they must understand that both parties will have to work on evolving themselves. They must both seek to embody the best parts of Pluto: purification of the unnecessary rather than destruction from rage or frustration; intense passion without jealousy or insecurity; power that does not make someone else feel bad about themselves. This will not be easy, and the M-type especially needs to shift their thinking from "this s-type is forcing me to change" or even "this relationship is forcing me to change" to "I choose to change myself because I'll be more effective if I do."

Pluto in the 8th House/M

Pluto in the house of sex, for the M-type, means that power over someone's sexual life is crucially important—and if they don't have that, they don't feel that they have any power in the relationship at all. Having a lock on the genitals, and on the choice of activities, is an absolute deal-breaker for them. In second place of importance is money, as this is the house of other people's money. Just be careful that both of these are done out of joy, and not out of deep-seated fear of being cheated, or cheated on. Taking control of an s-type's money is not something that should be done quickly; give them months or even years to feel comfortable with that. There's also the issue that if the relationship falls apart in the first couple of years, the s-type should be able to leave and support themselves.

People with this placement are all fascinated with Death, and anything that brings one close to it. While having life-or-death power over an s-type is not something that is high on the initial list for most M-types, the ones with Pluto here have probably brooded over that before they figured out how they wanted a potential slave to address them. This fascination doesn't mean that they are any more likely to harm their s-types; it may come across simply as "You aren't allowed to kill yourself, or do dangerous self-harming behaviors. I take that decision from you."

Pluto here can also mean, for some of these M-types, that taking power can become a spiritual act for them. Looking into writings about positive spiritual leadership may be worth doing. This is also the house of transformation, and they may have a desire to "Pygmalion" their s-type, to transform them into something else that they have designed. If the s-type is fine with that, the M-type can go ahead, but they must remember that this is a human being who had decades of programming before they came along. The M-type must not become upset if that programming is more resistant than they expected; this person is not a blank slate and cutting off parts of their psyche is not the way to change. Instead, the real work of transformation is to shift each part of the mind into a healthy mode and integrate everything.

Pluto in the 8th House/s

As we've mentioned with the M-types, people with this placement are fascinated by Death and all its trappings. This can sometimes create an s-type who is torn between the thrill of a dominant partner who can threaten their existence convincingly enough to allow them to imagine that they are actually flirting with oblivion, and on the other hand someone who will value and care for them. As you can imagine, this can go quite badly if they let the fascination run away with them. The perfect balance between loving dominant and sexy killer is hard to get right, but they will keep trying.

This placement can create an s-type who instinctively struggles for power, sometimes, just to feel their partner's strength when they clamp down. Hypnosis may be particularly alluring for its combination of helplessness and transformative potential.

If the fascination isn't with Death itself, it may be a search for the dominant partner who will transform them in ways that they haven't been able to do themselves. M-types who have a "savior streak" are particularly vulnerable to this, and should resist the temptation unless they are absolutely sure it is not above their pay grade, and possibly even then. Pluto is power, and sometimes it's better to lead a follower into developing the power to change themselves than simply manipulating them into changing. In addition, it may take a while for these s-types to be willing to give up control over their money, if they ever do; it would behoove the M-type not to push this point or they may face a defensive explosion from their partner.

Pluto in the 8th House in a Composite Chart

This is the house of sex, and having the planet of intensity and transformation here indicates that the sex will be very dark and intense — perhaps running to physical and emotional edgeplay — and that it will be the best vehicle for changing how each of you think. While some power dynamic relationships have good luck in using BDSM to release negative emotions between the M-type and s-type, many find it to be ineffective. You two, however, have a very good chance of finding this technique quite effective. Make sure that the emotions and the intent is stated clearly and honestly beforehand. You will probably also have a good deal of success in using dark sexuality to unearth and purify old wounds and repressive patterns around sex and intimacy.

It may feel very important to both parties in this relationship that the M-type has very significant power over both the s-type's sexuality and the s-type's money, and there may be some struggles over money or resources that the s-type shares with others outside the relationship. This may include control over the s-type's stepchildren or child support from a former marriage, if the M-type unconsciously sees either of those as objects or resources. This is also the House of Death; control over whether the s-type can take their own life, and under what circumstances, may also come up. While every power exchange couple or family should make arrangements for the s-type should the M-type predecease them, the s-type in this relationship may find this crucially necessary for them to feel secure.

Pluto in the 9th House/M

Traditional wisdom has it that the worst trait this placement can cause is some sort of religious fanaticism. Modern astrologers shift that over to fanaticism, period; the person with Pluto in the ninth house can make a sort of religion out of their conglomeration of beliefs, regardless of whether they see it as one. The ninth house is associated with Sagittarius, and one of the faults of that sign is that it wants to be Right. When a loved one disagrees with their world view and ideas, it can be seen as a kind of mutiny, to be put down at any cost. The worst of these individuals are not above vengeance aimed at anyone who questions the correctness of their doctrines.

One can already see how this might play out with a dominant partner. The M-type with this placement not only needs to work on accepting disagreements with maturity, they should also take care to look for an s-type whose beliefs are already congruent with their own, because shifting those beliefs at a later date may become a deal-breaking power struggle. This may include formal religious faith (ruled by the ninth house), or just general philosophy and world view. If the s-type turns out to differ strongly on these points, the M-type may never quite feel like they are in charge. Sending the s-type back to school to educate them (or re-educate them) may also please this M-type. Since this is the house of travel, they may see the willingness to pack up and move with them without complaint as a measure of loyalty and commitment.

On the positive side, Pluto here inspires an insatiable desire to Know, and these M-types will usually be willing to pursue their own education in how to manage a power dynamic skillfully. While they may have some set ideas and values, they are able to see where they lack specific skills, and willingly turn to books or classes on the subject. When they've gone further down the path (and when they've learned to be more tolerant of disagreement), they make good mentors for new potential M-types, as well as excellent "teacher-masters" for s-types who are looking for a "disciple" role.

Pluto in the 9th House/s

Just because someone desires a submissive relationship role doesn't mean that they won't have strong opinions about how the world works, and how things should be made to happen. S-types with Pluto in this house will not easily give up their ideas just because a dominant partner informs them that they are wrong, and such insistence is likely lead to a serious power struggle. Their best bet is to find a partner who already shares their world view, especially their religious beliefs (including not believing in religion, if this applies). Actually, their ideal would be to find someone who has the same views, but is more advanced in understanding than they are, so that they can be a wholehearted disciple. They may not feel able to fully surrender to someone whose ideas are too divergent from their own.

If they have a college degree, they may base a fair amount of their self-esteem on their training or academic background, and may balk at surrendering to an M-type who dropped out of high school and became a truck driver. They would secretly prefer to be out-educated by their dominant partner, and if the M-type can wrestle them into going back to some kind of school or new training, it's proof of real submission.

Their love of knowledge may drive them to collect books and seek out classes in power exchange, which they may prod their dominant partner to read or attend. Travel is important to them, and they may fight if they aren't allowed to take the occasional road trip, with or without the partner.

Pluto in the 9th House in a Composite Chart

With this placement, the biggest power struggles will be over who is more morally "Right", and whose worldview is more correct. At worst, both partners want to beat the other person over the head with their own personal ideals and hope that the head-beating will get it through their skull and cause them to absorb it. In real life, of course, this rarely works, even when the M-type does it to the s-type. Clashing moral values may become a huge issue. While power dynamic relationships generally require a higher level of initial compatibility than egalitarian ones, this is exceptionally true for the two of you, especially around your ideals, values, and how you believe the world works. If you are still in the early negotiating stage, figure out how different your values are before you go too much further.

Religious beliefs and practices may become an area of power struggle, as can higher education (whether it matters, and whether to get more of it) and travel, especially traveling alone. Consciously or unconsciously, the s-type in this relationship wants the M-type to be knowledgeable enough to trust with all those questions of values and world view, but the M-type is going to have to prove themselves worthy by the s-type's standards before that trust will be given over.

One issue with this placement is that both parties may spend more time finding outside information to prop up their views than actually looking at what works uniquely for the two of them. While getting outside education can be quite helpful, the end goal is to thoughtfully decide together whether it has any relevance to your own situation, and this point may often be missed. Spend some time actually looking internally instead of fixating only on externally derived rules.

Pluto in the 10th House/M

Having the planet of obsession in the house of career and public life can create a workaholic, or at least someone to whom their career is their lifeblood, and being seen and respected in that career is dearer to them than love or money. Traditionally, it's also said to indicate someone who is a serious control freak (I've always preferred the term "control enthusiast" instead, frankly), wants to oversee everything, and is often sorely tempted to fill any power vacuum in range. Sometimes they are not above creating power vacuums if there isn't one laying around to fill, which can be problematic with the billions of people who didn't consent to be their subordinates.

This means that the M-type with this placement who doesn't have a satisfying career into which to throw themselves may vent all the control urges that would ideally be spread throughout a company staff onto their hapless s-type. This can be a saving grace or crazy-making, depending on how honest both parties manage to be. Perhaps the most effective heart-gift a devoted s-type can give a dominant tenth-house Pluto partner with thwarted ambitions is their services in helping them to achieve better career options.

Controlling the s-type's career — and particularly their public image around that career, or lack of it — may be extremely important to this M-type's feelings of control and being in charge. This can range from pushing the s-type into a better and higher-paying career, encouraging them all the while, or it can be a demand to quit all work and stay home to be a house servant. They may feel much less in charge if those career decisions are out of their hands, especially if the s-type's career affects the M-type's life goals.

Pluto in the 10th House/s

The planet of power struggle in the house of career means that this bastion of independence may be the last area of authority given over to a dominant partner, if these s-types ever agree to that. Their careers are very important to them and their sense of identity, and unless they are snapped up straight out of high school, they are probably already ensconced in a profession and aren't generally willing to give it up to stay home, or wreck it to make the M-type's life more convenient. An intelligent M-type whose subordinate has this placement will let them have their head when it comes to their vocation, and consider it part of their mental health. If they agree to stay home and give up earning money, power struggles over hundreds of small issues will proliferate. Like a working dog who chews up the couch when it can't go out and herd the sheep, these s-types need meaningful outside work and a powerful public persona, even if they submit at home.

Since this is also the house of public life, the s-type with this placement will likely rebel against visible markings, or enforced public behaviors that violate their career persona. If the M-type wants them to be very public about the dynamic and the s-type feels that it will threaten their job, a giant power struggle may ensue. On the other hand, if their chosen vocation is their kink life, they will want a fair amount of public visibility in their local communities, and may be involved with running events and creating organizations.

Pluto in the 10th House in a Composite Chart

For this couple, having a strong practical objective is key to working out power struggles. The best objective, in this house of career and public image, is one that allows them to do community work together, being seen to make progress for others. While most composite Pluto placements are all about the private dance of power between two people, this placement by its very nature weaves the couple into the eyes of their community. Your power exchange will do better when ensconced in a situation where you can set goals together and help each other to achieve them, preferably where others can see and admire the work.

As you might expect, the careers of both people loom large with this placement. Power struggles may ensue over the s-type's career, including whether the M-type should have a say in it, or whether the s-type should have one at all. The M-type's career may also cause waves if it hinders the power dynamic; no matter how lucrative and important it is, if it requires an amount of stealth that affects the s-type's peace of mind in their role, fireworks will erupt. The M-type should take care to notice how their career affects or supports the relationship, and keep this in mind when making career changes or accepting promotions. The image the two of you present to your communit(ies) may be an issue as well; remember that in the long run, authenticity is better than secrecy and closets.

Pluto in the 11th House/M

This is the house of friends and groups, and someone with this placement is going to have extremely intense feelings about their community. As an M-type, it will be important to them to bring their s-type into their circle of friends, and their community if there is one. Ideally, they would prefer it if their friends became the s-type's close friends as well, although hopefully they will be evolved enough not to attempt to cut off the s-type from their own friends.

Pluto's not only power, it's also power struggle, so while the M-type with this placement will be grit-their-teeth loyal to their friends and tribe/community, Pluto will also bring drama into their lives in that direction. This might mean periodic blowups, walkouts, and/or breaking up and making up again with those friends and tribes; a wise s-type will be patient through the repeated process. It's also wise to work hard to become not only the M-type's lover and/or servant, but their best friend as well, if at all possible. That may give the s-type more "job security" than even being lover, spouse, or slave.

This house is also associated with one's long-term political and social goals, so finding an s-type whose political views are congruent with theirs is crucial. If the s-type is too politically different, it will be hard for this M-type to keep from constantly trying to control and change their minds on the subject.

Pluto in the 11th House/s

It's highly likely that this s-type will come with a wide variety of friends, ex-lovers who are still friends, temporarily-ex-friends with whom they have a continual combative fight-and-make-up relationship, interest groups, hangout groups, and support groups ... all of whom they will fight tooth and nail to keep in their lives. A wise M-type will not get into a power struggle over this tribe, even if they seem to occasionally take a higher priority than the M-type in the early days. The M-type should remind themselves that as soon as they have won the position of Best Friend In The World, they'll be at the top of that priority list.

It's also possible that the s-type with this placement has recently endured an explosive breakup with drama-ridden friends and groups, and is currently swearing that they will become a hermit. The best gift that the M-type can give to heal these wounds is to bring the bitter s-type into a group of loyal, down-to-earth, and caring friends, or a sane and positive support or interest group. On some level, the s-type may both want their authority figure to help vet stable and well-balanced friends, and at the same time hate the very idea of anyone interfering. It's a tricky balance.

This s-type probably also comes with political and social-justice ideas and opinions that they will fight tooth and nail to keep, and this can become an area of power struggle if the M-type has serious differences. It's best to have those out on the table on the first date or email, in order to evaluate initial compatibility.

Pluto in the 11th House in a Composite Chart

This is the house of friends and groups, and power struggles may erupt over whether the s-type gets to keep all their friends, spend lots of time on social media, or belong to political or interest groups that take the s-type's time away from the M-type. The friends you attract as a couple may be intense, dark, Plutonian types who fascinate and frighten you by turns. Be careful about getting into relationships with friends who insist on secrecy and isolation, and aren't honest about their motives. Be careful about groups who ask the same of you.

Like couples with a tenth-house composite Pluto, being part of a community may be wonderful for your ongoing power exchange, but in your case it's not about mutual goals but peer support. Getting peer support for your roles and their difficulties, both separate and together, can help iron out a lot of problems for you. If you do ensconce yourselves in a community, you will be doggedly loyal to them, and willing to put yourselves in difficult situations on behalf of your chosen family.

Having goals is also important for couples with this placement, but rather than practical goals, they should be humanitarian ones. How do you think the world ought to change? Work on that together. Doing political or social or environmental work together can be a bonding activity.

Pluto in the 12th House/M

Most of the astrologers I know agree that this is the most difficult and dangerous placement for Pluto, because it puts the planet of intensity and obsession in the house of the unconscious. Many people with Pluto here only have two types of strong emotions: the ones that are consciously repressed and the ones that are unconsciously repressed. The most repressed of all, of course, will be anger … until it suddenly explodes and blows everything up. People with this placement who have not worked tirelessly at self-awareness are notorious for shoving it down until it detonates, and then wonder what happened. For the dominant partner in the equation, this can be a dangerous quality. It's crucially important that they work at mastering themself before they go on to attempt the mastery of another ... and that they understand that simple repression is not mastery. The emotions need to be perceived, understood, accepted, and vented in a safe place that is not a vulnerable s-type.

On the other hand, these people also want to know everything that goes on in their partner's head, even as they are unwilling to share their own internal thoughts and processes. For an M-type with this placement, it's not only about learning the inside of their s-type's head, it's about wanting to use that knowledge to make changes. The s-type may be alternately flattered by their intense attention, confused by their constant interrogation, and disheartened by their refusal to show any intimate parts of themselves. Ideally the s-type could eventually earn the position of "safe space" where the repressed M-type could learn to open up and explore their feelings, but that would require both reasonable and achievable standards for earning that place, and patience and understanding from the s-type.

Pluto in the 12th House/s

Start with reading the description of the 12th house Pluto in the last entry, and then imagine how hard it is for an s-type to be living on top of that hidden volcano. Transparency will be extremely difficult for them, especially since they may be so used to hiding their intense emotions that they have forgotten what they are. All s-types are vulnerable to the early-stage temptation of hiding their negative feelings (including anger or irritation at the M-type) in order to pretend to be the "perfect slave", but usually they get over it in time, when the M-type earns their trust and shows the ability to handle their emotions. However, s-types with this placement need ten times the trust in order to reveal their consciously repressed emotions, and quite possibly outside help to get to their unconsciously repressed ones.

Transparency in these cases is possible, but it needs to be pushed for gently and patiently. When the s-type manages to reveal something — especially a negative feeling toward the M-type — it is extra important to praise them for doing so, even if the M-type is somewhat discomfited by it. (It's also good to emphasize how much this crumb of information helps the M-type to do their job better.) Continual positive reinforcement for honesty and self-awareness is the best way to go; a defensive reaction will just force them to swallow it again, and perhaps wish they had never spoken up. Pushing too hard will result in that explosive volcano erupting.

On top of this, the M-type needs to be careful with the information they are so painfully given. Using it to make major changes in the s-type's behavior should be handled gently, and with the s-type's full collusion and agreement. If they feel that their dug-up feelings have been used against them in a manipulative way, they will strike out and close up. Pluto guards those intimate feelings, and will not sell them cheaply.

Pluto in the 12th House in a Composite Chart

The house of the subconscious is a rough place to have explosive Pluto, because this placement can encourage both of you to repress your strong emotions, only to have them explode at some point further down the line. While this is bad enough in the M-type—exploding pent-up rage can terrify a vulnerable s-type—it's even worse when the s-type does it. Refusing to communicate strong and possible "unacceptable" feelings, perhaps out of fear of rejection or wanting to look like the "perfect slave", sabotages the M-type's ability to manage the situation. Regular honest communication is not only a good idea for the two of you, it's necessary for the relationship to survive. Transparency will also be crucial. In most cases, the s-type is required to be transparent while the M-type promises at least to be open about relevant subjects, but in the case of this composite placement, both parties should work toward full transparency with each other, if only to combat the constant urge to repress and hide anything painful or uncomfortable.

Of course, once you begin to resist the repression, this placement will uncover all the dark places within each of you. This is a relationship that will clean out and purify all the parts of both individuals that have been rotting in the psychic basement, and it needs to be accepted as such. Refusing to go along with Pluto's direction will just destroy the relationship, in time. Both should be willing to be open to sometimes painful purification.

Power struggles may erupt over whether one or both parties needs or should get or continue therapy, whether one or both should follow a personal spiritual path (and if so, what it should be), and what each of you believes your innermost weaknesses to be. Since this is the "house of confinement", one or both parties may desire to keep the s-type closely confined and isolated; be sure that this is a good idea before trying it, and make certain that some kind of trusted outside support makes regular contact with both of you, separately and together. If you haven't got anyone you both trust, make finding them a mission to attempt together.

Pluto in the Transposed Houses

When you take two people's charts and lay them one over the other, you'll see that one person's planets fall into the other person's houses, and vice versa. This makes Person A's planet light up Person B's house in the way specific to that planet, whenever the two people are together and interacting.

For example, my Pluto is in my natal second house, but it falls into my slaveboy's fifth house of romance and falling in love. He'd had relationships before he met me, but he was not prepared for the intense longing he felt when beginning a relationship with me. He thought of it as falling in love on steroids; I knew that it was just my Pluto lighting up that house for him. While we'd intended for him to be a service-only relationship, him falling madly in love with me ended up being a source of power over him that I hadn't anticipated. On the other side, his Pluto falls into my third house of communication, and while I'd been intermittently an author, teacher and speaker in the past, that career of mine took off like a rocket after he came into my life, in large part because his service enabled it to be so.

That's what you'll look for next. Check the sign and degree of the M-type's Pluto and see where it falls in the s-type's chart. That's a serious source of power over the s-type, but it should not be used without care and respect, nor should its complete withdrawal be used as a punishment. It's too "heavy" an area for that. Instead, use it as positive reinforcement when the s-type does something right, or is feeling in need of support.

Now check the s-type's Pluto—sign and degree—and see where it falls in the M-type's chart. This will be a place where the s-type's service—or in some cases, their mere presence—can have hugely positive effect on that area of the M-type's life, perhaps making it explode and take off like my teaching career.

We've been sporadically referring to the house indications throughout this chapter, but here's a quick reference list of them to use now and when you need to check other planets in transposed houses, or anything else to do with astrological houses in general.

1: Physical body, outward appearance, style and demeanor, how one walks and moves.

2: Finances, movable property, possessions, values in general.

3: Communication, reading, writing, speaking, computers and phones and the Internet. Short trips, local transit, elementary education, brothers and sisters, and the neighborhood.

4: Home (early and current), family (of origin and chosen), ancestry, inherited patterns of childhood for better or worse.

5: Romance, children, play, fun activities, creativity, art, gambling, self-expression.

6: Service, maintenance, scut-work in general, jobs that pay the bills, actually paying the bills, cleaning, hard labor, health and its necessities, and mentoring others.

7: Long-term partnerships, both of marriage and of business. Long-term enemies that you know about.

8: Sex, death, taxes, deep emotional bonding, psychic powers, the Deeper Mysteries, karma, inheritances and other people's money (given, lent, or owed).

9: Higher education, group religion, travel, philosophy, mind-expansion of any sort.

10: Career and public life.

11: Friends, interest groups, political groups, long-term goals to change the world.

12: The unconscious, where all one's repressed thoughts lie. Institutions, prison, monasteries, and any sort of confinement, voluntary or involuntary. Private, personal spirituality.

M/Pluto in s/1st House

When the M-type's Pluto falls into the s-type's first house, especially if it is near the Ascendant, the M-type has the strong urge to control the s-type's physical appearance—clothing, hairstyle, weight, body modifications, walk and movements, etc. The s-type may be put on a diet or given an exercise program. It's not unusual for the preferred new style to be more Plutonian in nature—darker, more intense or extreme or primitive in some way. The s-type finds themselves scrutinizing these aspects of themselves and discarding assumptions that are no longer necessary.

s/Pluto in M/1st House

This placement inspires the M-type to think deeply about their demeanor (including their physical appearance and personal decoration) and how it communicates their personal power and dominance. The s-type may have some ideas of their own about how the M-type should look, which may be taken into consideration but should not be adopted by the M-type just because the s-type is attracted to the idea, especially if it does not feel authentic to the M-type.

M/Pluto in s/2nd House

Controlling the s-type's money and possessions will seem very important to the M-type, and the s-type may feel just as intensely about turning them over, for good or ill. A concerted effort may be made to "clean up" the s-type's bad habits around money, budgeting, care of possessions, etc. Seeing the s-type as "property" may be very attractive to both people.

s/Pluto in M/2nd House

The relationship itself, and its circumstances, may push the M-type into the realization that their management of money and/or possessions needs some serious work. Getting that in line can become a significant focus for them. Using the s-type as a tool to help the M-type improve (if appropriate to the s-type's skills) is a better way to handle it than simply allowing the s-type to nag about it.

M/Pluto in s/3rd House

The M-type will have a strong urge to control the s-type's communications, perhaps with voice protocols, or perhaps just training them how to communicate in a respectful way while still being completely honest and open. This is the important part—the M-type's control of information exchange should make it clearer and wider, not block or discourage it. The s-type will be pushed to look at their communication habits and clean out old patterns that are no longer useful.

s/Pluto in M/3rd House

The power dynamic will force the M-type to think deeply about the way they communicate and how that aids or thwarts their effectiveness as the dominant partner. This can include how clear their orders are, or whether it occurs to them to give the s-type enough information about their priorities and preferences, or whether they remember to give verbal kindness and approval. The M-type should not resort to just doing things the s-type's way in the face of strong verbal emotions from that quarter. Instead, the s-type should be directed to render respectful services that help the M-type to improve.

M/Pluto in s/4th House

It will be very important to the M-type that the s-type moves into their home with them as soon as possible. This will not be a relationship that can thrive long distance for any length of time.

The M-type may also want to have control over the s-type's contact with their family, and if the two of them begin a family together, it will feel crucial to the M-type to set the tone and decide how the s-type will act as a family member. Digging into the s-type's past may also be a constant fascination. The s-type will probably be fine with most of this, although they may balk at the unearthing of past patterns. It will be good for them, although outside support may be necessary.

s/Pluto in M/4th House

The power dynamic may drive the M-type to examine their early childhood patterns, and their assumptions about family. Just by being themself, the s-type may trigger a great deal of hidden baggage in their dominant partner regarding their upbringing; if the M-type is willing to work with it, then the power dynamic will function more smoothly. Outside support may be useful for them to work through it all without reacting defensively to their s-type.

M/Pluto in s/5th House

The M-type will prefer to keep control of any children that they have with the s-type, the way that any romantic gestures are performed, and what both parties do for recreation. The s-type's creative activities may also be a target area, possibly with a mandate that the s-type will be diligent in those activities "for their own development". Since this is Pluto in the house of romance, the s-type is likely to swoon fairly heavily, with an intense sexual and romantic attraction for the M-type; they may fall in love very quickly and the fireworks will be easy to bring up again in difficult times.

s/Pluto in M/5th House

The presence of this s-type and this power dynamic will cause the M-type to examine and reevaluate their opinions and assumptions about romance, children, and creativity. This is also the house of risk-taking, and this placement may encourage them to take risks with an s-type who is not as compatible as they might ideally need. If the risk-taking goes south, they will learn a great deal about themselves from it. This placement can cause a huge upwelling of creative fire in the M-type, and/or a blinding romantic flame that should be carefully considered before taking permanent action.

M/Pluto in s/6th House

It may feel important to the M-type to control the s-type's health and medical care. Chore lists and household maintenance will also become a huge and scrutinized issue, with the s-type very invested in getting it done properly. They may find themselves wanting very much to render service to the M-type, especially of the domestic cleaning and organizing variety, even if they are not the most service-oriented person with others.

s/Pluto in M/6th House

This power dynamic will push the M-type to think hard about their health and how they manage it, and also how they render service (if top-down) in the relationship, and possibly to the rest of the world. The s-type may be very interested in the M-type being a mentor to them, teaching them about some way of being, and the M-type may find themself responding strongly to that desire. Chores and household maintenance will be a serious area for discussion, possibly used as a touchstone for how well the relationship is going.

M/Pluto in s/7th House

The M-type will find it important to control the rules around relationship commitments, including whether it will be monogamous or polyamorous. Also on the "serious table" will be how "partnered" both people look in public, and whether they do most things together or spend significant periods of time apart, doing their own thing. The s-type will feel driven to go along with the M-type's preferences on the matter, but it is important that they take a breath and make sure their own preferences are taken into account.

s/Pluto in M/7th House

This relationship will force the M-type to confront all their baggage around relationship commitments and how they ought to be designed — should one bow to cultural mandates or create one's own template? What is "proper" and what is an outdated assumption? What is fair and equitable, and how does that relate to a power dynamic? Whatever they decide, it should be done without feeling pressured by strong emotions on the subject from the s-type.

M/Pluto in s/8th House

With this synastry placement, the M-type will be driven to control the s-type's sex life, their money, and their resources, possibly also resources that are not necessarily rightly owned by the M-type, such as child support or personal loans from family or friends. The s-type will be strongly tempted to give in and give that up, but at least in the case of financial or physical resources, they should take a breath and focus on what is honorable. (The absolute worst-case scenario I've seen with this placement was the M-type who convinced his s-type to steal money for him.) Giving up control of the sex life will probably feel very natural and fated, however. As with all Plutonification of houses, think it through carefully.

s/Pluto in the M/8th House

This relationship will bring up all the M-type's baggage around sex, including inhibitions, secret unacceptable desires, and ego-propping illusions. Other ugly baggage that might rear its head might be around inheritances that went awry, financial or property that they didn't get, resources that were snatched away, and all the places in their life where they are powerless. This is the house of power, and they may end up cleaning out their entire concept of how power works. It's also the house of the Mysteries, and it can inspire them to look into new spiritual paths that may seem to hold answers to their old questions.

M/Pluto in s/9th House

This interaspect placement will inspire the M-type to want control over the s-type's religion (if they have one), whether or not they can travel alone, whether they should get further education, and their general view of the world and the cosmos. The s-type, for their part, may be completely mesmerized by the M-type's grasp of those areas, and ready to fall into line as a disciple. This house rules the teacher/disciple relationship, and that pattern can seep into this relationship, even without benefit of any religious beliefs on either side. The M-type needs to be careful not to let this go to their head, though.

s/Pluto in M/9th House

This power dynamic will inspire the M-type to revolutionize the way they think about their religious beliefs (or lack of them), their education level (or lack of it), their opinions on foreign cultures, and their general view of the Universe (and their place in it). This is the house of fanaticism, and when it gets Plutonified by someone else, the contacted person may have a reactionary battle going on in their head. They may perceive the s-type as expanding their mind and expecting them to keep up, and may get defensive about their conflicting ideas. It's best to breathe and talk to someone on the outside rather than striking out in that direction.

M/Pluto in s/10th House

This relationship will make the M-type want to control the s-type's career, even if that hadn't occurred to them before. The s-type, in turn, may be triggered into deep conflict about their career and whether it will fit into this power dynamic. Another area of control-grab will be how the s-type presents themselves in public, especially in influential groups. The s-type may fight this, or feel drawn to go along with it; at least one s-type that we knew gave up a flourishing career to be with their M-type and regretted it later when the relationship broke up and they had shaved their head, making it difficult to get rehired in their field. The risks should be assessed carefully.

s/Pluto in M/10th House

This relationship will inspire to M-type to reassess their career choices, and perhaps change careers to something more emotionally appropriate to their vision of themselves as a powerful person. They may find themselves longing to be in charge in areas outside the power dynamic, such as jobs and public volunteer work. Tenth-house interaspects tend to cause leaking outside the relationship, and the M-type needs to be careful and remember that employees are not slaves. The s-type may end up being the "career support" who encourages them to new ambitions.

M/Pluto in s/11th House

This interaspect can inspire the M-type to want to control the s-type's friends, and to bring the s-type firmly into their own circle of buddies and chosen family. They may also want to control the political or interest groups the s-type belongs to, and the s-type may be starry-eyed about entering their magic circle and be adopted in. A wise M-type will allow them to keep their social circles, as cutting off outside support can be cruel and unnecessary. However, Pluto here may inspire the s-type to purge friends and groups they didn't need anyway. On the other hand, conflict between the M-type and the s-type may trigger friends to take sides in the power struggle.

s/Pluto in M/11th House

This relationship will, just by being authentic, show the M-type who their real friends are, and who might better be purged from their life. The same goes for social communities, political groups, and interest groups. The M-type will end up questioning how these people do or do not support their path of mastery, and many of them may end up going by the wayside. The s-type needs to step back from feeling responsible; this is a process that needed to happen anyway, and being a catalyst is not always a bad thing.

M/Pluto in s/12th House

This is a rough interaspect, because the M-type's presence will bring up all the unconscious baggage that the s-type has been burying, especially anything about power and powerlessness, and the people who first had power over them (meaning parents) and the people who have misused power in their lives. The M-type may become a projection screen for the s-type's internal monsters while the s-type is forced to deal with them and clean out some of those issues. This is the house of imprisonment and monasteries, and Pluto here may inspire the s-type either to feel imprisoned or feel intensely positive about being in a restricted space.

s/Pluto in M/12th House

This one is just as difficult as the other way around, if not more so. The relationship will bring up a huge amount of the M-type's baggage around all the times they have felt powerless or trapped, and they may pour that out onto the triggering s-type by cracking down and leveling more punitive restrictions than may be necessary, or even healthy. If this interaspect is not handled well—perhaps by the M-type getting outside support for the struggle of cleaning all this out—they may fight for control of as much of the s-type's life as possible, projecting their own out-of-control psyche on the s-type. To make this power dynamic work, the M-type has to be very self-aware, and committed to that self-awareness.

Pluto Interaspects To Planets

Here we're going to talk about interaspects, which is a synastry term. When you lay one chart over the other, lining them up at 0° Aries, you'll notice that their respective planets make aspects to each other, just as planets within a natal chart will do. (If this is a new concept for you, get a computer synastry chart printed out, with lists of the interaspects so you won't have to determine them yourself.) Just as planets in aspect in a natal chart indicate internal arguments and gifts, planets between charts indicate areas of harmony and disagreements. In fact, most of your most stubbornly present arguments can be seen clearly as an interaspect between your charts (with the exception of the arguments which are actually composite chart aspects).

For a power exchange relationship, Pluto's interaspects show areas where the s-type is driven to give over power *to this one M-type*, even if it doesn't come all that naturally to give over power in this area. They also show where there may be a power struggle, possibly around their partner's ideas and preferences in that area. Any aspect between the M-type's Pluto and the s-type's planets will affect the flow of power exchange between them. Enhancing aspects (trines and sextiles) usually indicate areas of life where the s-type feels comfortable giving over power to this particular M-type, even if they haven't felt comfortable yielding up those areas with other people. Challenging aspects (squares and oppositions), on the other hand, sometimes have an ambivalent feel to them. Conjunctions—when one planet is right on top of another—are always a combination of harmony and challenge; they may lean toward one side or the other, or be both at once. If a planet isn't aspecting the M-type's Pluto, the s-type will neither feel strongly driven nor strongly ambivalent; it will be a neutral area.

It's important to emphasize that when it comes to squares, oppositions, and conjunctions, that the urge is still there, unlike planets that have no major aspects at all between them. (There are a number of minor aspects, but for the purposes of this book we won't be going into them.) It's just that with the challenging aspects, it's a little trickier. It can still work, but both people will have to put in more effort, be more honest, discuss it more clearly, and be more mindful of obstacles (unlike a trine or sextile where one can just "slide right in"). It is also important to point out that a harmonious aspect can also have the negative side effects of a challenging one; it's just that the two of you may be so busy humming along that you don't see it coming, unlike a challenging aspect where it may come up more immediately and need to be addressed. The cosmic wheels can be tricky that way.

Examples of the ambivalence around challenging Pluto aspects on the M-type side can include:

❖ I'm not sure if controlling this is the right thing to do.
❖ I really want to control it, but when I try, old baggage (mine or theirs) comes up and causes problems.
❖ I really want to control it, but they raise such a fuss that it quickly becomes not worth it.
❖ I'm scared of how much I want to control that, so I hold back.
❖ I control it, but I sometimes overreact and clamp down too hard because of a feeling that I'm constantly losing control in that area.

The s-type whose planet is being contacted by the M-type's Pluto is going to have a combination of "I want to give this to them! In fact, I want to feel them taking control of it!" and "This is really scary, and I need to back up and protect myself at all costs." It's fear that motivates Pluto power struggles, not any sense of practicality or what is proper (that's Saturn's department), although that can be used to disguise and excuse the fear.

In the other direction, when the s-type's Pluto is in aspect to one of the M-type's planets, it brings up an explosion of intense emotions about the areas of the contacted planet, and also a surge of power to do something about it. The presence of this s-type will evolve and purify those areas in the M-type, because that will be necessary in order to manage this particular power dynamic with this particular person. We may be practicing unequal relationships, but the planets affect us equally in both directions … as we do for each other.

One way to compare the two sides would be to say that the M-type's contacting Pluto causes a drive for *possession*, and the s-type's contacting Pluto causes a drive for *purification*. If this feels uncomfortable to the M-type, one way to get through it quicker is to use the s-type's service as a resource to aid the M-type in their struggle to evolve in these areas and become a better leader and Master.

M/Pluto in Aspect to the s/Sun

If it's a harmonious aspect, the s-type will feel more comfortable shifting their identity to be closer to the M-type's idea of who they should be. With a challenging aspect, the s-type will instinctively balk and struggle when pushed to change pre-existing aspects of their identity. Either way, the M-type will be drawn to changing the s-type's identity and self-image as a way to enjoy controlling them. Since Pluto uncovers dark qualities and exposes them to the light, this relationship may bring up all the s-type's issues about having a submissive identity. Also, changing how they think of themself is a long, hard road even with a particularly malleable s-type, and prone to backfiring, especially if the M-type is impatient and not willing to work at it gently over a period of many years.

s/Pluto in Aspect to M/Sun

Here the s-type's Pluto forces the M-type to confront all their ambivalences around being the dominant partner, especially if there are dark sadistic desires involved. This can be a cleansing process, or it can trigger their defensiveness, which can bruise the s-type and damage the M-type's credibility. Working through these issues can be transformative for the M-type and their reactions to confronting their own flaws; this process will be easier if it's a harmonious aspect and harder if it is challenging. Ideally this aspect will purify the M-type's understanding of who they are on a deep level.

M/Pluto in Aspect to s/Moon

This synastry aspect is infamous for obsession and emotional explosiveness. The M-type may be tempted or even driven to attempt to manipulate the s-type emotionally in order to control them; they need to work hard to resist this tendency and be honest, remembering that trust is imperative and if you're really in control, you should have no need to hide anything. The s-type will feel extremely vulnerable and their emotions may be more volatile than normal. If the aspect is harmonious this will feel like a relief and the s-type will be able to open up and offer their deep emotional vulnerability. However, if it is challenging the s-type may panic and fight any attempt at emotional control or (real or imagined) manipulation. On the positive side, this interaspect may manifest in the M-type wanting a very parental role, and showing their dominance through nurturing behavior.

s/Pluto in Aspect to M/Moon

This one is tricky, because the Pluto person gets under the skin of the Moon person, and the M-type may be triggered into more volatile emotions than they intended, which may make them feel out of control. The s-type may be desperate to get inside their head and heart, and may not feel safe or secure until that happens. It will take a very emotionally self-aware and self-disciplined M-type to navigate this combination, and it will involve setting and enforcing good (but not threatened or reactive) boundaries while still not withdrawing in a negative reaction to being challenged. If the aspect is harmonious, it will be easier to transmute this into self-awareness and self-compassion. Ideally, over time this relationship will purify the M-type's emotional competence, and the presence of the s-type will release not only the urge to do so, but the power to make it happen within themself.

M/Pluto in Aspect to s/Mercury

The M-type will be drawn to tinkering with the s-type's speech, word choice, writing style, and general thought process. They may fall into a "teacher" role, and may want to control the s-type's media-watching (TV, movies, Internet, books) as well as social media contacts. This connection may inspire the M-type to share their favorite fields of knowledge. Problems arise when they want to verbally censor the s-type to the point of shutting down emotional information; remember always that there *should* be nothing that can't be said, and there *is* nothing that can't be said in a respectful way. Another way this interaspect can manifest is in using consensual mental conditioning to literally "play with the mind".

s/Pluto in Aspect to M/Mercury

The presence of this s-type brings up all sorts of dark and ambivalent thoughts, and forces the M-type to deal with them. The M-type may worry about their sanity, or their ability to focus, or their thinking possibly being sloppy. They may feel driven to be more articulate, make more lists, read and research more, finish up paperwork, organize their libraries, and thoughtfully consider their words when they open their mouth. The goal of this aspect is to purify the M-type's intellect and mental processes, and with some creative orders they can use the s-type to help them with this struggle for mental clarity.

M/Pluto in Aspect to s/Venus

The M-type will feel very strongly about being the s-type's primary romantic partner, and possibly their only romantic partner. As Pluto is possessive by nature, it may become important for them to see the s-type enacting behaviors that say "romance" or even "love" only with them. On their part, even if the s-type is not very monogamous, they may feel "enchanted" by the M-type to the point of wanting to give that only to them (unless it is a challenging aspect, in which case they may want it half the time and resent it half the time). In addition, since Venus is aesthetics, the M-type may want very much to control the s-type's aesthetic style and dictate their beauty or grooming regimen, and perhaps "retrain" the s-type's aesthetic sense to find beauty in what the M-type sees as such. The s-type will feel compelled to go along with it, but may fight the compulsion if the aspect is difficult.

s/Pluto in Aspect to M/Venus

The presence of the s-type will bring up issues around how the M-type loves, and conducts love affairs. They may be driven to examine their honesty, commitment, kindness, and expressiveness around romantic relationships, and will find the power to change things for the better welling up in them. The eventual ideal of this aspect is to transform the M-type into someone who loves more cleanly and with more caring. It's possible to use the s-type to work on these issues, but be careful of their feelings, especially if the relationship doesn't yet know where it stands.

M/Pluto in Aspect to s/Mars

Mars is sex and controlling the s-type's sex life — not just who they have sex with, but what they do and how — will be very important to the M-type's feeling of possession and control. (In general, Mars/Pluto contacts of any sort are infamous for turning up the sexual temperature.) Sex will also be a strong way in which the M-type shows their dominance. Another point of importance will be the s-type's work ethic; the M-type may want to control day-to-day work decisions, just for the joy of it. The s-type may find themselves surprisingly energetic when it comes to work that the M-type asks them to do, even if they would drag their feet under other circumstances. If the aspect is challenging, however, they may have periods of argument and resentment between periods of a strong desire to get cracking on it. Since Mars is anger, it may become important for the M-type to put rules and protocol around how the s-type may express their anger; just make sure that they are still left a useful way to express strong emotions that will be heard.

s/Pluto in Aspect to M/Mars

The presence of this s-type will bring up all sorts of anger issues in the M-type, possibly showing a path where improvement needs to happen, and revealing triggers the M-type didn't know they had. This will probably not be intentional on the part of the s-type, and the M-type needs to remember that, even in the midst of being triggered. It may also bring up issues that need improvement around the M-type's process of taking action on an issue, and reveal areas where the M-type tends to be unrealistic about their ability to motivate themselves or take on tasks. If the aspect is challenging, it will take more patient intent to turn these fiery triggers into self-improvement. An enormous amount of intense sexual energy will be released regardless of the nature of the aspect, which can help during difficult times.

M/Pluto in Aspect to s/Jupiter

Since Jupiter is faith and trust and Pluto is naturally suspicious, this aspect between charts will trigger trust issues in the s-type, especially if it's a challenging aspect. The M-type may instinctively desire to clamp down on all the areas where the s-type gives themselves away for free—friends, family, children, community, volunteer organizations—with a motivation-mixture of wanting to protect them and possessively wanting the s-type's generosity all to themselves. The s-type may be torn between being moved to give it all to the M-type and losing the joy in helping others, and a power struggle may ensue. The wise M-type will fight their Plutonian desires and allow the s-type a reasonable amount of outside generosity, with boundaries set out of practicality and not out of jealousy. This sometimes manifests as a desire by the M-type to control the s-type's enthusiasms and overt emotional expression, perhaps making rules of decorum that dampen exuberant behavior. On the other hand, the M-type may also be moved to make a concerted effort toward raising the s-type's self-esteem. Jupiter is also religion, and controlling the s-type's religious beliefs or practices (or lack thereof) may loom large in the M-type's sights. In addition, the effect of escalating Jupiter on the M-type's Pluto can make all their territorial urges stronger; they may shock themselves with how strong they feel about controlling the s-type. This can exacerbate the s-type's trust issues, and the sensible M-type may want to build trust back up by showing how much in control they are of these urges.

s/Pluto Aspecting M/Jupiter

Trust goes both ways, and s-types must also earn the M-type's trust. This aspect can make the s-type extremely suspicious of the M-type's every move, and (if it is a challenging aspect) especially untrusting of their overall good intentions toward the s-type. Thought needs to be given as to whether the s-type's standards for trustworthiness are too high for a mere mortal to achieve. The s-type may secretly want to make the M-type their anchor of faith—religious or otherwise—and at the same time may see their every human error as a reason not to do so. The presence of this particular s-type may bring up issues around the M-type's generosity, giftedness, luck, ability to love unconditionally (or not), and possibly religious worldview (or lack thereof). These must be examined and cleaned up in order to successfully master this s-type.

M/Pluto Aspecting s/Saturn

Saturn is the planet of both discipline and obstacles, and this placement can send the M-type into a fury of imposing the former and trying to destroy the latter in the life of their s-type. Whether either line of offense is successful or disastrous depends on the M-type planning with humility, compassion, and a realistic attitude. Wielding Pluto's power with an attitude of arrogance and "I know what's best for you" without in-depth understanding of the s-type's actual limitations is bad enough. Unlike some other planets, however, Saturn is capable of holding its own against Pluto, and careless handling of the s-type's Saturn can cause them to dig in their heels and resist. A challenging aspect is particularly at high risk for this kind of behavior from both sides. The s-type may well desire the M-type to help them through their Saturnian obstacles and develop more discipline in the affected area, but that training needs to proceed with patience, encouragement, and gentle communication, rather than a heavy-handed approach. Changing one's Saturn areas can be one of the hardest things one ever does in one's life, and it will not be a quick process. On the other side, the M-type may well be feeling a Saturnian pinch on their passion and power, which can dismay them and set them off. They should use it as a chance to apply discipline to their dark, intense Plutonian desires, which will set a good example anyway. *(Check the Saturn chapter for the Saturnian side of this aspect.)*

s/Pluto in Aspect to M/Saturn

It's not only M-types who push for more in the face of an unsure partner. This interaspect may find the s-type pleading for *More, Harder, Faster, More,* while the M-type stands back in Saturnian caution. The M-type may find themselves constantly putting the brakes on the s-type's passions, and pushing them to discipline their unruly desires. On the other side, the power dynamic will force the M-type to do a lot of serious thinking about their own personal discipline, and whether it is solid or spotty at best. This aspect will push them to question their fitness for authority, and perhaps even rebuild that fitness from the ground up. Saturn/Pluto contacts are rough on everyone, but they are a superb impetus for carefully constructing a power dynamic with everyone's self-improvement in mind. *(Check the Saturn chapter for the Saturnian side of this aspect.)*

M/Pluto in Aspect to s/Uranus

Since this is the planet of freedom and nonconformity, this interaspect can be extremely explosive. The M-type feels driven to clamp down on the s-type's freedom in general, and specifically all the ways in which the s-type bucks the social order. Even if the M-type in question is no conservative and happily bucks the social order themselves, they will be sorely tempted to push the s-type to rebel in *their* way, and only against groups and cultures disapproved of by the M-type. With a harmonious interaspect, the s-type may be willing to give in and change, but if it is challenging, sparks will fly. The s-type will see the M-type as overly controlling, and the M-type may interpret the s-type as blindly unthinking. On the other hand, over time the presence of the s-type will spur the M-type to rebel against society in new and different ways. Since Uranus rules neurology, the M-type may also want very much to assert control over any neurological problems the s-type may have, and how they handle them.

s/Pluto in Aspect to M/Uranus

Clash of the opinions! Here the s-type's values that are based on personal passions, and the M-type's values that are based on intellectual consideration, smash into each other. The s-type will be pushed to learn about the wider world from the M-type, and at the same time will resent being pulled from their own stubborn views. The M-type may be drawn to use humor and perhaps even a bit of wackiness to poke holes in the s-type's darkness and let in some rational light. The s-type may find themself the possessive one for a change, clutching at a more eccentric and freedom-oriented M-type. (Disputes over monogamy and polyamory are common with Pluto/Uranus interaspects.) On the other hand, the relationship may force the M-type to clean out some old assumptions in their political and cultural ideas. If this is a harmonious interaspect, the couple will help each other to grow in understanding of the world; if it is challenging, many arguments may erupt over the kitchen table. This interaspect may also bring up the issue of any neurological problems the M-type may have, and may push them to handle those glitches more skillfully.

M/Pluto in Aspect to s/Neptune

This is the planet of power making an interaspect to the planet of sacrifice, and the s-type may find themself wanting desperately—and perhaps even surprisingly, if it's not their usual mode—wanting to just lay down and surrender to the power of Pluto. If the aspect is challenging, however, Pluto will pounce and grab, wanting to possess something deep and yielding in the s-type, and they will passively slip through the grasping fingers like a slippery fish. At worst, if the s-type has some sort of active mental illness, a challenging aspect here can trigger it; the M-type may want control over that, and should carefully examine whether it is within their abilities to skillfully handle. A harmonious interaspect can create a sense of the M-type protecting the s-type while not letting them get away with anything. This can inspire a strong spiritual theme in the relationship, although the M-type needs to be careful not to force their ideals on the s-type; Neptune contacts work better with gentleness. The M-type's convictions will encourage the s-type to clean out a lot of illusions and confusion from their life. (*Also check the Neptune chapter for the Neptunian side of this aspect.*)

s/Pluto in Aspect to M/Neptune

Harmonious or challenging, this is going to be an uncomfortable one for a power dynamic. The s-type's strong emotions hit the M-type in a very vulnerable place, and whether they show it or not, they will feel hurt and uncertain. They may feel pushed to give in to the s-type more often in the face of those emotions, which undermines the power dynamic and makes neither person happy. The s-type may resort to manipulation of the M-type, and then scorn them if it works. The solution for the M-type is threefold, although not easy. First, firm, consistent, and continual boundaries must be set regarding how the s-type is to treat the M-type; kindness and compassion must be stressed as their goal in these interactions., no matter what they are feeling emotionally. Second, as this interaspect drives the M-type to clean out their old unhealthy patterns and illusions, this process needs to be embraced actively by them or the tension will destroy the relationship. Third, the M-type needs outside guidance and aid with this purifying evolution, and appropriate support should be sought. The s-type will find that their strong emotions may be made more wild and confusing with this aspect, and they should probably have their own outside support to learn coping strategies. A strong spiritual path for both, and for the relationship, can make the difference in helping it to survive. *(Also check the Neptune chapter for the Neptunian side of this aspect.)*

M/Pluto in Aspect to s/Pluto

If the two individuals are very close in age and this is a conjunction, the interaspect will simply indicate that they have similar ideas about how power works and how passion flows. They will need to be a quarter-century or more apart for a harmonious sextile aspect, and almost forty years apart for the challenging square. These tend to turn up less about wanting specific areas of power, and more about just having possible differences about how power works—what makes one worthy or unworthy, what is owed or obligated for what, etc. These differences are mostly cultural and generational, and will require patience and generous listening on both parts.

Saturn: Authority and Discipline

In both people's charts, Saturn is the need for structure (or not!) and one's preferred style of structure. It's also how one reacts to authority, and being in authority. For the dominant, this is fairly obvious. The sign and house placement suggests not only the style of their authority but the areas in which having authority over the submissive will be particularly important to them. It may also reflect their internal ideas on the source of their authority — for example, a dominant with a fourth-house Saturn might feel that they ought to be in charge because they set the tone for the home, whereas a second-house Saturn dominant might need to make more money than the submissive in order to feel as if their authority was genuine.

However, Saturn is also the planet of our obstacles and limitations — the ones that aren't going to go away in this lifetime — and our job is to find ways to improve ourselves and compensate by using Saturn's first and best tool: self-discipline. M-types often have a love-hate relationship with Saturn-ruled areas. We often want to be respected as an authority for our achievements in this area, while at the same time it may be one of the places where we are struggling and perhaps failing. In the porn stories, M-types are all perfect paragons of personal discipline (when they're not portrayed as sadistic sociopaths), and this can shame flesh-and-blood M-types who are still working on those imperfect Saturn areas. On a spiritual level, a power dynamic can be used as an ongoing training ground to improve our Saturn wounds, so that we can eventually achieve real progress in these areas that are so important to us, and yet also so difficult.

Of course, s-types all have Saturns as well. Often their Saturns manifest as the places they want help with self-discipline, where they crave a competent and honorable authority, especially someone who will mentor them and set clear rules to keep them from running amok. Their imperfections in these areas can also be a source of shame, motivating a periodic urge to push for excellence against all odds. The M-type who tries to help the s-type improve in their Saturn area needs a great deal of (Saturn-approved) patience, because while victories here can be truly wonderful, these are actual blockages which have caused a lifetime of frustration, and cannot be handled quickly or easily. Sometimes the common bewildered M-type complaint of "I told my slave they were good enough for my standards in this area, but they won't accept my reassurance on this topic, and keep flogging themselves over it!" can actually reflect the torments of guilt that the personal Saturn snarls to them. A quick check of the chart can help the M-type to understand the problem better.

On the other side of that urge, the s-type's Saturn also informs their vision of the perfect authority figure — it probably resembles the sign and house of their Saturn in a lot of ways. They may subtly pressure their flesh-and-blood M-type to be more like that, while at the same time they want to become more like that themselves. When the same recriminations come up toward the M-type again and again, it's not a surprise when it turns out to be their dissimilarity to the s-type's Saturn image.

In moving from Pluto to Saturn, we have to compare authority and control ... which really means comparing the action of Saturn with the action of Pluto. For purposes of this book, *authority* means *the s-type has given the M-type the right to make decisions in this area*. Conversely, *control* means *the M-type has the means to effectively enforce this authority, even when the s-type is having trouble obeying*. Authority (Saturn) is based in the s-type's honor and willingness to discipline themselves to carry out an order, although they may ask for the M-type's help in achieving that self-discipline. Control (Pluto) is based in the M-type's force of will, although they may ask the s-type for aid in learning the best ways to leverage that willpower onto them. Authority may be granted; control must be built up over time. (Neither has anything to do with the swooning semi-surrender of falling in love, which is often mistaken for both or either.)

One of the biggest subjective differences between these two is that the Pluto force of control simply needs to seem powerful to hit the s-type's buttons effectively. The Pluto force in all of us doesn't care about social right vs. social wrong, proper vs.

improper, or practical vs. impractical. (Although it does care very much about mindfully clean vs. blindly unthinking.) When the mind starts to bring in *those* everyday wet-blanket details that get in the way of the delicious rush of power exchange, that's Saturn talking. Control needs only to be *powerful*. Authority, on the other hand, needs to be *Right*. The s-type will be extremely invested in the M-type being Right and having good judgment in their Saturn areas, and in any area where the M-type's Saturn touches their planets or houses. Of course, no M-type is Right all the time. We're human and sometimes we make mistakes. When we do, the s-type's Saturn areas will be places where our authority may take the most dents and dings in their eyes, if we can't fix things.

Saturn is also about structure, and the s-type's Saturn areas (sign and house) will be places where they desire structure the most. Many (though not all) s-types were attracted to power dynamics partly because the idea of a relationship with clear rules and structure appealed to them, and even those who just thought it was sexy will find they have some areas where structure means more to them than others. Similarly, the M-type's Saturn areas will be places where they will want structure in the relationship in order to make them feel more comfortable. So when we say, in the following listings. "The M-type will want authority over…" or "The s-type will be want them to have authority over…" you can also mentally add in, "…and will ideally want structure built in those areas, in order to feel better about the power dynamic and their place in it."

Ideally, both authority and control ought to be discussed on an ongoing basis throughout the development of a power dynamic relationship. In reality, many beginning couples don't understand the difference, and don't know what exactly they are granting and being granted. It's rare that each statement by the s-type of "I want you to be in charge of this area of my life," is followed up by the M-type asking, "…And what do we do when you are having trouble making yourself obey me? Let's think about that now."

If these relationships were all conducted like job interviews, without the added underlayment of hopes, fears, and sexual desires, we would all start with Saturn's authority exchange and slowly work up to Pluto's dance of power. However, it rarely works like that, and sometimes we leap into intense Pluto before tedious Saturn has been acknowledged, or even after authority has been granted but before trust has been earned. Saturn, however, will stand back tapping his foot while Pluto makes a mess of things, with plenty of "I-told-you-so"s afterwards.

So what happens if you're an s-type who ends up with the M-type who is nothing like your inner perfect authority figure? Well, you'll probably end up with some disappointment, as will the M-type whose s-type has an inner authority archetype who looks nothing like theirs. However, it doesn't have to ruin everything if you don't let it. Getting the ideal you desire is not the same thing at all — at least from an evolutionary point of view — as getting the person you need, the complex three-dimensional human being who will touch your soul and inspire you to grow. I don't look like my slaveboy's Saturnian fantasy, nor does that look like what I'm striving to become. (In fact, they're astrologically opposed to each other.) In the beginning, this triggered cascades of complaints and castigations from him. Eventually, he realized that I was who he needed for a wide range of reasons, and becoming my slave helped him to become a better and more tolerant human being.

I will admit, however, that I did work at becoming a bit more like his Saturn ideal, not because he was pressuring me, but because I saw that I could stand to at least improve a little in that direction. Doing so helped many areas of my life, not just the relationship. I also showed him the kind of authority figure that I continually strove to be, and he gained a new appreciation for me, my path, and that style of leadership. A little compromise can go a long way, even in a power dynamic, so don't give up if there are Saturn problems. Use them as an excuse for practice in excellence. That's what Saturn wants most, anyway.

Saturn in the Signs

Saturn in Aries/M

For this M-type, the ideal authority figure is bold, decisive, and something of a warrior. Military models may inspire their mastery style; the idea of being in charge of boot camp appeals to them. They will both strive to be this sort of person and secretly fear that they are failing at it; whether they are or aren't will depend on how much work they've done in the areas of their Saturn. They want to be respected as an authority because of these qualities, possibly spiced with some physical intimidation.

It's important to them to have authority over when—and whether—their s-type begins new projects, and how the s-type shows assertiveness or aggression, including through their appearance and manner. They find it fulfilling to provide discipline around courage and motivation—teaching the s-type how to make themselves do something, even when it is scary or they fear failure. While this can be useful, they need to understand that some s-types aren't meant to be warriors, and need a little more gentleness to achieve goals of courage.

Saturn in Aries/s

This s-type wants to be a warrior, or perhaps the servant to a warrior, or perhaps both. Their ideal internal authority figure is brave, risk-taking, aggressive, and hopefully can wrestle them to the ground when they feel they need it. They feel that they don't have the discipline to develop those qualities in themself, and they want their M-type to help them get closer to that ideal. They may criticize themself for not being brave or motivated enough in the M-type's service. The idea of an assertive bodyguard role may appeal to them, or the superhero's sidekick on an adventure, or comrades in arms. At the same time, they may have a tendency to pressure their M-type to be more like this model, or be disappointed in them when they aren't. They need to understand that there are many kinds of strength, that not all of them are the forward-momentum-at-all-costs sort, and that the qualities of caution and being unwilling to take serious risks are not necessarily humdrum and boring.

Saturn in Aries in a Composite Chart

When these two partners are together, they often fall into a crisis of cowardice when faced with obstacles, or just with the usual Saturnian drag of tedious adult responsibilities. The s-type may look to the M-type as a military-style commander, and be disappointed when the would-be drill sergeant slumps in despair when faced with the mountain of tasks. Both partners should work together to figure out a discipline of courage, something that they can do for each other in rough times that still keeps the power dynamic going. They need to remind each other of who they are in ways that are fiery and passionate, and consider protocols that harness both as warrior comrades-in-arms on an adventure. Physically exercising together can get them in synch. The ideal is for the M-type to be able to inspire the s-type to courage and motivation, but it can be useful to use the s-type as a tool to help the M-type to get to that inspiring point on a regular basis.

Saturn Taurus/M

For this M-type, the ideal authority figure is solid, reliable, consistent, and probably has a good amount of money and financial resources. They both strive to be this sort of person and secretly fear that they are failing at it; whether they are or aren't will depend on how much work they've done in the areas of their Saturn. It's important to them that at least some of their authority comes from their financial success—at the very least, they will want to make more money than their s-type—and how solvent and stable the material parts of their life are. They may "market" themselves as the one who can be relied on, whether or not that's true for them. They may light up at the fantasy of buying a slave at auction, or being the wealthy Owner with the mansion full of expensively dressed property.

It's important to this M-type to have authority over their s-type's financial plans, and possibly their money. They find it fulfilling to provide discipline around building a stable and solid life, making them keep a budget, working hard, and constructing practical plans and goals that will maintain material stability in later years. These M-types want to make the rules at the beginning of the relationship and be sure that they won't ever need to change, which may be building sandcastles against the tide. They need to understand that while these are all good plans, the world changes, people change, and they and their s-type will both change, so the most practical solution is to learn to roll with that.

Saturn in Taurus/s

With Saturn here, the s-type wants consistency, consistency, consistency. Part of what they love about power exchange is that there are rules, and the rules don't change even when they hurl yourself against them. Their Saturn also wants absolute consistency in reinforcing their personal discipline. The power exchange is, for them, a bedrock on which to rest and find that deep calm, in its very unchangingness. It's hard for them when the rules have to change, have a lot of exceptions that they're expected to reason out, or even when a new situation arises for which rules have not yet been made.

They may be looking for a dominant partner to help them manage the material parts of their life, and they may have a tendency to pressure their M-type not only to push them in this way, but to be a paragon of stability and financial common sense themself, and be disappointed when they aren't. They need to understand that sometimes Life sends us speed bumps that even the most competent of M-types cannot expect or cope with appropriately in under ten seconds. Also, sometimes things change—including the M-type—and rules have to change with them because they are no longer useful. This is always hard for these s-types, but it's a life struggle they're supposed to learn to cope with gracefully and maturely.

Saturn in Taurus in a Composite Chart

The power dynamic will work better for both partners if they work on solid, practical consistency, making sure all the rules are followed and the obligations carried out on both sides.

The problem is that these two may inadvertently sabotage each other on this, or their life together may provide all the sabotaging in spite of their best efforts. Start by reducing rules and protocols to the ones that work regularly, and examine what those have in common. Then add new rules or routines very slowly, one at a time, keeping an experimental attitude and troubleshooting when necessary. Drop what doesn't work, and focus on what the two of you can do together to build a solid foundation to lean on. Physical contact — regular snuggling, for example — that is non-sexual but very sensual will definitely help your bonding as a couple, and can help resolve emotional difficulties. This is not a relationship that can work without a binding commitment; the two of you are going to want to work for the long term, even if you started out thinking it would be a limited situation.

Saturn in Gemini/M

For this M-type, the ideal authority figure is brilliant, versatile, articulate, witty, multitalented, and able to be mentally one step ahead of their subordinates. They both strive to be this sort of person and secretly fear that they are failing at it; whether they are or aren't will depend on how much work they've done in the areas of their Saturn. They want their authority to be grounded in their intelligence, and ideally that they can outthink and outsmart their s-type; they tend to feel hopeless when this doesn't work. Teacher roles where they can show off their knowledge appeal to them, especially if they're mentoring the s-type as an older person would a younger person. They may be fond of "littles" and s-types with a childlike bent.

It's important to them to have authority over their s-type's ideas and thoughts. They want to fill the s-type's head with stories while they are admired for their many talents. The M-type may enjoy giving the s-type reading assignments and encouraging them in new studies — approved by the M-type, of course. These M-types find it fulfilling to help s-types polish their information-gathering skills and mental quickness, as well as their sense of humor. While this is wonderful, it's important to remember that not everyone is meant to be an intellectual, and there's a difference between impressing an s-type with your mind and making them feel stupid when you set them up for brain tasks they aren't able to manage.

Saturn in Gemini/s

These s-types worry that they're not smart and talented enough; they want a dominant partner who will teach them to be sharper and more articulate. Conversely, however, they desire that partner to be even more sharp and articulate than they are, and they are disappointed when the M-type fails in this way. They may beat themselves up for not being smart or talented or mentally organized enough, or for not being good enough at multi-tasking. When the M-type tries to help or guide them in this area, they might be grateful or they might be resentful or hopeless, possibly both by turns. (There's a fine line between "Help me be smarter!" and "You think I'm stupid!") They may be drawn to playing the role of a younger schoolchild — especially a mischievous one — with a dominant partner as the teacher, or possibly the older brother or sister who can mentor them into intellectual adulthood.

Saturn in Gemini in a Composite Chart

Clear communications will be crucial for this power dynamic to function properly. Both partners will be at high risk for misunderstanding and communication problems. It will be important for them to work out structures not just for orders, but for discussion, check-ins, and any other exchanges that are important to the power dynamic. The s-type is going to want the M-type to be smart, talented, and able to think fast on their feet, which may be easy for the M-type or may put immense pressure on them. On the positive side, the relationship tends to fall easily into a teacher/student model, and this makes training much easier. This couple will find that they have a good sense of humor between the two of them, which can help with the rough times. One subtle issue with this placement is a feeling that they are living double lives; this can either feel inauthentic or exciting, depending on your individual personalities.

Saturn in Cancer/M

Cancer is the most parental of all the signs, and when Saturn is in Cancer, the individual can't help but think of their ideal authority figure as parental. The problem is that their model for "parental authority figure" is based on their own parents. If the M-type's parents were kind, nurturing, disciplined, and honorable people, that's great—they will find satisfaction in being the Good Daddy or the Wise Mama. However, if they had a bad ticket in the parental lottery, the dysfunctional parents remain like a shadow over their authority style until they are able to reparent and free themself from the residue of their childhood. It's a life's work to relearn on a deep level what good parental authority looks like, and it may help to have a mentor who can gently embody an example of that.

Saturn here also causes blocks in the emotions and intuition, and the M-type who hasn't worked that out can denigrate and shame the s-type who is more emotional or intuitive. It's important to examine what they were taught about these ways of being, and learn how this can be useful in taking care of another human being.

Saturn in Cancer/s

As mentioned above, the Saturn in Cancer s-type will be, on some deep level, wedded to the idea that real authority is parental authority, and their first imprinting is from the parents who raised them. If they grew up with family dysfunction, they need to dig all that out and examine it before getting into a power dynamic, or they will project the bad parents onto the M-type. They might fear that the M-type will repeat their parents' bad behavior even when there is no good evidence for that, or they may reject an M-type who isn't "bad" enough to resemble their parents. In some cases the M-type can help them to reparent themself, but only if they do the groundwork themselves first.

This s-type may be somewhat emotionally blocked and may find it hard to depend on their intuition for discerning behavior in a given situation. They should not be shamed for their difficulties in that area, but instead given support to learn how to do better. They may desire to be "littles" or have a child role in a relationship, but may find themself acting out to test the authority of the parental figure.

Saturn in Cancer in a Composite Chart

Parental role models will be important for both of you in this relationship, clearing out the baggage of your various upbringings, and exploring together how the most positive parent/child relationship would look. This will hold true even if there is no obvious ageplay going on — there are a lot of ways to embody parental authority and childlike openness. Rules and protocols will be based on safety and security. They may conceive of themselves and their group of friends as family, clan, or tribe — the chosen replacement for the possibly faulty originals.

The s-type will expect the M-type to embody the parent in their mind, which the M-type may not be able to do. They might not actually know what that ideal looks like, if the s-type has been unable to communicate it clearly. In some cases, they may not want to copy that image, especially if it is the echo of an abusive situation.

Saturn in Leo/M

The ideal authority figure floating around in the head of the Saturn in Leo person is confident and charismatic, at home in the spotlight, and inspires others to follow with their flair. However, the M-type with Saturn here may both admire that model and feel they can never achieve it. They want to be admired and possibly even adored — this is the sign of royalty — and may react poorly if the s-type values them for reasons that aren't the ones that make them feel good about themself.

If they can find the s-type who will admire them like a King or Queen or superstar even if they are introverted and terrified of the group spotlight, or if they can gather their courage and learn to be self-possessed in public, all may be well. It may be important to them to have authority over the s-type's self-expression and creative urges, which can come back to that identity clash we've mentioned in other chapters. Some will want an adoring peasant before their throne, while others may encourage the s-type to think of themselves as a royal consort and move with dignity in public.

Saturn in Leo/s

This s-type's idea of the perfect authority figure is a charismatic performer, able to command the eyes of others with word and attitude, supremely self-confident and never thrown off their dignity. If their M-type is not able to live up to this role even a little bit, there may be disappointment. The s-type with this placement realizes that this way of being is not their strong suit, and they want to be subordinate to the M-type who will help them to be more confident in their self-expression, and to move easily in the public eye. However, pushing them into the spotlight too quickly, without a long period of training, can freak them out and cause a fearful push-back. They want someone they can admire and adore, and can think of as a superstar, so long as the M-type's ego doesn't make them feel uncared-for or bad about themself. Being trained for a "supporting role" in which they feel competent can give them a small amount of spotlight and the ability to hide behind the larger-than-life M-type when it gets scary.

Saturn in Leo in a Composite Chart

As a couple, you'll want to be seen in public together (possibly to have your power dynamic validated), but at the same time you'll have a love-hate relationship with the public scene. Both of you may find yourselves particularly susceptible to becoming resentful over any perceived criticism from outsiders regarding your relationship; take care not to read criticism into comments with no bad intention, or just someone having a rough day. Inside the relationship, you may both have trouble with self-expression. Perhaps you may get stuck in roles and protocols that discourage spontaneity or individuality. Remember that the roles of s-type or M-type must come to fit who you really are, including all the humor and spark inside, rather than you both damping yourselves down in order to fit in small boxes. You'll both openly or secretly believe that the M-type's authority comes from their ability to inspire rather than demand obedience, and discussion needs to happen around what inspires rather than demands.

Saturn in Virgo/M

For this M-type, the ideal authority figure lurking in their head is superbly organized, incredibly efficient, and able to multitask dozens of lists and keep all the details in their head. They desperately want to be this person, and want to be seen as an authority because their organizational skills are so excellent, but the likelihood is that they struggle dreadfully with keeping their own life organized, much less someone else's. Chaos looms constantly on their horizon, and Saturn makes them less able than other people to cope with it, or ignore it and work around it. As a result, having authority over the s-type's organizational process, and hopefully training them to be the perfect personal assistant, is very important to this M-type.

They get a great deal of fulfillment out of helping the s-type to get their life in order, and may often take on the sort whose life is a dumpster fire, just for the satisfaction of sorting them out. (It's always easier to clean someone else's house than your own, after all.) This can work miracles or end in disaster, depending on how badly they want to fix an unrealistic prospect, and whether they indulge in the Virgo Saturn's nastiest quality — constant picayune criticism that can inadvertently undermine a partner's self-esteem. Underneath, this M-type secretly wants to have authority over an s-type who will help *them* stay organized, but even if they manage this, they won't really feel like a proper authority until they have been able to polish their own skills. It may be best to train a realistically talented s-type both to do the job for them, and to help them to be better about it themselves.

Saturn in Virgo/s

This s-type's dream is a highly organized leader who appreciates detail and polish, and is perhaps just a little on the obsessively neat side. They swoon over the M-type who wants all the silverware lined up perfectly, and who dictates the number of ice cubes which should be in a glass. Their part of the dream is to be the super-efficient personal assistant to this paragon of order, but they know that Saturn gets in their way, miring them in a swamp of chaos out of which they must continually dig themself. They want the M-type not only to surpass them in organizational ability, but to be able to train them past their obstacles and messiness. They are disappointed in a slapdash M-type who can't be bothered with details or a clean house, much less micromanaging their s-type into a state of executive perfection. On the other hand, when they actually get such an M-type, they may find themself crumbling in a morass of self-loathing if the training shows off their biggest difficulties and assumes that this ought to be simple for them. (Saturn problems need to be approached both firmly and compassionately.)

One of this s-type's most unpleasant qualities is probably their constant stream of mental criticism—of themselves, of others, and especially of their M-type. While the M-type needs to honestly listen to their critical subordinate, they also need to have the self-possession to shrug and say, "Yes, we're all imperfect, I hear you, but this is not a priority right now, so drop it."

Saturn in Virgo in the Composite Chart

For both people with this placement, being organized, precise, and efficient, and also getting all the details straight will be extremely important, especially when it comes to the M-type proving their worthiness as an authority figure. If they were both rather sloppy before, the mutual urge to "tighten up" and work toward a discipline of being neat and orderly in as many ways as possible may surprise them both. Of course, both parties have to work at this discipline; even if the M-type is giving all the orders, they still have to keep on top of the long view and make in an efficient plan for the next day's work, and the future. The pursuit of excellence will be a disheartening mountain that each may despair of getting over, but it will also be extremely attractive. Remember that Virgo is the sign of small moves—taking one tiny step at a time and not worrying about the final goal. Take all power exchange goals in finite, manageable steps, breaking those down as small as you need to keep from being overwhelmed. This is particularly important for goals that are at risk of perfectionism being projected all over them.

The big problem with this combination in a composite chart is that both partners tend to revert to criticism — and sometimes cutting and nasty criticism — when stressed. It may be that the best discipline to work on together is one of remembering to frame problems kindly and compassionately (perhaps making "we" statements or using neutral ways of describing situations), apologizing when either gets too critical, and trying hard to rephrase those ugly darts. Even difficult complications can be described considerately.

Saturn in Libra/M

The ideal authority figure in the mind of this M-type is a gracious, civilized, people-manager who is never unfair or unjust. They want to be this person, and to be seen as this person, but they secretly feel that they constantly fall short. (It's so easy to take sides in arguments and be less than pleasant in the face of unpleasant people.)

M-types with Saturn in Libra want very much to be seen as fair, even while they're getting what they want. Sometimes being the s-type can feel rather unfair, and the M-type simply pronouncing "Well, you agreed to this," is not helpful, does not address their feelings or help them to find a way to get a better attitude, and does not convince them that you are being fair.

On the other hand, Libra also has a problem of wanting harmony and peace badly enough that they will sometimes go into a spiral of indecision about whether to be fair or to wreck the atmosphere, which is also not helpful, especially if you do not let the s-type know what is spinning in your head. Indecision can freak out your s-type, but so can constantly giving in to them in order to keep the peace. Breathing exercises can calm you down and help you to focus; this is an Air sign problem.

Saturn in Libra/s

This s-type wants an authority figure like the one described above — scrupulously fair, gracious, charming, unerring in taste and sophistication, and able to manage difficult people with a smile and a well-modulated voice. In fact, they hope that their M-type will be able to work this magic on them, and eventually teach them to be more like this Libran ideal. The problem is that they often get stuck on either the side of justice — demanding that everything should be fair even when they have agreed to a subordinate role that is, by its nature, unfair — or on the side of harmony, hiding their negative emotions to keep from rocking the boat and stirring up conflict. Their M-type needs to learn to read that fixed smile and pry out what's going on underneath. Conversely, the M-type also needs to remain calm and urbane when the s-type begins their unfairness rant, and serenely point out over and over that they agreed to this negotiated dynamic. Libra is ruled by Venus, and this s-type may wistfully dream of the M-type who will take charge of the unsophisticated ugly duckling and transform them into a graceful swan.

Saturn in Libra in a Composite Chart

Both parties secretly or not-so-secretly want the relationship to be run by an authority figure who is like the one described above: gracious, charming, and always fair. The M-type will find themselves wanting to be that person, and the s-type will find themself wishing that the M-type would try harder to be that person. However, sooner or later they will run into the Libra dichotomy that all Libra planets share, but that Saturn displays at its most frustrating: the opposite poles of harmony and justice.

Most humans don't want pure justice; they want mercy, and to be allowed to slide when they behave badly. The more just the M-type is driven to be, the more the s-type may feel oppressed; the more the M-type tries to bring peace and harmony in the relationship, the less fair it becomes, in one direction or the other. Resolving this dichotomy will require a careful balancing act, one that the M-type cannot do alone. The s-type needs to take responsibility as well, and the two negotiate out a situation that is balanced between authoritative fairness and domestic harmony. In the process, they will learn more about the true nature of the give-and-take of relationship, regardless of who is leading or following.

Saturn in Scorpio/M

This M-type's secret ideal of an authority figure is someone who is iron-willed, highly moral and incorruptible, has beaten their internal monsters, and wields a great deal of raw power. They wish that they could be respected for these traits, but at the same time they secretly fear that they will never grow to be that person. It is important for this M-type to cultivate enormous self-honesty, and work on controlling themself and their compulsions. Water-sign Saturns all combine strong emotions with blockages around understanding emotion on a deep level, and as such are the most at-risk for lashing out at an s-type.

This placement gives an attraction to dark aesthetics, especially when feeling down; the depressed M-type with Saturn in Scorpio may dress in black gothic splendor with all the heavy eye makeup. They want to crawl inside the heads of their s-types and learn all about them, and may push transparency too quickly on an uncertain subordinate partner. The secret under their close interest is plain fear; they want to find out how to control and possibly manipulate their partner before their partner can do something to hurt them. If they manage to get through their own baggage, they can be powerfully compassionate people who are not frightened or disturbed by anyone's darknesses, which can be a boon to the s-type who is insecure about their own socially unacceptable desires.

Saturn in Scorpio/s

In their secret soul, this s-type dreams of an M-type who is the Dark Knight on the black horse, as implacable and iron-willed as their armor, unswerving in their honor, filled with dark passions but never letting them out of control ... and who can teach the s-type how to build an iron will strong enough to keep their own dark emotions from getting out of control. They want their

M-type to do whatever it takes to get inside their head, even when they are fighting or hiding to keep them out. They also want the occasional moral takedown—a sharp correction about their ethical behavior from an M-type whose own behavior in that area is stubbornly beyond reproach. It's often said that one must master one's self before one can master another human being, but the literal reality of that statement is more important to this Saturn sign than to any of the others, largely because mastering one's unruly emotions is such a challenge for this sign, and so crucial for their survival.

This s-type does have a tendency to push for takedowns just to make sure that the edges of power and control are still where they were yesterday. This bad habit isn't limited to this combination, but these s-types are definitely at a high risk for it. The M-type should calmly call them on it when it comes up---"Are you doing that thing again? Let's talk about why." This will drive them crazy, but if they can get past their fury, it will help them in a practice of mindfulness, and show that the M-type is less manipulatable than they thought.

Saturn in Scorpio in a Composite Chart
The two of you both see the ideal authority figure as an implacably self-controlled figure who cannot be bribed or cajoled, and does not waver in the face of temper tantrums from subordinates. At the same time, that authority figure should radiate a dark sexuality which may seem barely contained but is actually impeccably boundaried. Sound like something from a romance novel? In real life, it's important to cut the M-type enough slack to be human and vulnerable; this placement tends to create assumptions that are pretty rough on the M-type. As a result, some M-types in these relationships feel compelled to hide their inner selves, their errors, and their misunderstandings, and in desperation sometimes even lie about them. This has an unfortunate effect on trust when discovered. The M-type needs to work on viewing being honest about frailties as a strength, and communicate that to the s-type. Conversely, the s-type needs to work on seeing all the M-type's faults clearly and compassionately, with

no inhumanly ideal standards, and respecting them anyway. On the positive side, this placement will bring up both parties' tendencies toward emotional imbalance, and push them to encourage each other in self-discipline around those issues.

Saturn in Sagittarius/M

The ideal authority figure dancing in the subconscious of this M-type is an optimistic adventurer who attacks the search for Truth with idealism, is philosophical in the face of disaster, and has an avuncular tolerance of all people, even the annoying ones. They would love to be that person, but in reality they may often be dragged down by pessimism, fear of risk, and getting trapped within their dogmatism and short-sightedness. If they've worked on their Saturn issues, they may have become more tolerant of others just through having to face their own flaws. Like Saturn in Capricorn, it's important to these M-types to be seen as Right, and to be followed not just for their position but because they happen to be Right about the situation, whatever it is.

They may find it useful to have their s-type take on the role as "enthusiastic optimist", especially when they are having trouble being optimistic about anything. (Of course, this will depend on the s-type's ability to do that themself.) If this can happen, the s-type can not only be an auxiliary ray of sunshine, they can be a quiet role model for the M-type to learn from when it comes to relaxing and not sweating the small stuff. This is especially important if the M-type is pushing back at their fear of risks and taking the s-type with them on adventures, including travel to new and unknown places.

This is the sign of Trust, and this placement is one of several that scream "Trust Issues!", especially in the general goodness of human beings. Oddly enough, this M-type may trust too much and too little by turns, not sure where to place their investment. If you fear all risk while occasionally blindly defying that fear, you don't learn how to realistically assess it. They might benefit from outside aid and training in this skillset.

Saturn in Sagittarius/s

In Sagittarius—the sign of the adventurous and the religiously faithful—Saturn creates barriers to jumping into adventures both physical and spiritual with both feet and an open-hearted spirit of discovery. The s-type may long to climb a mountain or take a leap of faith, but that Saturn voice (and the Saturn voice in all of us) often starts with "…You're not good enough to…" or "…You don't deserve…" and they pull back, unable to make the leap. They may secretly be terrified of taking risks, and long for an M-type who can drag them along into an adventure by force of will. Unfortunately, Sagittarius is also the sign of Trust, and Saturn here creates huge and sometimes pathological barriers to trust. In some cases, the partner could stand on their head and it wouldn't help, because they're reacting to the memory of someone from long ago. It's worth it to do a lot of internal work—perhaps with a therapist—about what it would really take to trust someone, and make sure that goal is achievable and doesn't require the M-type to be superhuman.

Sagittarius is the sign of religion, and attempting to push this s-type into religious practices that they do not believe may result in violent reaction. Travel, too, is a sticking point, and if they can't get regular trips away (perhaps even alone, to pursue their hobbies) they may feel trapped. This placement gives a strong Saturnian feeling that things Must Be Done Right, and these people often have intense but unexplainable feelings that if they don't do certain things exactly the same way each time, bad things will happen. As with all things Saturn, they get better about this as they grow closer to old age.

Saturn in Sagittarius in a Composite Chart

Conflicting values can create trouble here, especially values about large, complicated, overarching issues, the sort that drive philosophers to drink. "Is vengeance ever acceptable?" "Is it ethical to manipulate people into doing the right thing or improving themselves?" Questions like these will become arguments quickly, because this placement wants to nail down Truth. A good mantra for this couple should be, "There are many truths, and we don't have the objectivity right now to see beyond our small ones to the greater ones, so let's wait and be patient." Which is not Sagittarius's strong suit, but it's worth focusing on.

Both people want to see the perfect authority figure as fiery, adventurous, and above all Wise and Right. There is a strong drive for a teacher/student relationship, but not in the elementary training of Gemini. This is the higher-education sign and the s-type wants to absorb the M-type's wisdom about the world, and expand their mind. However, they may trigger each other into remembering all the times when education went wrong and made them feel stupid or incompetent as teacher or student, and it is important to extend compassion in both directions.

The problem comes when the M-type is wrong, which they will inevitably be. Both people will be disappointed beyond what is reasonable at every error; they both need to breathe and realize that this an opportunity to work through it and gain more trust, not a negative point to be stacked up in an ongoing pile of resentments for not being inhumanly Right. With the planet of obstacles in the sign of Trust, they will find that trusting each other is both crucial and very easily lost. Finding ways to actively build up trust again every time it is lost, and not giving up hope in that process, is the way to build something lasting ... but both people have to be willing to take that leap, as many times as it takes.

Saturn in Capricorn/M

The M-type with Saturn in Capricorn wants their s-type to see their knowledge, skills, ambition, and hard-won wisdom about how to make it in the world as the main reason why they are worthy to lead. This is especially true if those qualities have given them some kind of status in their community; they want the s-type to be impressed by this and see the opinions of others as an integral part of their worthiness to be followed. They want to be seen as Right, and for the s-type to bow to them because they are Right, not just because they are dominant. The problem comes, of course, when they are not Right, a situation which will periodically arise because they are human. With this placement, they may have a hard time backing down and admitting error, because on some level they fear that admitting error will damage their dominant standing. Personal discipline is very important to them, whether or not they're good at it, and they will want to impress this on their s-type. Be careful to actually walk the talk here, and not just expect of the s-type a higher level of personal discipline than they exhibit themselves. These M-types may be very attracted to "traditional" formal protocols, however they define those.

Saturn in Capricorn/s

Openly or secretly, this s-type wants to follow a leader with community status — and preferably one who is ambitious, disciplined, and savvy in the ways of worldly power. The public in question can be a small community or subculture, but they want their dominant partner to have real, concrete standing among the people whose opinions they value. They want to be the servant to the Prime Minister, to follow behind the person who is bowed to by others. It will be difficult for this s-type to properly respect a hermit with no public ambition enough to submit to them.

Part of why they want this is because they desire someone who will give them status as well, as they ride in on their M-type's coattails. They enjoy it when their dominant partner trains them in how to function smoothly and be seen as competent in their community milieu, and they are happy to be arm candy if it will get them seen by others who may eventually be useful to them. (This goes especially if those others are a little envious of the s-type, their partner, or the relationship.) This s-type would also love an authority figure who could mentor them in their career and teach them how to achieve their goals. Since these s-types are likely both secretly ambitious and not-so-secretly incredibly uncomfortable with ambition, they seek a partner who can teach them how to motivate themselves to climb that mountain.

Saturn in Capricorn in a Composite Chart

Status is very important to this couple, or rather the M-type's status in whatever community or groups in which they may be invested. The s-type's status will depend on the M-type's, and both partners want it that way. Capricorn is Saturn's own sign and it enjoys being there; this will be a relationship where discipline and rules are emphasized, more even than in other power dynamics. The couple may be drawn by formal, dignified settings — perhaps even of the sort labeled "butler porn" — where people with wealth, prestige, and cultured tastes engage in a graceful dance of service and privilege. Even if they live in a trailer park, they may scrape to get an echo of old-fashioned manorial living into their power dynamic. They may judge each other as dominant and subordinate partner, at least a little, by how well they manage to enact this energy even in a less-than-ideal situation. The quest for polished excellence will entrance them both, although they may have their own private standards for what constitutes excellence.

One drawback to this placement is a tendency to depression for both parties. Find ways to build joy into the relationship, or it will become all drudgery and no spark. Don't downplay the value of humor and play; even Saturn can't be in authority all the time.

Saturn in Aquarius/M

For the person with Saturn in Aquarius, the ideal leader is a brilliant, eccentric revolutionary who changes minds and comes up with ground-breaking ideas. The M-type with this combination wistfully wants to be this person, to be seen as such by their s-type, and respected as a worthy leader for doing that so well. The problem, as usual, is when they don't quite manage it competently and feel like a failure. Saturn, in the end, is about disciplined competence, Here Saturn tries to find a competent balance between flaunting public opinion and doing things one's own way, and alienating one's self from other people by one's opinions and eccentric behaviors.

This M-type will want their s-type to be their biggest cheerleader in their struggle against whatever unfair social enemy is on their dance card this month, and agree with their current pet peeves about how things are done by Everyone Else. They may have unusual ideas about how to run a power dynamic, and may reject others' ideas on principle, because if it's been done often enough it must be tired and old. This can be brilliant or clumsy, depending on how much information they are willing to secretly absorb before coming up with their Grand Plan. If their ideas are not immediately accepted by others, they may retreat into solitude and avoid their peers. It helps for them to find peer support in the form of other M-types who are also known for unusual new ideas and bucking the system.

Saturn in Aquarius/s

The ideal leadership archetype hiding in this s-type's head is the brilliant but misunderstood revolutionary, ahead of their time, bucking the system and giving the finger to stodgy current norms. They can be disappointed with the M-type whose beliefs are too average and unconsidered; the M-type can even hold surprisingly conservative beliefs with the s-type's admiration so long as they can reframe them as some sort of brave fight against encroaching liberalism, but just absorbing ordinary media without debate or rebellion will disenchant the s-type.

The underlying reason they want this sort of M-type to admire is that they want to learn these qualities themselves, and have someone sufficiently brave and rebellious from whom to absorb them. (It's also sometimes easier for an s-type to defend unusual beliefs and practices if they are simply enacting their M-type's orders.) However, in their quest for the Weird And Different, they may mistake instability for eccentric brilliance and snub someone more practical and sensible. On the positive side, they tolerate an inconsistent M-type better than other Saturn signs, and don't care if their M-type resembles nothing in any power exchange community.

Saturn in Aquarius in a Composite Chart

Whether or not they think of themselves this way, a power exchange couple with this placement will want to buck the system together, and will get a thrill from doing it. They might try it in any number of ways—alternative relationships (obviously, if they are reading this book), alternative careers, radical politics, unusual sexual or gender expression, etc. The image of ideal authority in both their minds is the radical genius who has their own crazy way of doing things, and holds to it in the face of all social disapproval. The M-type will want to be that, and the s-type will want to follow that. Of course, their idea of what is radical and unusual will be hand-picked from their own combined values and cannot be generalized; the whole point is that it doesn't fit in a box.

Or does it? This is Saturn, after all, and Saturn loves to put things in boxes. That's why the main danger of this placement is becoming extremely rigid in one's differences, working so hard at resisting social pressure that one closes one's ears to any other opinion and begins to believe that one's way is the Only Way. While it's difficult enough to be the "different ones" in a group, being the different ones who think they've got the Real Trip and everyone else is deluded is especially problematic. Saturn in Aquarius is all about having trouble with friends and groups. (It doesn't help that Saturn is also the planet of You're Not Good Enough, and the couple who are heavily invested in being The Different Ones can also end up agonizing over whether they are radical enough, or whether they are selling out every time they do something "average".)

At its worst, Saturn will herd them into a paranoid hermit-hole where they will avoid peers and community ... which is not the point, as Aquarius is all about peers and community. The goal of this sign, when on the planet of authority, is to uphold one's beliefs while connecting with and learning from many, together as a team. It is accepting that beliefs become more nuanced over time with new information, then showing your community that what you do works, not through preaching but through your clear and obvious joy in each other and in your dynamic. On the interest side, you may both be enamored with technological aids to power exchange and service, long-distance and "virtual" dominance and submission, nonsexual service relationships, and unusual family structures in a dynamic.

Saturn in Pisces/M

This is one of the hardest places to have Saturn, especially for the M-type. Pisces is ruled by Neptune, the planet of sacrifice, surrender, and spirituality, which wants to blend and merge as much as Saturn wants to structure and crystallize. The M-type with this placement may have a hard time, in the beginning, even consciously accessing a satisfactory mental leadership archetype, except possibly one that sacrifices for their followers and feels responsible for everything in a fifty-foot radius. As their mastery matures, however, they begin to understand the Saturn in Pisces concepts of spiritual discipline, or compassion with boundaries, or structured mysticism. Their ideal authority figure resolves into a compassionate, responsive leader who inspires by the discipline of self-awareness and quiet understanding that they are willing to suffer to cultivate. Their ideal leaders look more like Gandhi or Pope Francis or the Dalai Lama than any fierce, sexy warrior, and they may believe that no s-type would follow those strengths. If they already have the bad habit of trying to save problematic s-types who may be above their pay grade to handle, they may secretly feel like a failed messiah, someone who can't save anyone and would be better off alone.

The first key is to apply as much compassion to themselves as they can call up for others, which is its own kind of constant discipline, and learn to set good boundaries from that place of self-compassion rather than fear or exhaustion. The second key is to learn that their job is not to save people but to inspire them—to be an example of personal evolution in action, and if people don't see it, well, those aren't your followers. These M-types often have better luck from s-types who pursue them than any they attempt to pursue themselves. Eventually, they learn that the more open and honest they are about their struggle to discipline their own internal roiling cauldron, the more respect they will gain from the right people.

Saturn in Pisces/s

On some level, this s-type wants a spiritual leader. They may not use the word "spiritual"—in fact, they may hate that word — but it comes down to the same thing. They want someone with near-saintly compassion and understanding, who has disciplined themself into self-awareness, and could guide the oversensitive or under-sensitive s-type to that place. They know that they have problems with boundaries — either not setting them soon enough and being taken advantage of, or surrounding themselves with a psychic fortress through which no pain (or much of anything else) may pass. They may not be able to articulate it, but they want the M-type who can teach them the trick of setting balanced boundaries competently — but teaching in a way that does not threaten their flinchy inner selves. If their M-type is clumsy or callous or fails to see past the walls they erect, they will be disappointed.

This placement has a hard time with transparency, because they have generally been hurt and don't trust easily, and because they have a fatalistic view of the world that assumes they will have to suffer to get anything decent out of life. They may shrug and say nothing about all the little hurts until they pile up, then utilize the Neptune-ruled Pisces strategy of just walking out and vanishing with no explanation.

A wise M-type — and this s-type desperately wants a wise and kind M-type more than a domineering or even a powerful one — will build exercises of self-awareness and self-compassion into the mastery of their subordinate partner. For example, the M-type could say, "Thank you for trusting me," every time the s-type asks for a limit or speaks up about a problem; the M-type could also use those moments to focus the s-type on seeing these as acts of compassion (or self-compassion). This is another interaspect that encourages a disciple relationship; note how similar that word is to *discipline*, Saturn's stock in trade, but put through the Neptunian sieve of Pisces.

Saturn in Pisces in the Composite Chart

Both partners in this relationship will have the urge to sacrifice for each other, to be Givers in a big way. This can be wonderful, or it can go very wrong in a number of ways. Either might find themselves giving past their comfort zone because they feel that they "ought to", and resentment may ensue. Either may get too used to being coddled, and get out of the habit of being a responsible adult. The s-type may feel uncomfortable with the M-type giving so much, as they may feel that it is their job, or they may enjoy it when the M-type is more selfish. The M-type may worry that the s-type is sacrificing too much and never challenge them or push them toward excellence. Honesty, and self-honesty, are needed to make sure that no one is giving inappropriately, or giving out of old misguided baggage rather than realistically assessing the situation.

For both partners, the fantasy of ideal authority is someone compassionate and understanding enough to handle a sensitive follower, and yet self-controlled enough to be wise in the ways of emotions. In fact, *wise* would be the single word to sum them up. The M-type will want to be that person, and the s-type will want them to be that person. Pisces' keyword is "I Believe", and the s-type desperately wants to believe in the M-type, their judgment, and their goals. Of course, no one is wise all the time, and some are actually rarely so. This placement sets a high bar for the relationship, but on the positive side, both partners will have a deep fund of sympathy for each other. That's good, because they will need it in order to help each other evolve toward their own wisest selves.

SATURN IN THE HOUSES

Saturn in the 1st House/M

This is the house of the Body, and it rules one's physical appearance, clothing, mannerisms, body movement, and everything else that makes up your public persona. The M-type with this placement may have a vision that an ideal authority figure first establishes influence over the s-type's physical body. This can include having authority over the way they dress, accessorize, wear their hair, speak in public, sit, walk, and carry themself. A program of exercise and diet — physical discipline — may be on their list, although unlike a "health house" placement, this is less for health and more for maintaining a certain look. Uniforms of various sorts may also seem attractive, as may body modifications such as tattoos, piercings, or cosmetic surgery.

How they look themself is also an issue. Saturn in this house sometimes portends some sort of physical disability, or in some cases extreme difficulty in gauging how one looks to others, so these individuals often feel awkward and unsure of their image. They may throw themselves into a Saturnian physical discipline in order to maintain a certain "look" which helps them to feel worthy of dominance, or else cultivate a dignified and precise attitude that does not depend on physical image to indicate their authority.

In some cases, the M-type may actually find it important to their sense of authority that they can physically restrain or wrestle down their s-type. If physical play of this sort is an important part of reminding both parties of who they are to each other, thought needs to be put into how that will change when both grow old and the M-type may not be able to manage this any longer.

Saturn in the 1st House/s

With Saturn in the house of the body, the s-type may want a dominant partner who can overpower them physically, being able to wrestle them to the floor. Another possible way this can play out is wanting the M-type to be more physically attractive or fit than the s-type. This can be accompanied by a desire for the M-type to manage their body be decreeing disciplines of hygiene, dressing, makeup, hair care, exercise, dieting, movement, etc., possibly with a hope of the M-type turning their "ugly duckling" into a swan. As Saturn in the first house often comes with physical disabilities or at least a difficulty in gauging how others see you, this can be a goal that not every M-type necessarily wants to take on. However, the s-type may be disappointed if they don't.

The s-type may have high standards for the M-type's appearance as well, and may turn down less physically gifted types in order to find someone whose exterior matches their fantasy. Socially-acceptable attractiveness aside, it may be important to the s-type that the M-type has the bearing of a proper authority figure, or in other words, that their external mask embodies Saturn, ideally but not necessarily in its most positive form. M-types that are more laid-back, mischievous, or otherwise lacking in obvious stern dignity may not make the cut. However, even an M-type needs to let their hair down sometimes, and when this happens, the s-type may be slightly scandalized. It can help if the M-type stresses how much of a privilege it is to see them like this.

Saturn in the 1st House in a Composite Chart

Saturn in the house of appearances can indicate that people look to you as authority figures when you are together; just be careful to be the benevolent authority rather than the forbidding one. Saturn here can also indicate that the two of you have difficulty figuring out who to "be" when you're together in public; if your roles and relationship don't translate well to your social circle, you may be very uncomfortable showing your power dynamic in public. It indicates that the public "face" of your relationship can be awkward, and you both tend toward formality when together in public in order to cover that awkwardness. It's also possible that one or both of you is visibly disabled.

There's a pull in your relationship to mutual physical discipline for body shape and health; even if your bodies aren't great, having a regular physical discipline of some kind will be good for you. Motivate the s-type with the M-type's orders (and perhaps a chart to be checked off) and motivate the M-type by having the s-type on orders to encourage them and make exercise and good diet easier.

Saturn in the 2nd House/M

This is the house of possessions and resources. Traditionally, people with Saturn in this house were characterized by financial obstacles early in life, having to work hard for their money and assets, and having nothing in that area come easily. Wealth of any kind is a painful subject, and one which they might react to with greed and hoarding, in fearing that it will all slip out of their grasp, or conversely living a spartan life so that they won't have much to lose. What they don't have is an easy attitude toward their property, and if we're talking about an M-type, they may have those attitudes toward anyone who ends up being their human property.

These M-type may feel that they aren't a convincing authority figure unless they have money — preferably more money than their s-type — and if they have become reasonably wealthy, they may be tempted to use that as a handle, becoming a "sugar daddy" and supporting their subordinate partner. They will probably want authority over the s-type's finances, and might prevent them from working, or possibly send them out to a job in order to bring more money into the house. They may want an Owner/property relationship very much, but they need to make sure that they aren't pushing for that out of fear that their valuable partner will slip through their fingers. That's not a clean motivation, and it can set up a spiral of greed and desperate possessiveness that undermines their own self-control. On the positive side, once they have their issues better sorted, these M-types can be excellent at coaching an s-type through budgeting, investing, and making the most of their money. They are usually very good about building a fund for their subordinate partner in case they exit life first.

Saturn in the 2nd House/s

Most of the s-types I've met with this placement have lived with financial hardship, have a difficult time hanging onto money and property, and very much want an M-type who can support them financially. Some are aware of their financial clumsiness and would like to be taught better. A few that I've met are the opposite — fiercely financially independent, usually because they've been down, clawed their way back up, and don't ever want to risk that again. However, this s-type's mental image of the proper authority figure definitely includes financial solvency and competence; it's unlikely that they would consider the M-type who is living on welfare or disability. Even if they have their own money, they would like their M-type to have more of it.

They may have a love-hate relationship with seeing themself as property. On the one hand, they may find it extremely compelling; on the other hand, their ambivalent history around keeping and losing resources may make this role fairly daunting, and they may reject it and keep most of their autonomy. Their picture of submission likely includes the M-type controlling their finances and personal property, but at the same time they won't turn that over unless they feel completely secure in the relationship and their M-type's competence.

Saturn in the 2nd House in a Composite Chart

Composite Saturn in the second house usually signifies money troubles—and certainly fears about money. Finances may always be a difficult problem for you, and you need to start saving now. Any tendencies for impulse buying as a couple need to be stomped on, because this is not an area of life where you will be lucky. Instead, Saturn here indicates that you will both have to work hard for your money, although if you are careful and persistent there is no reason why you shouldn't be able to amass a comfortable sum. Saturn is the old taskmaster here, decreeing that boring financial responsibility is your hardest job as a couple.

Also, you will be wrestling with values around rules and authority. What does positive authority look like? What sorts of rules are good and what sorts are soul-oppressing? What kinds of structure works and what kind is outdated? What values are inappropriate for a leader to hold? Can the leader force their values on the follower? These questions will need to be worked out the hard way in your relationship.

It's also possible that there is some kind of obstacle to having an Owner/property relationship, where one of you is literally owned by the other. If that's not your wish, then it's no problem. If it's something you want, you both may have to work to overcome some serious roadblocks, whether internal or external.

Saturn in the 3rd House/M

This placement traditionally indicates obstacles in the ability to communicate, in some cases due to learning disabilities, neurological issues, or just an upbringing where clear and direct communication was not rewarded. The M-type with this placement is going to have to work hard to give clear and concise orders, be able to explain their reasoning to a confused subordinate, listen thoughtfully to the s-type's problems and respond appropriately, and teach skills and pass on knowledge in a way that works for the s-type's learning style.

The problem is made worse by their internal idea of the ideal authority figure as being someone who has those skills. It may be that they ran into someone in a leadership role who excelled at them enough to draw out the would-be M-type's fumbling communications, and they may feel as if they will never achieve that goal. Formal structures and rituals for communicating may help them to find their footing, as may getting some outside training in teaching and leadership communication. Talking about their emotions—and understanding and responding usefully to the s-type's emotions—will be particularly challenging and may need external training to work through.

Saturn in the 3rd House/s

Not all s-types come to a power dynamic with good communication skills, sharp memories, and excellent problem-solving minds. Some come assuming that a power dynamic will allow them to bypass all that talking and thinking, and they are often disappointed when they discover how wrong they are. With this Saturn placement, the s-type is going to have trouble communicating, particularly about how they feel. Since this placement sometimes indicates learning disabilities, neurological problems, or a childhood full of being told that one's opinions were unwanted and useless, it may take a lot of time and patient training to get them to open up and give honest updates on how the relationship and the power dynamic are working for them. Emphasizing how withholding information can sabotage the M-type's job can help motivate them. Their mental processes may be a bit erratic, and it's helpful for their focus and peace of mind to require that they keep their personal environment as orderly as possible, as clutter can be extremely distracting for them. On some level their ideal of an excellent authority figure is one who can communicate with them through their mental blocks, guide them into focused thinking and working, and always phrase orders in ways they can understand. That may not come quickly and easily, and both parties must be patient and work to comprehend each other better.

Saturn in the 3rd House in a Composite Chart

This placement indicates that the two individuals are going to have communication difficulties, due to opposing mental processes. One or both may have neurological or learning disabilities, or perhaps they grew up speaking different languages or dialects. They may clash over cultural values on book-reading, education, or intellectual prowess. Both must learn the other's language as best they can, and remember to speak in it when discussing important things ... or, as another option, both can adopt specific protocols around how to articulate concepts and issues. The protocols can reinforce the power dynamic, and remind the two of you who you are to each other. However, the M-type will have to work as hard as the s-type on this — it can't all be one-way.

Keeping your home environment — and especially any "work environment" in your home, such as a home office or library — neat and orderly will help, as will making sure that any books, computers, paperwork, or other media materials are well-organized and easy to find. This is because your conflicting ways of thinking can create chaos when allowed to get sloppy in the same space, and keeping a general sense of order around your mind-things can help. You may both be interested in the M-type having authority over the s-type's speech and access to media, but the M-type also has to work to discipline themselves around that area.

Saturn in the 4th House/M

For this M-type, having authority over the s-type's domestic service around the house is very important to them. Actually, having the s-type right there in their home is important to them as well; like those with Pluto and Neptune in the fourth house, they will not do well with long distance relationships. (On the other hand, Saturn is the planet of obstacles, and it's possible that the Universe may throw up blockages such as an s-type who can't move in for some time.) This is the house of family, including what you inherit from them in the way of difficult assumptions and dysfunctional patterns, and the M-type with this placement is going to have to work very, very hard not to wake up one day and realize that they have become the problematic authority figure of their childhood.

The best way to prevent this is to do a lot of mindful work, perhaps with outside help, to outline what that trap looked like, so that the edges are clear and the M-type won't mindlessly fall into it. We are all born into power dynamics with flawed human beings, and we need to work out the cracks and scars we inherited before we can cleanly become an authority figure ourselves—and for no Saturn house placement is this truism more important. In a sense, whatever discipline the M-type may level onto the s-type, this is the one they must take up themselves: to be mindful of their old baggage and to prevent those old ghosts from speaking orders through their mouths.

Since this is also the house of ancestry, one useful inspiration might be researching the ways people held honorable power in history. (Yes, there were some!) It's also a good way to note historical mistakes, as well. M-types with this placement might also be drawn to adult/child roleplay and prefer a very parental role, where they can strive toward being the good parent, Saturn-firm and fourth-house-nurturing, perhaps the one they never had themselves.

Saturn in the 4th House/s

This placement puts up a lot of obstacles to domestic service. These s-types may have associated it with political oppression or emotional degradation due to an upbringing that was spent either watching a parent resentfully dragged down by it, or being forced to do it themselves to an extent that was not appropriate to their age, perhaps due to a parent's inability to take care of it. Either way, if they're asked to be the full-time housekeeper, something in them runs into a wall. Since these more "menial" jobs tend to fall to s-types in a relationship, they will either need to find an M-type who doesn't want them to be the housekeeper (perhaps because they M-type can afford a professional, or enjoys doing it themselves, or the s-type ends up being the full-time breadwinner, or is too physically disabled to do it themselves), or else they'll have to learn to get over it.

Since Saturn is also the planet of discipline, it might help to have the M-type treat it as an exercise in discipline. No, that doesn't mean punishment for slacking off; I'm talking more about a situation where the M-type makes regular inspections, encourages the s-type to excellence even when it's hard, and perhaps comes up with a system of small rewards for making it through another week of cleaning and maintenance. In addition, if the s-type has a strong say in the decorating of the home, they'll probably also have more investment in caring for it.

This is also the house of old childhood patterns, and home-and-household issues need to be watched for those old patterns cropping up, even if only inside the s-type's head. This is especially true for Saturnian feelings of "I'm not good enough." The M-type needs to know about them, and know the signs of the s-type unthinkingly reacting from that place instead of from the reality of their adult situation.

Saturn in the 4th House in the Composite Chart

This placement sometimes creates problems with living together. The couple may decide not to share a home, or there may be financial concerns that get in the way for a long time. When they do get a place to live, it may be a bit of a financial burden. On the other hand, this is the house of early family life, and it can also apply to issues of mutual childhood difficulty. It may be that living together triggers all the wounds from each of the partners' pasts, and in order to make their home something other than a constant rough therapy session, they will both need to be very aware and conscious of these land mines, and figure out practical protocols to cope and comfort each other when the inevitable explosions occur—and even more important, immediately and diligently figure out how to prevent each one from happening again. Power exchange often brings up these old patterns, because we are all born into a power dynamic (healthy or not) and it's the first thing we learn. If the partners find themselves repeating old patterns, it will be up to them as a couple to make each other aware of them, and enlist each other's aid in breaking out. "Are you listening to me and hearing your mother again? I'm not her, you know. I'm coming at this from an entirely different space, don't stick the Mom mask on me!"

They may find that the Saturn influence makes them put up with a very spartan home with few luxuries. Bother to paint and make the place beautiful and comfortable, even if there's a Saturn voice in your heads saying, "You can't afford that, and it's not important anyway!" If nothing else, it's important not to let that voice go unchecked. Saturn in the house of home and family can mean that the M-type is extra harsh and demanding when it comes to how the home is kept. Rules seem to keep piling up around housework and they seem more upsetting when forgotten than rules in other areas. It's important that none of the rules are being made in an unthinking reaction to old childhood patterns, but are clearly and reasonably thought through for their sustainability.

Saturn in the 5th House/M

This is a hard place to have Saturn in most relationships, because it's the house of romance, love-struck fireworks, and play. Saturn here can make someone feel like they are no good at that sort of thing. It's actually likely that their idea of fun may be introverted and solitary, whereas romance may seem like a foreign language that they despair of learning. However, a certain percentage of power dynamics are highly structured and somewhat more formal than egalitarian relationships, and the 5th-house Saturn M-type may find themselves much more comfortable in these heavily negotiated, systematized interactions. The behavioral rules and expectations can be worked out in a straightforward manner, and no one has to guess what anyone is feeling … assuming for a compatible partner who is honest and comfortable with this kind of candid dynamic. Romance, this M-type may find, is an art that can be filtered through rules and protocols, and this may make it seem a lot more doable. It does mean that they'll want to have authority over how affection and emotions are expressed; as long as the system is set up so that no content is excluded, however difficult, they may find a power dynamic to be the fun that they never thought they'd have.

Saturn in the 5th House/s

This is the planet of obstacles, and having it in the house of romance means that these s-types may feel rather awkward about their ability to be romantic on demand. However, there's a benefit to being the s-type in this situation because it gives options. Saturn is also the planet of discipline, and they can work toward being a polished, M-type-approved version of the "perfect companion", a slave who acts like a lover instead of a lover who acts like a slave. One male s-type I know with this aspect refers to himself as a "boy geisha". Making a discipline of being pleasant, cheerful, and doing exactly the romantic gestures in which one has been trained can sidestep awkwardness. Of course, the M-type has to be into it, and not be put off by a perceived lack of spontaneity, which can be seen by the insecure as a lack of sincerity.

This is also the house of creativity, and they may appreciate a dominant partner who both encourages them in creative pursuits and sets limits when they take on too much, or use it to avoid practical responsibilities. They may be at their most creative in projects with strict boundaries. In the house of children, Saturn here can indicate sterility or other difficulties in having children.

Saturn in the 5th House in a Composite Chart

Anywhere that Saturn falls in the composite chart, there is likely to be a sense of duty and obligation, and you can imagine what a wet blanket that is in the house of romance, children, gambling, and joy. This often makes a romantic relationship feel like a dutiful arranged marriage rather than an explosion of rosy fireworks, and it usually means that either there will be no children for external reasons or that the offspring situation will be fraught with difficulty and disappointment somehow. Infertility is common with this placement, as is a general sense of one person feeling responsible for the other one, and not always in a pleasant way.

One feeling often expressed in relationships with this placement is that if it were not for special external circumstances, this couple would never have chosen to be in a relationship of any sort with each other. Of course, power exchange can sometimes be those special circumstances; both may be keenly aware that if not for the power dynamic, they would never have chosen a romantic relationship with each other, and indeed the only "romance" may be that of master and slave. They can make an effort to form bonds based on the hardships they have endured and survived together, and focus on the romantic actions of service, control, and surrender. Orgasm control may be particularly interesting as a discipline for them, but they should not push it to the point of robbing the relationship of a useful tool of positive reinforcement. If they choose an ageplay relationship, the Daddy/Mommy may have to be careful not to be too harsh to the "child".

Saturn in the 6th House/M

This is the house of scut-work, maintenance, health ... and service. It is service that we are most interested with these relationships. Before we get to that, it must be said that having the planet of obstacles here will sometimes make someone extremely wary of sixth-house activities like organization, management, and scut-work. Sometimes these people will dislike being in the workplace enough that they will slack off and leave every job before long. If the M-type has this problem and it doesn't look like they are going to get over it any time soon, then their best bet is to find the s-type who will support them financially, and structure their management in a way that is effective and efficient but as unlike the nasty workplace as possible, so that it won't trigger them.

They will be very focused on getting good service from the s-type, and will want complete authority in how those services are performed; for people who seem not to care about details in their everyday life, they can suddenly become very interested in every detail of how the s-type does things, particularly around the house. The s-type's health may become an issue, and the M-type may want authority over that. The s-type may be willing, or may be torn about it; tread carefully on this subject. At the same time, people with this placement are infamous for not taking proper care of themselves, and the s-type may become scared and upset if they see the M-type risking their health. (We recommend getting other M-types that the s-type respects to talk to them about how to handle one's health issues in a dominant, take-charge manner that enlists the s-type has a tool to make that process easier.)

Saturn in the 6th House/s

This s-type wants very much to render service to the M-type, but they have a number of organizational blocks to doing it competently without some routines and structures, which they may find uncomfortable even if they are necessary. This placement traditionally indicates someone who has a lot of insecurities in their job, and in a power dynamic, the duties they are assigned by their M-type definitely fall into that "job insecurity" danger zone. They may be wary of trying new services because they fear failure, and may have given up too easily in the past so they don't have a mental track record of seeing themselves practice until they get it right. However, once they get on track, they find great satisfaction in performing service correctly.

They may also have trouble with organizational structures; lists, Post-It notes, and technological aids are a good thing here. This is the house of mentoring, and these s-types may very much want the M-type to mentor them in "adulting", including ways to find motivation for those necessary activities.

Since this placement indicates people who have a rough time with taking care of their health, they may want the M-type to take over and handle those decisions, or they may suddenly become Saturn-stubborn and refuse to give up that area. This may depend on how much competence the M-type shows with their own health.

Saturn in the 6th House in a Composite Chart

In a power dynamic, Saturn in the house of service can mean that the two of you take service very seriously. That's a good thing, but the problem is when you take the goal of perfecting service so seriously that it loses its charm and becomes mere drudgery, or worse — a thorn in the foot that constantly galls because you can't get it perfect. Remember that the worse you feel about service, the more the performance will decay, because part of good service is the love you put into it and the satisfaction it gives you. If one or both partners are beginning to hate or fear it, they need to stop and start over. They should reconstruct the place of service in their life, and examine each service rendered to see if it's working. If it's not, throw it out and find a more satisfying one.

Having composite Saturn in the house of Duty can make it feel easy, or make it feel like drudgery, depending on how well both of you deal personally with the concepts of Duty, Responsibility, and Work. Saturn likes being in the sixth house of Service, because Saturn is all about the above qualities. However, Saturn here can also push the two of you into thinking that everything has to be all Duty, all the time — including the work of ironing out the million problems in the relationship and in yourselves. Saturn here turns this into a work relationship to one extent or another, for good or ill. It's a great placement for a professional relationship, but it can be hard on a romantic one, because Saturn clamps down on spontaneity and demonstrative affection. The key is to deliberately build in times where, no matter how much work there is to do, the two of you take time to have fun together.

This is also the house of health, and with Saturn here, the M-type may want to have authority over the s-type's medical care and how they handle their body maintenance. Of course, the M-type's health may come up as an issue as well, with the s-type becoming frightened and nagging, which never helps. Utilizing the s-type's services to help make health care less of a drag can help the M-type to motivate and take care of their body.

Saturn in the 7th House/M

These M-types either want very much to Get Married Immediately, because they do actually see the wedding ring as a ball and chain—on the s-type, that is—or they are wary of marriage and find reasons to put it off. There may actually be good reasons, for that matter, like another spouse or a nonsexual power dynamic. Once married, they may emphasize how much marriage is a Duty, rather than a romantic adventure. Actually, they don't need the marriage license to emphasize that; they can point to whatever form the commitment takes and talk about Duty.

In a sense, they don't expect commitment to be much fun, so when they make one with all due seriousness and forethought, they are quite willing to work to make it function. Work is what they expect here. These M-types will shoulder the burden of responsibility and slog through without stinting. The hard part for them is getting over their assumptions and finding a way to make the commitment into a romantic adventure. Periodically playing with sexual scenarios around having just met (or just been captured) can be rejuvenating to them.

Saturn in the 7th House/s

This s-type's ideal authority figure is someone older than they are (and for whom they are The Special One, not just one of many), who is good at one-on-one relations of all sorts, and who Keeps Their Commitments—and isn't afraid to initiate them. A dominant partner who isn't interested in a committed relationship—of the sort with joint bank accounts and house deeds—will not hold their interest for long. While we often see this placement as indicating the right commitment coming at a later time in life, the other way it can manifest is taking up with partners who are significantly older, and this is something I've often seen in s-types with this placement. The s-type will want to give over the relationship commitment and structure to the M-type. Sometimes this can manifest as the s-type waiting patiently for years for the M-type to propose marriage, while the M-type thinks they're just fine without a legal commitment. Sometimes this involves the s-type going along with a relationship structure that wouldn't be their first choice, and making that sacrifice to stay in the relationship. A thoughtful M-type will stay on top of the s-type's feelings, and get them peer support from other s-types who have been in the same situation.

Saturn in the 7th House in a Composite Chart

Traditionally, this placement meant that the couple would not be allowed to marry due to outside circumstances; we have seen this placement in s-types who are not the primary nesting partner of their M-type, or with M-types who could not reconcile "slave" and "spouse". It also comes up sometimes in couples who get together at much older ages. Traditionally, Saturn here gives a very strong sense of duty in the relationship, indicating attachments other than emotion and attraction that keep the couple together. This placement does not prevent emotion or attachment, but it does mean that these passions, however lovely, are not the foundation that holds the couple together. In a power exchange relationship with this placement, it likely indicates that the bond of dominance and submission is the foundation; they will be Master and slave — or however they label it — first, and all else second. Their pledges of honor will keep them together, and all the emotions and passions are simply frosting on the cake.

Saturn in the 8th House/M

The eighth house is the house of sex, death, the hidden mysteries, deep emotional bonding, and other people's money. Saturn is the planet of obstacles, and the individual can expect to find those in most or all of these areas. One of the biggest problems with this M-type is their difficulty in opening up emotionally to a partner and bonding deeply to them. This can happen to other M-types as well, but this placement really puts the walls up, usually due to past trauma or wounds. It can also sabotage the ability to make a lot of money (at least until late in life), so any s-type needs to understand that they won't be getting a good meal ticket and will probably have to pitch in and work as well. This placement tends to tends to impair the M-type's ability to change themselves, at least in the early stages, but by the time they reach their second Saturn return they have generally become wizards at that process out of sheer self-defense, and can help others to change as well. They have to go through their own hard, ugly transformation first, though — possibly a few of them.

Sexual problems are common with this placement, either for psychological or physical reasons; this is the house of transformation, so using sex (and possibly unusual sex that doesn't hit the triggers) as a catharsis can help transform those iron bars. These M-types have a mental image of an authority figure who is mysterious, magical, shrewd about how people tick, and able to whisk money out of thin air; they may feel a fair amount of shame when they fail at being this person. On the other hand, as they get older (Saturn rules old age) they may well mature into being just that.

Saturn in the 8th House/s

This is the planet of obstacles in the house of sex, and the first ugly truth we much face with this placement is that they are at high risk for sexual problems. For some people with this placement, these are deep-seated psychological repressions; for others, they are physical or hormonal or chemical disabilities. Some of these Saturn obstacles can eventually be overcome and others can only be worked around and compensated for. Patience and flexibility in this area will be necessary for the M-type in this equation, especially since these s-types tend to imagine that the right M-type will be able to transform them into people who don't have these problems, and they will want a trusted person to have authority over their sexuality.

Saturn isn't something that you just get over, though. Nobody gets a Saturnectomy, much as we might like one. This placement demands discipline and boundaries; it demands that you build the crutch and the wheelchair instead of whining that you can't walk. This is the house of transformation; sometimes a power dynamic relationship can help transform the s-type's sexual boundaries, and sometimes it can only be the useful crutch. (Kinky sex and BDSM can often, although not always, be of service here.) This is also the house of other people's money, and the s-type may be very willing to turn their money over to the M-type; or if it is a challenging aspect, they may balk with Saturnian stubbornness. Whether it is sex or money, the s-type with this placement resists emotional intimacy, and it will take a lot of patience and safety for them to open up.

Saturn in the 8th House in a Composite Chart

This is the house of transformation, and any major planets found here indicate that the relationship will transform you both. In the case of Saturn, it will transform you in Saturnian ways — making you both more disciplined, more solvent, and more able to persist in the face of obstacles. However, when Saturn does the transforming, it's usually pretty uncomfortable. The planet of "Eat Your Vegetables and Do Your Homework", the sensei of the Dojo of Hard Knocks, can be unpleasant enough to make a couple instinctively resist those changes. *That's all right,* says Saturn. *Things will just keep going wrong until you get the picture. I have all the patience in the Universe. I can wait.*

Power dynamics need Saturn more than egalitarian ones, because Saturn is the master of boundaries, and power dynamics with poor boundaries tend to go very badly. Power-over is dangerous, so we need strong tools to handle that power safely, and we need the skill to use those tools. With this placement, the partners will need to make a joint commitment to having better boundaries, better discipline, and better self-control — and then commit to helping each other with that joint transformation. If Saturn issues are going wrong, they will know because this is also the house of sex and other people's money, and both those areas will start to go downhill. On the other hand, sex can be a wonderful tool in the transformation process — as long as it's eighth-house sex, which is deep and intimate and soul-penetrating and isn't afraid to rip across taboos. If these partners can play/work with formally or ritually incorporating those Saturnian qualities listed above into their sex life, it can be the key that opens the magic box of darkness.

Saturn in the 9th House/M

This is the house of philosophy, religion, higher education, travel, and worldview, and the classic experience of this placement is that the individual first experiences dogmatic teachers in their youth who push closed-minded ideas on them, either from religion, higher education, or the family philosophy. The Saturn person then rejects these ideas and sets out to create their own worldview, which they do ... and then they become just as closeminded and dogmatic about their ideas as the people they rejected, because they have still absorbed the form if not the substance. Age eventually loosens them up enough to become more open-minded, as Saturn loosens its grip on the decades.

What this means for the M-type is that while they may reject "traditional" forms of power exchange, they may also reject everyone else's ideas (even that of the s-type) and feel the need to go through it all experimentally and reinvent all the wheels. This can be rough on the s-type who brings home ideas from the book or support group and finds them rejected on principle. (If someone with this placement is reading this book, it's probably because their partner asked them to, and they already dismissed it as nonsense in Chapter 1.) Like all Saturn faults, it's a combination of fear and habit, and the M-type should seriously think about their motivations. If they're still determined to do it blind, great. At least they'll know themself.

This M-type will find it important to have authority over the s-type's higher education, possibly paradoxically making them go back to school — or perhaps the M-type themselves is providing a sort of higher education. They may want to have authority over the s-type's religious practice and whether the s-type is allowed to travel alone.

Saturn in the 9th House/s

The s-type with this placement may want very much to be a student of life with the M-type as their teacher, and/or a traveling companion on adventures. Their ideal authority figure is the sort of person who has been all over, done thousands of interesting things, and can hold forth about any of them — you come away from their conversations having learned a lot, and they may whisk you off to a new mind-expanding experience at any moment. The ninth-house Saturn s-type is generally timid about adventures, has bad luck with travel, cringes at the thought of going up a mountain, and resists new ways of looking at the world ... but, on some level, wants an authority figure to push them through their fears and mental resistance.

Of course, that doesn't mean that they will be easy to lead down the path to new ideas and world views; Saturn in the ninth makes them balk and shy away, and even if the M-type is persistent, it may take a lot of convincing and trust. The s-type will be disappointed in some way if it doesn't happen, though, even if they dread the idea. If they trust the M-type, they may be quite willing to hand over the difficult but fruitful areas of higher education, religious practice, and where they can travel. If the M-type wants to be their teacher, the s-type may do better with informal teaching rather than anything that resembles a classroom, so that it doesn't set off their fears and insecurities. It's also easier to absorb new world views and philosophies if they are tossed off by someone you trust and care about in a way that is confident and self-assured.

Saturn in the 9th House in a Composite Chart

This placement indicates that you are both very opinionated people with your own entrenched world views. It's difficult for you to get past that in order to see and appreciate each other's views, and in the places where you do actually agree with each other, it will be a challenge to keep from falling into a rut together where no new information about anything will be accepted. It's worthwhile to work on learning new things together, and trying hard not to be judgmental until you know how the new information might work in your life.

The s-type will want the M-type to be extremely knowledgeable about many areas of life, however — rather like a college professor — and won't mind the lectures as long as they prove the knowledge base. If the M-type isn't this sort, the s-type may be disappointed. The M-type can help this a bit by sending the s-type off to classes, as this is the house of higher education. Travel will be challenging for the two of you, and the M-type may want to limit the s-type's ability to travel alone, in order to keep them home and at hand. If the s-type balks, it's worth it for the M-type to let them out, as their solo travel will ultimately make traveling together easier and more fulfilling.

Since this is the house of religion, it's possible that this relationship is based on strict religious principles, and religion may be a deal-breaker (which can be a problem if it starts out nonreligious and then somebody "gets religion" at some point down the road). It's also possible that there will be religious differences. The best way to handle this is religious structure and discipline on the part of both parties — find the spiritual viewpoints that you have in common (if there don't seem to be any, perhaps consult a neutral spiritual counselor) and make them into regular and consistent rituals that both can find gratifying. Ideally, the power dynamic should be worked into these rituals, so as to both reinforce it and make the rituals more satisfying to both partners.

Saturn in the 10th House/M

With the planet of obstacles in the house of career, many people with this placement either never really get off the ground with their career, get to a high place early in life through sheer willpower and then crash and burn due to outside circumstances, or spend decades mucking around at the bottom until finally making it big in old age (Saturn's time). Saturn in this house makes it very difficult for them to succeed, and even diligence can't make up for the continual hindrances that Saturn slings at their path.

Their mental image of the ideal authority figure is not just someone who rules over a single s-type at home, but someone who rules over a number of people in the public world — in other words, someone in a high position in their career, with numerous subordinates who acknowledge their real-world power. This generally comes with the idea that the ideal authority figure ought to be the one bringing in the biggest bacon and supporting the s-type(s), and they may feel like a failure if they can't do that.

Whether they are successful or not, they will likely want authority over the s-type's own career, which can lead to arguments (especially if the aspect is challenging). Some of these M-types may decide that if they can't get off the ground themselves, they will be the "internal power behind the external power" and push their s-type to succeed and bring in enough money to support the M-type in a style that reads as social success, if only by partner proxy. This can be a great service if they can offer it cleanly and not as a projection, trying to live their own unfulfilled dreams through the s-type. If they do have an s-type who is willing to support them financially, it might be best for them to concentrate on a career of volunteer work that isn't bound up with finances, and make their success that way.

Saturn in the 10th House/s

While it isn't always the case, this placement can be the hallmark of the s-type who wants to be supported as a stay-at-home slave because they feel like they have failed in the workplace. With this ulterior motive, of course their ideal authority figure brings home the bacon, and is ideally quite successful in their career, so as to bring home a great deal of bacon. They can dismiss M-types who don't make enough money to satisfy their fears, or possibly be willing to "sell" themselves for a comfortable situation with the wrong partner.

If they are actually working at a career, the M-type should understand that Saturn is the planet of late bloomers, and encourage the s-type to continue their career — it could support both parties when they are older and the M-type wants a turn to rest. People with this placement who seem unambitious are really just scared and insecure about their abilities, and should be fortified by the M-type's positive reinforcement rather than be allowed to just give up. If there are good reasons to keep them at home for a time (such as children), make sure that there is a plan for returning them to a career road in a decade or so, perhaps with side education and preparation in the meantime.

The s-type will probably be happy with the M-type's authority over their career path if they haven't been doing well, but if they have an established career path, they may balk at changes. They will also want to see the M-type's track record of career success before they will happily accept advice.

Saturn in the 10th House in a Composite Chart

This placement traditionally indicates that the two of you will have to set concrete goals—for the relationship, for the household, for any personal development that you can help each other to achieve—and work toward them, step by step. It may also indicate a relationship where the two of you are in the public eye in some way, perhaps working together in a community, and usually holding some kind of outside-world responsibility. In addition, this is one of the aspects that traditionally indicates the two of you will be given a lot of burdens, and have to work through them. It's important to keep each other in good spirits in the face of this.

It may feel very important to the two of you that the M-type is successful at their career, and has some kind of authority that is seen in public by others outside the relationship. At the same time, Saturn won't allow any luck in that area; the M-type may have to work hard to succeed and acknowledge where it isn't possible, establishing their authority in other ways or finding outside authority in places other than a career. The more the s-type aids them in this, the more likely it is to happen, as the two of you must become a solid working team together. The s-type may need to take up some kind of paying work to help, or be an unpaid employee for the M-type. Your power dynamic may end up structuring itself in a way that feels more like a professional relationship (boss/employee or CEO/COO) at least part of the time. There's nothing wrong with that, but do make time for (perhaps deliberately scheduled) romantic times, as well as small personal acts of dominance and submission scattered throughout the days and weeks to keep the flame going.

Saturn in the 11th House/M

Having the planet of obstacles in the house of friends and groups makes someone a loner. They might have a few close friends — and even then they might go into social retreat for months on end — or they might have none at all. At the same time, they feel lonely and cut off from the crowd, scorning banal small-talk circles and wanting something deeper, but feeling too distrustful to seek it out. The M-type with this placement may dream of absconding with their s-type to a little world all their own, where they never have to see any other people again. In fact, part of why they secretly want an s-type is to have a best friend who can't run away and leave them.

Their hidden ideal of an authority figure is someone who is well ensconced in a loving tribe of people, with a full contact list and social capital everywhere. Since this is also the house of interest and/or political groups, part of this imaginary authority figure's clout is that they are accepted as some kind of authority (or at least as some kind of worthy person) by groups of people as well. As the M-type with this placement may find this terribly difficult, they may be subtly disappointed in themself, and may keep asking for reassurance from the s-type that their mutual isolation is all right. The s-type who needs social contact may have to seek it alone — and the wise M-type won't prevent them from doing so — or the M-type may ask them to be their social arbiter, as a service. The s-type can pick out and invite home carefully chosen potential friends while being a barrier against the unsuitable and annoying. Group involvement may also be somewhat limited, with the s-type being the group member and reporting on activities to the M-type, who may occasionally bestir themselves to go.

Saturn in the 11th House/s

Like their M-type counterpart, this is someone who has great difficulty with social situations, has few or no friends, and feels lonely and outcast. In fact, part of why they may seek to be in a power dynamic may be that they believe on some level that it will solve their need for a friend who won't go away. They're willing to give away a lot of their autonomy if they can get that from their M-type, which means that one of the most effective holds the M-type can have on them is to be their best friend as well as their dominant partner.

The secret ideal M-type in their minds is a member of a big rollicking tribe of people, who will both bring them into the tribe and make an automatic place for them by way of the M-type's social clout, and also protect them from an overload of group interaction. In addition, since this is the house of groups, it helps the M-type's authority if they belong to and are important in various solid political or interest groups, and/or do a lot of activist work to change the world. The s-type with this placement will enjoy trailing after them, or perhaps serving quietly in the background, letting the M-type handle the small talk while enjoying membership that doesn't have to be justified with a lot of chatter about nonessentials. They may especially enjoy groups of power dynamic people, where it's acceptable for them to have a Saturnian standard of behavior—quiet, formal, useful, in the background, and with a clear purpose. It's good if their M-type arranges for them to have practical tasks to do at group gatherings—perhaps lending them to the kitchen staff or having them do coat-checking—and it's also good if the M-type arranges for positive but honest feedback from group members about their service to the group.

Saturn in the 11th House in a Composite Chart

The planet of obstacles in the house of friends and groups can indicate that the two of you will have few friends as a couple, and not be joiners of groups, nor much interested in the outside world and what goes on in it. The two of you may perceive the lack of friends and groups as a failing of the people you are around, but in actuality it's due to the two of you structuring your life and relationship in such a way that it tends to rigidly exclude others. This can be modified if you can find the roots of fear (Saturn is always bound up with fear in some way) that the two of you subtly encourage in each other, and address those in a way that allows you to let others in. It may also be useful for you to form your own groups, where you can be the authority figures, but be careful about being too authoritarian or the people will walk away.

At the same time, the M-type will be judged more than the s-type (by both partners) if they don't have any social capital, and their authority will feel more honest and complete if they do the work to gain contacts and earn their way into some kind of tribe, or perhaps begin one. Setting it up like a disciplined situation where they can get to that point step by step can help, although since this is dealing with other human beings, allowance must be made for their personal anomalies. The s-type's job in this is to offer service and aid to the M-type in whatever way is needed to achieve this. If one partner has mental or neurological problems around social contact, structures should be worked into the power dynamic to both protect them and help them to make at least some of it possible.

Saturn in the 12th House/M

The twelfth is the house of sacrifice, of escape, of the collective unconscious, of self-sabotage and of moving beyond the ego. It is a place of solitude, and to have Saturn here is not an easy situation. People with this placement often had too much responsibility foisted on them when young, and as an adult they decided to avoid it. Escapism is a big problem with this placement, and you can just imagine how that works out with a power dynamic. It's sadly common for someone with this placement to want to be a master because they believe it will be magically easier than having a "real" relationship. They usually don't last long when faced with all the work and difficulties of real-life mastery.

We've all heard the (very Saturnian) maxim about having to master one's self before one can master another, and that is more true for this Saturn placement than for any other (except possibly Saturn in Pisces, which is the sign essentially associated with the twelfth house). The would-be M-type with this placement needs to have some kind of spiritual discipline in place before they can successfully handle the responsibility of a power dynamic. By "spiritual", we don't mean that it has to do with any religious beliefs, or belief in unseen entities. It simply needs to be a discipline that touches you in deep, profound ways, and helps you to evolve as a person. It can be based around art, creativity, mindfulness, self-awareness, compassion, music, or any number of things, but the M-type with this placement will find that they handle being realistic and responsible, not trying to escape into fantasy, much better once they have developed this skill. On a secret and possibly unconscious level, their ideal authority figure is the wise, compassionate figure who can lead them gently through illusion to reality, while being understanding of why they don't want to go there. They also believe that they can't be that person, and feel guilty about that. However, they need to become this person with themselves first, and then their authority will have real ground behind it.

People with this placement are notorious for not wanting to talk about their feelings or ask for help, which can be isolating. These M-types should make the effort to reach out to others; Saturn here may encourage isolation, but at the very least they should be able to talk honestly to their s-type. It's best if they have at least one other person who understands these things and with whom they can share their private selves in safety and confidentiality.

Saturn in the 12th House/s

If it's easy for a potential M-type with this placement to think of a power dynamic as an escapist fantasy, imagine how much easier it is for an s-type. There's all that supposed leaving behind of responsibility, only being a passive "thing" who need do nothing more than blindly obey orders, kept in an enclosed safe space and sheltered from the burden of the real world in every way. In reality, of course, living a power dynamic in everyday life isn't like that. No matter where you are, you bring your internal demons in with you, and still have to struggle with them. In addition, Life has a way of bringing challenges into the most sheltered existence. (Not to mention that most M-types aren't independently wealthy and living in old castles with lots of servants or secret underground bunkers with dozens of faceless minions.) It may be a terrible disappointment to this s-type to find out that even being a full-time slave requires responsibility and dealing with mundane duties.

Like the M-type with this placement, the s-type unconsciously longs for a wise leader who will gently guide them through learning to cope with the very reality they fear and avoid. This is a big hat for their M-type to wear, and they will be subtly disappointed if it doesn't happen. It may be that the wisest thing the M-type in this situation can do, if they don't feel up to being such a guru, is to outsource the problem and find the s-type a number of other teachers to help them through this growth, including possibly a therapist. Enforcing a spiritual discipline of some sort is also a useful maneuver.

Two other obstacles to a healthy power dynamic that this s-type may have are unwillingness to admit their problems and ask for help with them (thus the fantasy of the magical telepathic M-type who can read their mind), and also a deep sense of guilt over almost everything that goes wrong. The M-type may find it useful to institute a policy of skipping blame and going straight to problem-solving in order to keep the s-type from beating themselves up over every failure. In addition, the M-type may need to work harder to instill enough trust to get the s-type to report problems. Emphasizing that disobeying this order sabotages the M-type's job can help some with this problem, if only by enlisting that guilt in the process.

Saturn in the 12th House in a Composite Chart

The biggest problem with this placement is that both partners, by just being who they are together, trigger each other's unconscious "programs", the reflexive learned patterns that we all do without thinking and then wish we hadn't. This means a lot of hurting each other without intending to do so, and a lot of wondering on both sides why one said or did that thing. The only way to work through this is to become aware of those "programs", aware enough that both partners can name them, label them, realize when they went off and apologize, and eventually see them coming and head them off at the pass. Having an outside source of perspective can help.

In general, having the planet of discipline in the house of all things hidden means that regular rules and disciplines will take extra work to keep up with, and they may tend to fall away when attention is not paid to them, perhaps leaving things in chaos. The twelfth is a very spiritual house, so integrating some spiritual disciplines as an "underlayer" may be useful to build practical disciplines on top of. Both partners will have trouble talking to each other about emotional or critical subjects, and extra work needs to be put in here as well. In order to make this work, especially as a power dynamic, both partners must cultivate a great deal of patience, compassion, and humor about each other's mistakes, and not take them so seriously.

Saturn in the Transposed Houses

You've already read (hopefully) about Pluto in the transposed houses, so you know what to look for now. Each person has a Saturn, and they drop that Saturn into some unsuspecting house of every person with whom they have serious interactions. When this happens, Saturn points out all the ways in which the second person is not living up to their potential in the ways of that house, and pushes them to discipline themselves and do better. It's not a comfortable feeling if you're someone with an allergy to self-discipline, and Saturn contacts are very often the bad guy when someone in an egalitarian relationship cries out, "You're trying to tell me what to do!" when the other person actually wasn't doing that at all.

However, in power dynamics, one person actually has been given the right to tell the other person what to do, at least in some areas, and the M-type can check to see where the s-type is feeling the push of the M-type's Saturn and make that a formal and aboveboard discipline, rather than a vague nagging feeling. On the other side, if the M-type feels vaguely pushed to improve in the area of the s-type's transposed Saturn, rather than fighting the inevitable (which is going to happen with any relationship), they can formally enlist the s-type's aid and service to help them in the way that will be the most effective for them. To give a crude example: "I feel strangely embarrassed about my spelling errors since I've taken up with you, and not just because I'm comparing my writing with your perfect spelling and grammar ... and I see your Saturn falls in my third house! Guess what, slave — you're going to be my editing service and clean up all my emails from now on."

In our case, my Saturn falls into my slaveboy's eleventh house of friends and groups. He's always been an introvert, happier to sit alone in a room and play on a computer than to be around social groups, but I noticed that the longer he went without social contact, the worse his social skills became. It was as if he lost his tolerance for people. I drafted him into the church choir, took him to events as my personal assistant, and set up weekly "playdates" for him with friends who hold regular gaming sessions. These social events are scheduled, time-limited, built around a purpose, and take into account his limited resources (all very Saturnian) but his social skills have improved significantly.

For myself, his Saturn falls into my second house of finances and resources. This has manifested in two ways. First, while I was never particularly irresponsible with finances, once he'd given over his money and income to me, I discovered that being responsible for two peoples' income required more diligence than just my own. I enlisted him to help by taking care of the ordinary bills, while I oversee purchases with what is left. Second, we have an Owner/property relationship where he has actually become my most valuable resource, and I've had to learn to assess and allot his time, energy, and focus, while taking into account a brain that works very differently from my own. This has given me useful practice that I've used effectively in other areas of life.

M/Saturn in s/1st House

When the M-type's Saturn falls into the s-type's first house, especially if it is near the Ascendant, the M-type will want to have authority over the s-type's physical appearance — clothing, hairstyle, weight, body modifications, walk and movements, etc. Sometimes the M-type comes up with a personal discipline for the s-type to maintain their body and appearance; sometimes the s-type asks them for it, particularly if this has been difficult for them in the past. The s-type is inspired to pay more attention to, and polish, details about their appearance and style.

s/Saturn in M/1st House

This aspect inspires the M-type to pay attention to and spruce up their demeanor (including their physical appearance and personal decoration) and add structure to their personal grooming routines. The s-type may encourage them to work on this, or may simply be a more outwardly polished person themself, and may inspire the M-type to "match" them. This can be great so long as the M-type is not feeling pressured by the s-type to live up to a particular ideal, but chooses to improve out of their own interest. The s-type can render services such as encouraging and assisting the M-type with maintaining routines of hygiene, clothing care, exercise, grooming, etc.

M/Saturn in s/2nd House

Having authority over the s-type's money and possessions will seem very important to the M-type. The s-type may also desire to turn over those resources, but only if the M-type can prove their ability to handle money and possessions with self-discipline. A concerted effort may be made to "clean up" the s-type's bad habits around money, budgeting, care of possessions, etc. Seeing the s-type as "property" may be very attractive to both people.

s/Saturn in M/2nd House

Like transposed Pluto, the s-type's transposed Saturn may push the M-type into the realization that their handling of money and possessions needs some serious work. This is especially the case if the s-type has given over authority for their own money and possessions. Saturn will inspire the M-type to be more disciplined, and set up structures for this purpose. Using the s-type as a tool to help the M-type improve (if appropriate to the s-type's skills) is a better way to handle it than simply allowing the s-type to be disapproving about it. Training the s-type to give good service by handling more of the finances in the way the M-type wants it done can be quite useful.

M/Saturn in s/3rd House

The M-type will want authority over the s-type's communications, perhaps with voice protocols, better discipline when writing or communicating, or just better handwriting. There will probably be an emphasis on respect and courtesy. This is the house of mental processes, and the s-type may be pleased at having structure around how they think and speak and problem-solve, or they may feel repressed and rebel. While showing respect is a good thing, care must be taken to make sure that the s-type can still express all the information they may need to get across. Any feelings of not being able to speak should, ironically, be communicated as soon as possible.

s/Saturn in M/3rd House

The power dynamic will inspire the M-type to put more structure into their communications, and develop more personal discipline around how they give orders, impart information, follow up on standing orders, and correct unacceptable behavior. They may take on new tasks that involve writing or communicating, and work to gain new skills in that area. The M-type should not resort to just doing things the s-type's way in the face of disapproval from that quarter. Instead, the s-type should be directed to render respectful services that help the M-type to improve. These can include organizing; helping with scheduling, calendars, and reminders; making phone calls and returning emails; and doing necessary research.

M/Saturn in s/4th House

This M-type is going to want the s-type to be living with them as soon as reasonably possible; they will not be interested in a long-distance relationship. The M-type may also want to be given authority over the s-type's contact with their family, and if the two of them begin a family together, the M-type will want to be the head of household, set the tone of the home, and decide how the s-type will act as a family member. This is the house of ancestry, so it may be important to them that the s-type keep ancestral traditions with them. The s-type, on the other hand, may associate some of the M-type's domestic rules with older negative patterns from childhood. This is the house of past programming, and they may find themselves rebelling in a way reminiscent of their adolescent revolts. Letting the s-type have some say in how the home is decorated or used can help with these feelings.

s/Saturn in M/4th House

The power dynamic may drive the M-type to examine their early childhood patterns, and their assumptions about what is considered proper, stable, and healthy as a family. Their relationship may also trigger a great deal of hidden baggage regarding the M-type's upbringing; the M-type needs to refine some self-discipline and work with the memories, or they may start seeing the s-type as the cause of their discomfort. The s-type can be perceived as disapproving or nagging about the home and its condition. If they do the domestic chores, the s-type may think of the home as their territory, and subtly make the M-type feel like a guest or even a problem when home. It is in both people's best interest to be aware of these issues before they become an obstacle, and find ways to make the home welcoming to both. Special services the s-type might try include making healthy comfort food, decorating the house in a meaningful way, and making small romantic gestures that call up the positive parts of the M-type's history.

M/Saturn in s/5th House

This M-type will want to be given authority over any children born to the union, and may want to regulate romantic and affectionate gestures. Saturn likes things reserved, and if rules are introduced around romance and touching that seriously repress the s-type's style, they may rebel out of sheer need. If the M-type prefers it this way, it may be useful to find them other outlets for those needs. The M-type will also want authority over recreational activities, and what is considered "fun" between them. They may want to help the s-type be more disciplined about their creativity, and the s-type may actually become much more productive in this relationship. However, the s-type may also chafe under too much work and not enough play.

s/Saturn in M/5th House

This power dynamic may cause M-type to feel that they are taking on a great deal of responsibility, and that it is putting a damper on expressions of love, affection, and romance. They may become more cautious and less willing to risk in everyday life, and they may feel pushed to develop self-discipline around child care and finding time for creative work. The s-type may have a lot of emotional needs that feel like a burden, or may suffer from depression that also depresses the M-type, or there may be some reason why children or romance does not feel appropriate to either partner. On the positive side, mindfully creating protocols and schedules that make space for recreation can enlist Saturn in making things better.

M/Saturn in s/6th House

The M-type will push to improve and polish the s-type's service to them, perhaps instituting rules that emphasize self-discipline. Chore lists and household maintenance will also become a huge and scrutinized issue, with the s-type very invested in getting it done properly. Even if they aren't particularly into service, they will want to give it to this specific M-type. However, the s-type may feel that they can never be polished enough, so the M-type needs to be compassionate about making sure they both have reasonable standards. Disciplines may also be leveled over matters of health and self-care, and the s-type needs to decide whether to give that kind of authority over to the M-type.

s/Saturn in M/6th House

The s-type has the chance to render service to the M-type that helps their health and self-care, and helps them to become more organized and self-disciplined. However, the danger with this interaspect is that the s-type may spend too much time nagging or complaining about the M-type's organizational ability, health care, or lack of either, rather than respectfully offering to help. The M-type may be less willing to ask for service from them if it will not be rendered in a respectful way. The s-type needs to take a breath and remember that disapproval is less useful than offering aid in a pleasant way. On the positive side, if the M-type is willing to accept help, they can slowly learn to be better at everyday maintenance of life. Possible services for this situation are aiding with health care (find ways to make it interesting and fun) helping with organization, and working on anticipatory services, if desired.

M/Saturn in s/7th House

This M-type will want to be given authority over the rules around relationship commitments, including whether it will be monogamous or polyamorous. These rules may take into account how the relationship looks to others, which may discomfit the s-type if the s-type is used to not caring about appearances. Saturn here can mean more time apart, or looking reserved rather than affectionate in public, which can also make the s-type feel like they are not fully valued as a partner, unless the M-type goes to the trouble to find other ways to show that. Marriage may also not be on the table for some time, perhaps for external reasons. The s-type needs to make sure their own needs are getting met, but if it's worth the obstacles, they can turn the difficulties into a place for developing personal discipline and patience.

s/Saturn in M/7th House

This interaspect traditionally meant a partner who was a burden or difficult in some way, and the s-type may sometimes feel to the M-type like more of a responsibility than anything else. This tendency can be moderated if both parties work on developing the s-type's service in such a way that it encourages smooth partnering. The s-type can learn the job of being a "charming companion" on demand, like a geisha or courtesan, and be able to shift from one role to another as the M-type needs it. The s-type may press for marriage, and the M-type may be reluctant; if the M-type can come up with a reasonable goal to achieve that will make marriage work for them, the s-type will throw themselves into that process, and learn a fair amount of self-discipline from it.

M/Saturn in s/8th House

With this synastry placement, the M-type will want authority over the s-type's assets, and the s-type may or may not be willing to give this up. Financial authority may come to be a gift given when emotional bonding has gone to a deep enough level to make the s-type comfortable. The M-type may also have opinions as to the management of assets that are not necessarily theirs, such as child support or personal loans from family or friends, and s-type will need to consider this and make a fair decision. This is also the house of sex, and the M-type may be drawn to putting sexual restraints or disciplines onto the s-type, and the s-type may find themselves wanting to give sexual service and polish their sexual skills.

s/Saturn in the M/8th House

This relationship may inspire the M-type to discipline their own sexual urges as well as those of the s-type, perhaps because responsibilities leave little time for sex, or because they want to dole out sex as a reward. The s-type may also inspire them to look into spiritual disciplines, or may need to place heavy limits on the amount of power that the M-type can have in the s-type's life. In addition, the s-type may have a situation where they cannot turn over their finances, or cannot afford to bond deeply and emotionally to the M-type until certain obstacles are overcome or certain goals met. This interaspect will teach the M-type how to wait and work patiently for as long as it takes to achieve the goal, if they are sure they want it. Service the s-type can render to help include sex (lots of it, if desired); help with managing investments, child support, small business payroll, or other money that the M-type must handle that is not their own; and help with spiritual disciplines.

M/Saturn in s/9th House

The M-type will want authority over the s-type's religious decisions, if any; if they are religious, they may want an s-type of the same faith, and if not they may simply discount the s-type's faith and require that it not inconvenience them. Struggles may ensue over whether the s-type can travel alone, and how often; this interaspect may make the s-type may feel a bit stir-crazy if they don't get out regularly, or get vacations. At the same time, the s-type may feel obligated to stay home for the sake of the M-type or their duties. The M-type may want the s-type to continue their education, one way or another. Arguments may also ensue over differences in world view, with the M-type wanting the s-type to respect their authority because of their knowledge base. This house rules the teacher/disciple relationship, and that pattern can seep into this relationship, even without benefit of any religious beliefs on either side. The M-type needs to be careful not to let this go to their head, and the s-type should have alternate outside views to compare with as well.

s/Saturn in M/9th House

Saturn transposed into the house of world views can sometimes make the Saturn person (in this case, the s-type) seem disapproving of the house person's views, and the house person (in this case, the M-type) will get all Saturnian about it (that is, rigid and authoritarian). Arguments may ensue, with both sides trying hard to change the others' mind. Special focal points of arguments, besides general how-the-world-should-work discussions, may come down on religion (anyone's), other cultures, higher education, and traveling to strange places. In spite of themselves, the M-type may perceive the s-type as expanding their mind and expecting them to keep up, and may get defensive about their conflicting ideas. It's best to breathe and talk to someone on the outside rather than striking out. The s-type can render useful services of helping to plan for trips, creating calm space for the M-type to do homework, and assistance with religious groups (if applicable).

M/Saturn in s/10th House

The power dynamic has the potential to cause blocks in the s-type's career path — perhaps due to moving, or perhaps the M-type wants the s-type to give up or cut back their career and stay home more often. At the least, the M-type will want to be given authority over the s-type's career, and the s-type will feel at least somewhat obligated to do so, although they will need to seriously consider what is right for the long term. A more positive way this interaspect can manifest is the M-type pushing the s-type to do better in their career, through rules and personal discipline. Another area of desired authority will be how the s-type presents themself in public; Saturn transposed here usually means the M-type will encourage them to dress and act more conservatively, and may level rules to that effect.

s/Saturn in M/10th House

The s-type has the chance to render service to the M-type that will help them in their career, whether this is being their personal assistant, an unpaid employee, or just the person who makes calm space for them to work and takes extra responsibilities off their hands. On the other hand, the s-type — or the relationship — may interfere with the M-type's career, or push them into work areas that feel like drudgery to them. The M-type has the chance to turn the drudgery into an exercise in self-discipline and "master" their career path, and should use the s-type as much as possible to assist in that goal. Tenth-house interaspects tend to cause leaking outside the relationship, and the M-type needs to be careful and remember that their authority is limited outside the relationship.

M/Saturn in s/11th House

The power dynamic may end up limiting the s-type's interactions with friends and groups, either due to the M-type's wishes, because the s-type's friends disapprove of the relationship, or because the s-type gets so caught up in the M-type's life that they let their social life slip away. The M-type will likely want authority over the s-type's social life anyway. However, because peer support is a useful thing, the M-type might find it wise to make positive rules around who the s-type can see, pushing them to have a social life that balances giving time and energy to the relationship with a good dose of friendly peer activity. Bringing them into the M-type's own circle of friends, or looking together to find new friends and interest groups, can help as well. Differences in politics can be a problem here; rules can be made which let both parties have their particular interests without rubbing it in the other person's face.

s/Saturn in M/11th House

It's possible that this relationship will have a pruning effect on the M-type's social circle. That may be because the M-type's friends don't approve of the s-type or the relationship, or because absorption in the power dynamic causes the M-type to let outside connections slip away. It is also possible that the M-type retains their social connections, but the s-type doesn't want to have anything to do with them, and only attends as a requested service to be a "charming companion" during social events. This is a service they can render—hanging out with friends with whom they wouldn't otherwise spend time—and they can also add to the M-type's social circle by seeking out compatible friends and groups as a service.

M/Saturn in s/12th House

This is a particularly difficult interaspect, because the M-type's presence will bring up all the unconscious baggage that the s-type has been burying about authority figures in their life (which includes parents), and they may use the M-type as a projection screen for those early bad experiences—or even good experiences, which will be haloed in the light of memory and the M-type may have trouble living up to them. The s-type needs to achieve some self-awareness around those issues in order to function well in this power dynamic. Useful disciplines the M-type can level to help the problem might include mantras ("My M-type is not Evil Person X, they care about me and want to make my life better..."), breathing and meditative exercises, tools to stop negative spirals, and anything that helps stress relief and clear objective thought ("What story are you telling yourself right now?")

s/Saturn in M/12th House

This one is just as difficult as the other way around, if not more so. The relationship will bring up a huge amount of the M-type's baggage around any of their limitations that prevent them from being a perfect M-type, and they may respond to perceived disapproval from the s-type by being overly authoritarian and seeing disrespect in every question. Just as the s-type in the last entry might well use personal disciplines of de-stressing and pulling themselves objectively out of emotional postholes, the M-type whose s-type's Saturn is continually poking their dark basement should take these on themself. The s-type can render service by encouraging whichever disciplines the M-type chooses, respectfully reminding and accompanying, and being cognizant of what behaviors make things worse.

Saturn Interaspects

When the M-type's Saturn connects with the s-type's various planets, it gives both parties a strong feeling that the area(s) symbolized by the planet is important to hand over to the dominant, if at all possible. It may feel "natural" to give over authority to make decisions in those areas, or take it. This doesn't mean that authority over other planetary areas can't be taken; however, it is usually more of a conscious process of "I give this to you" and less of an "Of course you can have that." In a total power exchange and/or Owner/property relationship, the master will have full control over all planetary areas of the slave's life, but these sorts of relationships take time to develop, and in areas where the M-type's Saturn has no contact, while authority may be given, it may take a lot longer to settle in easily.

This urge is true even if the contact is a challenging angle; however, with a square, opposition, or even the ambivalent conjunction, the s-type may be quite conflicted about giving over that authority. They want to do it, but when push comes to shove, it's difficult. The point given in the Pluto chapter around challenging aspects being more difficult and requiring more mindfulness to get right applies here; so does the point that they are not impossible at all, just not easy …and Saturn is the force in the Universe that points out how much more rewarding something when you have to put in effort to get it.

An example might be a Master whose Saturn has a square angle to the slave's Venus; the slave may feel instinctively that it is the Master's right to control their appearance and general aesthetic, and even get a submissive thrill from it, but at the same time they might be irritated and discomfited by the dominant's choices about their new style—"She wants me to dress in an all-black Scorpio kind of way, when I'm really a jeans-and-T-shirt Aquarius Venus type!" On the other hand, the discomfort can come from the dominant partner's end—"She wants me to take over control of her day-to-day actions and decisions (Mars) but that sounds like a lot of work and I'm not sure that I want to do that!" The M-type may also feel more easily threatened in their authority in these areas, and be more likely to overreact to that feeling (which, we have to say, makes one look weaker, not stronger).

Power dynamic relationships may be one-way in terms of the flow of power, but astrological synastry is always two-way. The s-type's Saturn contacts the M-type's planets as well, and we've noted two separate effects from these contacts. First, the s-type's need for structure (their Saturn) affects the dominant in some way, if only subtly, because the M-type has to stretch themself to provide it. If they can't provide it for some reason, this will negatively affect the relationship and thus involve their peace of mind. Either way, becoming the Master that is necessary to fully and skillfully handle this particular submissive will be a growth experience. (This is true even if it is the Master's twentieth slave, because each new person challenges us to grow in a new way.)

An enhancing (trine or sextile) angle will make that growth process easy; a challenging (square or opposition) angle will make it a struggle, but a necessary one. (As always, a conjunction can go either way, and sometimes both at once.)

In addition, these are areas where the s-type is strongly moved to give the M-type practical, useful (Saturn!) service, perhaps in order to make their lives run smoother. However, if the aspects are challenging, it may be a place where the s-type requires clear, detailed instructions in order to provide service properly. These can also indicate, in some cases, that the M-type is uncomfortable receiving service in these areas.

Again, the urge is present for the challenging angles as well, but the s-type may lack the aptitude to do it well. For example, my slave's Saturn is conjuncting my Mars/Uranus/Pluto stellium, trining my North Node, and sextiling my Mercury/Neptune conjunction. He is naturally able to give me easy and skilled service in sex and problem-solving (Mars), dealing with technology (Uranus), kink and intensity (Pluto), helping me achieve my life goals (North Node), formatting my manuscripts and being a good conversationalist (Mercury), and assisting me in my spiritual duties (Neptune). However, his Saturn is squaring my Moon and Venus; he is very awkward around emotional expression, so offering emotional support (Moon) and making gestures of love (Venus) do not come naturally to him at all, although he very much wants to give them to me. We solved the problem in a quite Saturnian way by coming up with very specific actions that he is to perform at very specific times; they may not be spontaneous for him, but I know he is being obedient and doing his best to express love and care in a way he knows will work for me, and at least I have authority over how I receive support and actions of love.

Were I the sort of person for whom natural, spontaneous gestures in these areas were emotionally important, this would be a much bigger problem. However, you have to master the slave you own, not the fantasy slave you wish you had, and the one you own is going to have their fair share of limitations you'll have to work around. If your s-type lacks natural talent in a particular area (or the way they do it isn't your first choice) there is more honor in training them to follow specific rules to produce an adequate if not inspired result than in berating them because they aren't the wishful-thinking fantasy in your head. That's Saturn's take on it, anyway. Saturn also encourages you to remember that you're just as imperfect when compared to the fantasy M-type in your submissive partner's head.

M/Saturn in Aspect to s/Sun

The M-type wants authority over the s-type's sense of identity, possibly even wanting them to decide that being subordinate to the M-type is at the center of their identity. If the interaspect is harmonious and the M-type is careful to be kind, this can help someone to find and improve themselves. If the interaspect is challenging and/or the M-type is not thoughtful and considerate, it can feel like the worst of that painful authority-figure baggage around "Who you are isn't good enough." The s-type may, however, be extremely willing to center their identity around their role, without thinking about whether it is what is best for them in the current situation.

s/Saturn in Aspect to M/Sun

Planetary influence goes both ways, and this interaspect can make the M-type feel like the s-type is constantly disappointed in them, no matter how hard they work to be good at their role. The M-type may struggle with the question of whether to be themself — even if that means being a less effective manager for this s-type — or to attempt to change themself to be more like what the s-type needs, thus potentially undermining their feeling of being the one in charge of the relationship.

M/Saturn in Aspect to s/Moon

The M-type wants to have authority over the s-type's emotional expression. Like the Sun/Saturn interaspects, this can be gently but firmly guiding the s-type to mindful awareness of their emotional expression and enhancing their ability to modulate that expression at will; or it can be a continual brutal message of "You shouldn't have those feelings." The M-type can help by validating the s-type's right to have whatever feelings arise (which is not the same as validating the target or associated thoughts) while gently guiding them to shift attention, and the s-type needs to work on being willing to acknowledge that emotional expression can be a useful tool rather than a storm they can only endure. At the same time, the s-type may go overboard and hide emotions, which the M-type needs to gently pry back out by emphasizing transparency. This interaspect may motivate the M-type to control the s-type's interactions with their family of origin, especially if they are not always healthy for the s-type; if this is the case, the s-type will probably be very much in favor of the M-type running interference.

s/Saturn in Aspect to M/Moon

With this interaspect, the s-type can be so afraid of any negative emotional expression from the M-type that they put great subtle pressures on them to never express negativity in any but the least personal way. This can push the M-type to hide their emotional self from the s-type, which—in some cases—can actually be exactly what the s-type prefers, even if they protest otherwise. This practice does discourage intimacy; if this is what the couple agrees on and both want, it can work so long as the M-type has another outlet for intimacy and expects nothing more of that sort of thing from the s-type. If intimacy is wanted, then the s-type needs to practice finding ways to cope with disapproval toward them, as well as negativity toward other targets which they must not take personally. The M-type needs to be brave and express themselves, and remember that they should not be submitting to the s-type's fears and insecurities.

M/Saturn in Aspect to s/Mercury

The M-type has a tendency to intimidate the s-type into not talking, perhaps in subtle ways like dominating conversations or cutting them off in mid-sentence, perhaps in regulated ways like imposing voice protocols or taboo subjects, or at worst just making sure that nothing good comes of the s-type bringing up personal or uncomfortable issues. While helping someone to discipline their speech is not a bad thing, it is important to prevent that discipline from edging over into repression, or a lack of information can cause trouble. M-types with this placement may want their s-types to write more concisely as well — one M-type with Saturn trining their s-type's Mercury would not allow the s-type to text in anything less than complete sentences and accurate grammar.

s/Saturn in Aspect to M/Mercury

There's definitely one way that an s-type can end up inadvertently forcing their M-type to be more disciplined about their speech, and that is when the s-type is unable to understand the M-type's orders unless they are communicated precisely. Another possibility is an s-type who is so afraid of a harsh tone that they quail unless the M-type speaks gently. Either of these, and other subtle prods, can come out of this interaspect. The s-type needs to learn to take the M-type's communication style as it is, and not try to change them in a sideways manner. The healthiest way that this interaspect can manifest is if the M-type actively and openly uses the s-type as a tool to polish their communication style, setting it up in a way that makes the M-type feel helpfully assisted rather than nagged.

M/Saturn in Aspect to s/Venus

This M-type wants to have authority over the s-type's romantic expression. It may be that they don't want a romantic relationship, or that they want one but only certain ways of expressing it will be allowed, usually for their own emotional comfort. Some s-types might be fine with this; others might feel oppressed and lonely. Some might even persist, even after being told not to fall in love, in accidentally doing it anyway. As this is the planet of beauty, the M-type will probably also want authority over the general aesthetics of the s-type's look and style, especially when in "role" — is the "uniform" a frilly French maid or a monogrammed polo shirt? Again, this will depend on the flexibility of the s-type, the compatibility of both partners' ideas of beauty, and whether the aspect is harmonious or challenging. It can still work with the latter aspects, but it will take a lot more work, trust, and negotiation.

s/Saturn in Aspect to M/Venus

Sometimes it's the M-type who falls harder than the s-type, and this is one way that this difficult interaspect can manifest. Another might be conflict between the s-type who idealizes a very formal dynamic where affection is limited to a dignified pat and compliment and the M-type who wants a snuggle-pet on demand. Usually the s-type wants the M-type to discipline the ways in which the s-type loves, perhaps making sure that they don't fall for the wrong people. They likely also want the M-type to control their aesthetic appearance in some way, or at least help them to do so, but if the aspect is challenging, there may be a lot of struggle before ironing that out. If the s-type has an artistic talent or hobby, they may want the M-type to take authority over that in order to push them to do better.

M/Saturn in Aspect to s/Mars

While many s-types imagine that submission will be a life of passivity and no decisions, the reality is very different. While the M-type may push with the force of their personality in some cases, from day to day it's usually the s-type forcing themselves to follow the rules, and motivation is an important part of that. With this interaspect, the M-type will very much want to have authority over the s-type's motivational process, perhaps because they feel the s-type could use some improvement in that area. They may also want to train them to make better decisions, and how to manage their anger in the M-type's presence. Mars is the planet of sex, so control over the sex drive will be important to them; some M-types may get off on keeping the s-type in partial or complete chastity.

s/Saturn in Aspect to M/Mars

This can be a difficult aspect even in its harmonious form, because the s-type can set their standards so high that the M-type works themself to exhaustion trying to live up to them. Because inspiration is not just one way, this aspect will often inspire the M-type to try to meet those standards of mastery, leadership, dominance, and perfect decision-making, even if on some level they know it's not possible. It's especially common for those standards to include near-flawless control over Mars's more inconvenient manifestations, such as anger or bestial passion. The best way to handle this is for the M-type to set realistic boundaries on what they will or won't do, and to use the s-type as a tool as often as possible to aid them in self-improvement, emphasizing that the best tools are helpful and nonjudgmental and act as an extension of the Master's will.

M/Saturn in Aspect to s/Jupiter

On the positive side, the Saturn M-type can direct the Jupiter s-type's enthusiasms and exuberance into productive channels, and give them a sense of purpose. On the negative side, this combination may make the s-type feel like the M-type is always cracking down on them and raining on their parade, possibly making them feel like they can never do anything right or have any fun. The M-type may see the s-type as frivolous, and treat them like an errant child. If it's a challenging aspect, both partners will have to work hard to be patient with each other. The M-type may particularly want to have authority over the s-type's religious practices and ability to travel alone, They may want the s-type to get more higher education of some kind, and they will want to be able to crack down on how generous the s-type is with their time and money

s/Saturn in Aspect to M/Jupiter

Here again we have the problem of the Saturn person wanting to discipline the enthusiasm of the Jupiter person ... except that when the Saturn person is the s-type, it's not so easy. The M-type may find the s-type too hesitant to take risks or try new things, and the s-type may feel like they are hanging on for dear life on a wild bobsled ride down a mountain. If both work together, they can create a strong sense of purpose in the relationship, but the M-type has to listen to the s-type's concerns thoughtfully — they might have useful ideas. Reminding the s-type that the M-type's job is actually Jupiterian broad planning while the s-type's job is Saturnian details can help. The s-type may feel the urge to get more outside training, and be guided by the M-type in matters of philosophy.

M/Saturn in Aspect to s/Saturn

The M-type wants to have complete authority over the basic structure and rules of the relationship, and of their daily life. The s-type wants this too, but would prefer that the M-type choose rules and structure that the s-type would have chosen, and argument may erupt if these are too different. Challenging aspects are especially hard on the s-type, because it means that sooner or later they will run into a boundary that the M-type will not cross with regard to this subject, and the s-type will have to back down and accept the M-type's rules or leave. On the positive side, both partners will be strongly interested in personal discipline, and willing to help each other to pursue it.

M/Saturn in Aspect to s/Uranus

The M-type will have a large investment in deciding how much public unconventionality the s-type will be allowed, and the s-type may find themself willing to go along with a more conservation appearance and demeanor even if they were fairly radical beforehand. The M-type will also want some say about what friends the s-type may have, whether they will be allowed (or be pushed into) an alternative relationship style, and also their political views. This may become uncomfortable to the s-type, and the M-type should take their preferences into consideration in these areas. Uranus rules neurological symptoms, and we've seen M-types put a fair amount of investment into trying to control symptoms of neurological problems in the s-type, which should be handled carefully and with outside help.

s/Saturn in Aspect to M/Uranus

The s-type may find the M-type odd, radical, or extremely "alternative" in some way, which may or may not have anything to do with relationship structure. The s-type may find this unsettling, erratic, or alarming. They might not actually balk when faced with these potentially socially unacceptable behaviors, but their fear may inadvertently put a damper on the M-type being able to get what they want, and they will have to work through it. The s-type may want to place limits where the M-type wants freedom, which can create angry, jealous scenes. On the positive side, if the M-type has any neurological disorders, they may find it very useful to use the s-type as a tool to help control and compensate for them.

M/Saturn in Aspect to s/Neptune

If the relationship has a spiritual facet, the M-type will want to have authority over the s-type's practice and views, at least to some extent. Without a spiritual focus, the M-type will still want to spend time teaching the s-type how to live. They may see the s-type as being vague, directionless, and in need of guidance. The s-type may respond enthusiastically and very much desire a spiritual teacher or life coach, or they may rebel against what they perceive as too much rigidity. Since Neptune rules mental illness, the M-type may want to have authority over the s-type's mental health care. *(Also check the Neptune chapter for the Neptunian side of this aspect.)*

s/Saturn in Aspect to M/Neptune

This may be difficult for the s-type, because they may see their M-type as being unworldly, vague, and lost in a fantasy world. They may love the fantasy, but sooner or later their perception of the M-type may segue into "naïve and impractical", and they may question the M-type's judgment. (Sometimes this ends up with the s-type becoming a sort of protector-servant.) This aspect works much better if the relationship has a strong spiritual aspect, because then it is more likely that the placement shows the M-type as a spiritual guide through the s-type's obstacles and rigidity. If the M-type suffers from any kind of mental illness, the s-type can be used as a tool to help them manage it. *(Also check the Neptune chapter for the Neptunian side of this aspect.)*

M/Saturn in aspect to s/Pluto

The M-type will want authority over the s-type's expressions of intensity — whether they are allowed to yell or even argue loudly, what loaded words can be used, if they are allowed to storm off, etc. (One friend referred to this as the "Calm the fuck down!" interaspect.) It does guarantee a certain amount of power struggle, if only on an instinctive level, but the s-type wants the M-type to wrestle them down and win, if only partially. Having authority over their sexual expression is probably also a serious interest, as much or more so as a Saturn aspect to the s-type's Mars. This may be as much out of possessiveness as out of the joy of being in charge. *(Also check the Pluto chapter for the Plutonian side of this aspect.)*

s/Saturn in aspect to M/Pluto

This is another aspect where the s-type's fears may get in the way of the M-type's desires. The M-type may want to explore all their darkest corners and have a safe space to let their inner monsters loose, but the s-type will have a hard time providing that, for physical or psychological reasons. The M-type may have to put a disciplined break on their passions in order to interact with the s-type, which may make the s-type feel like they are bad at their role. The M-type can be resentful about this limitation, or see it as good practice in personal discipline. Slowly bringing the s-type past their limitations (if possible) over a long period of time can also teach the M-type discipline, as well as patience and precision. *(Also check the Pluto chapter for the Plutonian side of this aspect.)*

Neptune: Surrender and Sacrifice

Neptune is probably the most difficult planet in the solar system to nail down when it comes to associations, because by definition Neptune rules all that is vague, boundaryless, merging in and out of other areas, confusing, distorted, and also all that is transcendent, boundless, and ecstatic. Neptune rules mental illness and unconditional love, illusions and delusions, altruism and ultimate compassion. It rules all acts of sacrifice, because that is giving of one's self to a point beyond ordinary boundaries; and surrender, because that is putting aside one's ego to merge with a greater force.

If one doesn't believe in any kind of higher spirituality, Neptune is terribly problematic, and (in the eyes of some astrologers of that persuasion) almost entirely negative. It is in the pursuit of that higher spirituality that Neptune comes into its own ... and, in my own experience, in the soul of the s-type who has come to a place of peace and fulfillment with their role in a power dynamic. Neptune underlines the similarity between a content slave and a content monk or nun or sadhu.

When I wrote the Saturn chapters, I found myself writing very concisely. That's what Saturn likes. Neptune likes poetry, so I'm throwing out a poem to begin this part. There's a line in a prayer I wrote for my slave, and it goes like this:

> *Let me be like the ocean's water,*
> *Which, when struck, does not strike back,*
> *But yields, and is unhurt,*
> *And moves again to fill all space.*

Just as Saturn is the secret Authority Figure in each person's head, so is Neptune their secret ideal of the Contented Follower. Since Neptune is always confusing, many people aren't in touch with this internal archetype, or demonize it in some way, especially if their own Neptune is afflicted. For those of us who are drawn to power dynamics, Neptune is the image of the perfect slave in our heads, whether we lean toward that side or its opposite.

When I was a child, I loved watching *I Dream Of Jeannie* (already well into old reruns by the time I came around), although I couldn't have articulated exactly why I liked it. I fell in love with a toy based on the show, a Jeannie doll with her own dollhouse, shaped like her bottle, that opened up into a sybaritic nest of exotic luxury. Later, I was to find other models, but now I look back on that early obsession and I realize that what I loved was the idea of a magical slave, a powerful sorcerer who could do all sorts of mysterious things, but was entirely under one's command ... and came with a beautiful little home which could be invaded at will by the sorcerer's Owner, and to which the magical slave could be banished at will. I can see the tracks of my Neptune in mysterious Scorpio, in the fourth house of home, in that early attraction. (Now I own a Scorpio who lives in my home and does wonderful, magical things with those mysterious computer-gizmos. Go figure.)

On the other hand, my slaveboy with his eighth-house Sagittarian Neptune was at one point obsessed with the concept of the sacred prostitute, the servant who generously gives tolerant and transpersonal love (Jupiter-ruled Sagittarius) through sexual means (eighth house). It was difficult for him that while I could see the value in that sort of servant, it wasn't what I wanted from him. As with Saturn and the ideal inner archetype of authority, sometimes the inner Neptune slave doesn't match. Like the Saturn situation, that doesn't have to end the relationship, or the power dynamic. In the beginning, I arranged for him to have some experiences in line with his Neptune service fantasy, which showed that I saw and valued him as he was. Eventually, he decided that he didn't need that any more, and learned to appreciate — and become — what I wanted. Again, the slave in your head is not necessarily the slave you need, or need to be, in order to move further down your path.

Neptune isn't all doe-eyed passivity, though. The deep-sea planet is the place in each of us where we excel at passive resistance, and slippery escape. While we hear a lot of stories about s-types who left in a storm of argument, we also hear plenty about s-types who vanish without explanation, like a fish slipping out of someone's grasp and back into the water. When I hear this, I know that this is the s-type whose Neptune finally had enough, and did not get what it needed to sustain its ongoing surrender.

On the other side, if the M-type's Neptune becomes too disillusioned, they can also play that game and start becoming avoidant. Of course, difficult outside circumstances can also make them avoid not just their s-type, but everything in life. However, if the s-type notices that the M-type tends to regular evasion with them when certain situations occur, it's a good guess that their Neptune is unhappy.

As with Pluto in its prior chapter, we won't be going through Neptune in every sign. Neptune is so slow that some sign-generations are long dead, and we won't see them again for centuries. Also, I have opted not to write about the still-adolescent Neptune in Aquarius generation, because honestly we need a few years to watch them come into adulthood before I can write about how they will find their way through power exchange. Perhaps in a future edition I'll have enough information to work with.

Neptune Through The Signs

s/Neptune in Libra

Venus-ruled Libra is bound up with beauty, grace, and harmony. This was the generation who came of age in the 1950s, where the ideal housewife was an attractive (but not overly dramatic or slutty), gracious woman who brought peace and harmony to every household, soothing hurt egos and troubled minds, always fair to others and yet never complaining about the unfairness visited on her by society. Gender aside, this "perfect wife" archetype with her string of pearls lurks in the mind of every s-type born with Neptune in peace-seeking Libra. This is also a sign very concerned with aesthetics, and these s-types may have deep insecurity about not being physically attractive enough. It's not that s-types with other Neptunes don't worry about that as well, but it can be a serious sticking point with the Libra Neptunes, to the point where I've known some who wanted to quit being a slave because they were getting old and grey and it "wasn't fair" to their M-types (none of whom were interested in losing them). It's important to remember, however, that Libra is Justice as well as Harmony, and that their Neptunian exit is often caused by a perception of extreme injustice in the relationship, not so much about what is asked of them so much as seeing the M-type shirk their own obligations.

M/Neptune in Libra

Like the s-types, the Neptune in Libran M-types still carry that "perfect charming companion" we referenced above in their heads, regardless of gender combinations. If the s-type can't live up to that—and sometimes that includes physical aesthetics, other times it includes social graces—then they may be disappointed. They may expect the s-type to be the social intermediary for them, so that they can settle down in the comfort of their neat, elegant, peaceful home and have the s-type screen out anyone they don't want to deal with. (This job also comes with being charming to anyone the M-type *does* want to deal with.) Obviously, this job requires a certain level of social skills, which not all s-types have, and it may be important to either get them some training or cut them some slack. That slack is also important when the s-type gets old and grey and doesn't live up to the earlier aesthetic ideal. These M-types need to work a little harder to appreciate the internal qualities of the s-type, as they tend to be distracted by external looks. However, they are generally quite capable of grasping the idea of *equity*, even in unequal relationships—this isn't something for nothing, it is responsibility in trade for that surrender. The 1950s ideal husband does work hard to put bread on the table and money in the bank, and the Libran Neptune understands the concept of the fair trade of effort.

Neptune in Libra in a Composite Chart

It's likely that you are both close in age, due to the makeup of the current Neptune generations, and so the Libra Neptunian ideal of the gracious homemaker-slave who is also a charming companion is something you both grew up with. Your assumptions around what should be sacrificed, and what would justify mutiny, are culturally similar and you'll be largely on the same page about how a power dynamic should go.

s/Neptune in Scorpio

Just as the Libra-Neptune stylish wife looked down on the sexually open, drug-taking, mystery-chasing hippie woman, so the age of Neptune in Scorpio shaped the sixties and seventies, and the children born then. The Neptune in Scorpio slave-ideal is openly sexual — perhaps exaggeratedly so — and is comfortable in dark, mysterious settings that reek of underworld power. This is the era where gay leather and underground BDSM clubs began to come into their own, and the pearl necklace (or nice suit) were replaced by black leather corsets or chaps in the Neptune archetype of dominance and submission. (They were not a new trope, but this was the era that entrenched them in the demographic.)

The Scorpio Neptune doesn't worry about being attractive so much as being straight-out sexy. This s-type views surrender as walking into the underworld. Like the underworlds in all the myths, it's a place of terror and a place of ecstasy, of sorrow and of deep understanding where you find the core of your soul. Where Neptune in Libra surrenders in the name of peace and harmony, Neptune in Scorpio surrenders in the name of self-realization, of penetrating the veil of the mysteries — and what they want is the M-type who can take them there, who can play the guardian of the gates of the underworld, and the Dark Presence in the center.

Pluto-ruled Scorpio wants the deeper experience, and to use the power dynamic for deep, intense intimacy that explores and brings to light both people's darknesses. When this s-type decides that there's no more point in staying, it will be because they haven't been able to get this part of the relationship, and they feel that it's too tame and shallow.

M/Neptune in Scorpio

This M-type is excited by the dark, the dangerous, the hidden that can be torn away to reveal secret knowledge. While the shallower M-types of this generation may simply be in search of something to control, the wiser ones are, on some level, using the power dynamic as a force of intimacy that can stare at all the flaws of both parties and forge a closer connection through that scrutiny. Most would not acknowledge that they are groping for deeper intimacy, but the urge is there, underlying their constant pushing at the boundaries, diving into the darkness (and dragging their s-type with them), and tipping over the whole applecart because they are sure there's a rotten one somewhere underneath. This constant digging can ruin the peace and stability of a relationship, but then anything in Scorpio is not looking for peace and stability.

This aspect can indicate a desire for visible surrender, especially if there is a certain amount of conquering going on. Someone who quietly submits isn't as satisfying as someone who fights — at least a little bit — and then is passionately and loudly conquered. The Scorpio Neptune wants to watch that descent. They may not require extreme sacrifice, but they are incredibly touched by it, and find it highly romantic.

What they want of their s-type is someone who will fearlessly accompany them to their forays into the darker parts of the human psyche. What they also want is someone who can see their internal monsters and love them, not turning away in fear and disgust. However, sometimes they come on too strong and frighten people off, or the s-type becomes tired of the constant "soul-searching with a scalpel", as one friend put it, and slips away. These M-types believe that they don't need gentleness in their lives, and are surprised when getting some from their s-type feels so good. Eventually some of them actually learn a little gentleness themselves ... if only from the example in front of them.

Neptune in Scorpio in a Composite Chart

In this era, most of the people whose composite Neptune is in Scorpio are simply age-mates who both have it themselves, and are on the same page about the satisfying risks of using power exchange for deep self-actualization and intimacy, even if they aren't consciously aware that this is what they are chasing on some level. A small percentage of people, however, will have a much larger age gap between them, and may have Neptunes in Libra and Sagittarius. In these cases, they will be fairly surprised to discover how their relationship drives them together down into a dark intensity they didn't know they wanted. If they can accept the quest together, it can be worked out. If they can't, it will be the s-type who suffers first from this Neptune problem, as they will be locked out of the deep intimacy they crave, and may eventually become disheartened and leave.

s/Neptune in Sagittarius

This placement indicates someone who, under all their other personality traits, is secretly a dreamer and an adventurer, or at least wants to be. Where Neptune in Scorpio wants to go deep into the darkness, Neptune in Sagittarius wants to go wide, seeking for truth. The planet of spirituality in the sign of the wandering seeker, ruled by Jupiter the planet of religion, invokes the relationship of spiritual teacher and disciple. In the s-type, this suggests that their ideal of submission looks a lot like the disciple archetype. This is true even if they don't have any actual interest in religion or spirituality. What they want from their M-type is to have someone to believe in, and what they want to be as the s-type is the one who is learning to trust — in themselves, in another, in the world and the Universe, regardless of how they picture it.

This placement tends to make someone freak out regularly over how the real world does not measure up to their ideals, and the Neptune in Sagittarius s-type wants the M-type who can guide them through these emotions while showing their commitment to their own ideals.

For any planet in Sagittarius, trust is based on truth. Honesty is very important to them, and the sin that is most likely to send them drifting away from a power dynamic is dishonesty on the part of the M-type. This can include obvious self-delusion on the M-type's part. Once the Neptune in Sagittarius s-type matures past their own illusions of perfection, most would rather have the M-type be honest about their struggles than maintain an all-powerful mask.

M/Neptune in Sagittarius

The M-type with this placement wants the s-type who will be one-part adventuring sidekick and one-part wide-eyed adoring disciple—someone they can teach about how the world works and take them on a fascinating tour of it. If the s-type is hesitant about adventuring, resistant to adopting the M-type's world view, or unimpressed by the M-type's array of exotic experiences, then disappointment and doubts about their suitability can ensue. Since this placement also tends to make someone fly into a fury about the injustice and ugliness of the world, we can add one more job for the s-type: cheerleader for the M-type's opinions. In this case, a serious value difference, or a refusal to be a tolerant supporter, can undermine the M-type's faith in the s-type.

Honesty is very important to this M-type, and thus transparency is as well, since it is the most direct route to honesty (assuming that a transparency rule is actually being followed). Unless there are paranoid factors in the chart, this Neptune placement can make the M-type surprisingly trusting, assuming that a command of total honesty and transparency will of course be obeyed immediately, even to the point of a relatively new s-type being open and straightforward about their most sensitive feelings. When this instantaneous unfolding doesn't occur, or when it is found to be only partial, the Sagittarius Neptune M-type can feel betrayed. It's important to keep in mind that trust must rest on trust, and it is the M-type who must build the trust to inspire that opening.

Neptune in Sagittarius in a Composite Chart

The art of building trust will be a primary concern in this couple's relationship—but they have to remember that one does not improve without practice at facing complications. The art of building trust comes into its own when trust has been broken.

This is not Saturn, emphasizing structure and rules; this is Neptune that wants to go by instinct. In the sign of Truth, the best way to appease Neptune is for both parties to speak their truth, both as vulnerably and as compassionately as possible. Truth spoken kindly will heal all wounds in the end for these two. Dishonesty will be a cardinal sin, and the most likely road to breaking up.

Both tend to fall into seeing the ideal of submission as someone who—as we've said before—is one-part cheerful sidekick on whatever adventures the M-type leads them into, and one-part adoring disciple who wants the M-type to teach them all about the world and share their philosophy. Care must be taken to let the s-type know that they can have bad days where optimism wanes and focus fails, and there is no energy for adventuring or learning. Care must also be taken to let the M-type know that it's all right to admit to still being a seeker on the road, rather than someone who has "arrived" in wisdom.

s/Neptune in Capricorn

Neptune is the most elusive and unclear of the planets, ruling such conundrums as imagination, illusions, mental illness, psychic sensitivity, and religious transcendence. Capricorn is a worldly, sensible, ambitious sign ruled by as-different-from-Neptune-as-possible Saturn. When this generation started entering adulthood, astrologers had all sorts of theories as to how these two opposing forces would combine. What seems to have manifested is a generation that wants approval—from each other or from some Authority—and validation that they are Doing It Right. On the other side, they want to hold others to high standards as well, and their most prominent complaint—to government, bureaucracies, and culture itself—is Do Your Damn Job Already!

This attitude passes into power exchange as well; the "perfect servant", according to Neptune in Capricorn, is someone who Works, who Does Their Job With Excellence ... but more specifically, does that job according to standards set by outside Authorities whom they respect. The s-type with this placement may be torn between respecting and following the standards of their M-type and the outside standards of people who claim to be in the know about how power dynamic relationships work. While they strive for excellence (and are sometimes frustrated by how far short they fall from their polished ideal), they also want (secretly or not-so-secretly) to gain some kind of outside status for their pursuit of excellence — to be *seen* to be excellent — and the sole gaze of the M-type may not be enough. A wise M-type with this s-type will find ways for their subordinate partner to shine in public. In fact, the Neptune in Capricorn s-type who is kept in a closet and not allowed any public acclaim or approval may start drifting away from the relationship. Setting them up for success in this way may alleviate some of the arguments over whether the M-type should adopt the ideas of higher-status people in their community, a place where the M-type should take a stand and reinforce that they, not Master Important Person, are the most important Authority Figure in this relationship. Formal rituals mean a lot to this s-type, and make them feel comforted, so it's a good idea to build plenty of these into the dynamic.

M/Neptune in Capricorn

Like the s-type we just discussed, the M-type with this placement will have a strong desire for public status and acclaim, and in turn a compulsive tendency to want approval from the people they respect. These M-types may growl that they don't care what anyone else thinks, which probably means that they are embarrassed by their desire for approval and acclaim, and/or they don't believe that they can get it, so they slump back into a resigned silence (a very thwarted-Capricorn response) while surreptitiously checking people's opinions. Most M-types have worries and insecurities about their mastery and leadership — that's normal — but for Neptune in Capricorn, it's all about the invisible people judging them from behind the bathroom mirror. "What will people think of my dominance?" is a thought that harries them.

This, of course, leads to "What will people think of my s-type?" Their ideal of the perfect servant is one who constantly strives for the fantasy of the ideal super-competent assistant and sidekick, but they can drive the s-type too hard and too harshly if they are caught up in vague worry of how their behavior will look to others. It's important for this M-type to breathe and remind themself that bottoming to the standards of others is giving up your power to them. This is different from taking the useful standards of others and making them your own, in which case you are the only final arbiter of whether they are achieved, and it's no one else's business. Once the other people's judging faces are out of the way, it's easier to scrape off the unrealistic bits from the fantasy and figure out what is actually achievable with this particular s-type. If they don't turn out to be someone who can gain the M-type public status from being on their leash, that doesn't mean they're not valuable, and their value needs to be calculated by a different standard.

Neptune in Capricorn in a Composite Chart

The "dream" of this relationship includes a set of concise standards for excellence in the dominant and submissive roles—probably drawn from a number of well-researched outside criteria—and a commitment on the part of both people to follow them like a spiritual discipline, as dedicated and graceful as monks raking circles in a bonsai garden. Neptune does rule spirituality, and even a power dynamic couple who have no use for "weird woo-woo" might find it useful to look into the techniques used in monastic personal discipline, which puts the "dream" within very strict boundaries. Both may also be drawn to very formal practices with a "high-class" ambience, such as formal dinners, high teas, personal valet service, or cigar service.

As a couple, belonging to a group of respected peers—and gaining your own respect within that group—will be particularly important. Just be careful not to compromise what actually works for the two of you in order to claim that you do Protocol X or Discipline Y or Service Z, which is being touted as Correct at the moment. Take the most appropriate of what you hear, and don't feel like it's a blot on your ability to handle a role if some practices turn out to not work for your lives. Help keep each other from falling into the trap of using others as an unachievable example by reminding each other that you are unique, and so is this relationship.

Neptune in the Transposed House

Neptune in the 1st House/s

There's something dreamy and chameleon-like about people with the planet of confusion in the house of the body and outward style. The s-types with this placement have an innate ability to read other people's body language on a subtle, intuitive, and possibly unconscious level, and they will adapt themselves instinctively to be what the M-type they're looking at seems to want ... on the surface, anyway. Getting deeper underneath can be a harder job, because it's like fishing around underwater, or waiting for the tide to turn and reveal the rocks and seaweed and scuttling crabs beneath the glittering waves.

For them, the ideal slave image is someone who can do just that — adjust at will to the partner's desires, only even more skillfully. They may have spent so much of their lives being a chameleon (particularly if they got a lot of positive reinforcement for it) that they haven't ever had a chance to really figure out what their actual unique surface identity really is. One of the kindest things the M-type can do is to encourage them to find at least a little of their own style, and add it in even if it's not exactly what the M-type wants in the moment. This may bewilder the s-type, because they aren't used to people wanting them to be themself, but in the end it will make them more whole as a person, and more willing to pull back the tides and offer their authentic selves. On the other hand, if they are encouraged to constantly "chameleon" into something they are not, they'll try hard, but eventually the strain will start them doing the Neptunian drift away from the relationship.

Neptune in the 1st House/M

While this placement may seem like it produces someone more externally suitable to be an s-type, this is erroneous. One doesn't have to be loud and aggressive to be an effective dominant partner. One only has to know how to take charge, and that can be a much more subtle process. M-types with this placement do come across as gentle and sensitive; they certainly are sensitive, because Neptune here is like having antennae that pick up what other people want. How gentle they are in the end, however, has a lot more to do with the rest of their chart. Becoming — or appearing to become — what people want, if only for the moment, can be an instinctive surrender of one's identity, or it can be a power play to get the other person into a particular headspace. After all, who has the power in a session with a skilled therapist? It's a delicate, understated influence, but it can work just as well as any other mask of power, and possibly even go deeper, because they don't expect it. Since their internal ideal s-type is someone who can do what they do only from a submissive space, one problem may come about when the s-type isn't much good at assessing and shapeshifting.

Another problem comes in when the M-type isn't using that skill cleanly. If they spent the early part of their life being disempowered and don't have a firm sense of their own power — if they are still riddled with insecurities and pushing desperately against slipping into that instinctive chameleon mode — then those uncertainties will come through eventually. S-types spend a lot of time watching their M-types, and eventually they will figure out that what's on the surface isn't always what's real underneath. Ironically, it may be even harder to convince the M-type that what's authentic is actually what's wanted, given the current narrow social assumptions about what is acceptable for that role. Truly desiring what's under the mask — and then still desiring it when it's seen — can be the most wonderful service the s-type can render.

Neptune in the 1st House in a Composite Chart

Having Neptune in the composite first house traditionally indicates a danger that the two of you have different ideas as to what the relationship is about, and have not clearly negotiated enough to really understand what your expectations are—which means being taken by surprise in the future when you figure it out. You will both have to work hard at being realistic with each other, and not falling into dreams about how things ought to be rather than seeing how they actually are. You might want to take the time to write up a contract, not necessarily to be a stick to beat each other with, but simply as an exercise to help you both get on the same page with what is expected of each other.

Since the first house is how you are perceived, people may be vague about what kind of relationship they actually believe that you have. This may mean that you'll have to make decisions about how public you want your dynamic to be. You will have to take into account that people may well pick up on at least one part of it, whether you want them to or not—the s-type's willingness to go out of their way and sacrifice more to their partner than would normally seem healthy to outsiders. You can arrange things so that this shows less, but that will have to be done actively and thoughtfully. (Or you can decide that it doesn't matter.)

This placement puts Sacrifice and Surrender front and center in the relationship. The s-type may feel strongly pushed to surrender and sacrifice themselves, possibly sooner than they are comfortable; care should be taken to make sure that the s-type is given time to think about their feelings and acquiesce from a mindful place. Conversely, the dominant party may feel pushed by guilt or circumstance to ask for less control than they really want, sacrificing their own needs (probably silently) for the s-type's comfort.

Neptune in the 2nd House/s

The materialistic second house is a hard place for wistful Neptune to be, and traditionally this placement indicates someone who is fairly bad with financial judgment, as well as losing or hoarding their material possessions. At the same time, these s-types truly believe, down at the bottom of their deepest fantasies, that the perfect slave is one who turns over everything in their lives to their Master, including (and perhaps especially) their money and possessions, and also aligns their values with those of the Master. They may be disappointed with the M-type who wants them to retain more of their independence, especially if the M-type does not feel ready to take over the s-type's financial responsibilities. Since the second house is all about values, it's important for both parties to be patient during the early phases, and watch carefully to see if the s-type can adapt to the M-type's values. In general, however, financial instability is a cue for them to start emotionally drifting away.

Neptune in the 2nd House/M

Dreamy Neptune doesn't like being in the material second house. Traditionally, this placement means carelessness and poor judgment with finances, and unbalanced attitudes toward property (negligence or even hoarding). This all comes back to the values of the person with this placement; they value that concert more than the electric bill. In some cases, they may handle this struggle by giving it all up and living in deliberate poverty or simplicity, openly valuing not allowing possessions to get a hold on them.

When it's the M-type in a relationship who has this placement, it can be frightening for the s-type to follow, fearing that their material security is at risk. This is generally not helped by the M-type's ideal fantasy s-type being someone who will turn over their money and possessions, and align themselves with the M-type's values. If the M-type has managed to get a handle on their ambivalent relationship with money and physical objects, then all can be handled. If they haven't, then the best idea may be to order the s-type to take care of the finances and allot the M-type a certain amount of spending money. This placement may also make the M-type desire a complete Owner/property dynamic, and assume that a "real" s-type would immediately submit to this. However, if they actually get one, they may find that it is far more responsibility and work than they expected.

Neptune in the 2nd House in a Composite Chart

Having the planet of illusion in such a down-to-earth house as the second one suggests the need to beat out illusions about money and finances—where to get it and how to handle it. The desire to pretend you have more than you do (or will) and live beyond your means in a financial fantasy will always be creeping about, and you will have to do your best to root it out whenever you see it. Remember that any fights over finances or property, including whether the s-type should be allowed to keep their own property, are really covering up differences in values. Each of you may have the unconscious idea that if your partner really loved you, they'd sacrifice their own values for yours, in order to have harmony in the relationship. When it comes to values, you need to be absolutely sure that your values are based firmly in your mutual ethical/spiritual/cultural path, or you may fall into comfortable illusions about what they ought to be.

Just as the two of you may be vulnerable to get-rich-quick schemes, you may also be vulnerable to romantic tales about Owner/property relationships, and the s-type may be tempted to sacrifice themselves in this way (as well as their finances) without due diligence and the slow building of trust. You might want to have people with whom you can "reality check", whose spiritual knowledge you respect. Even if a full-on O/p relationship doesn't turn out to be practical for you (or perhaps not in the cards just yet) the whisper of "Mine!" will be very helpful for the s-type to surrender. Playing with objectification—"My thing!" may also be satisfying, if there are no psychological speed bumps around that.

Neptune in the 3rd House/s

Traditionally, having Neptune in the house of communication and the brain meant a vague, dreamy mind that was always off fantasizing, missing cues and instructions because of inattention. It can also indicate a problem with direct honesty, in that they are at risk for editing their memories, or speaking in particularly vague ways that aren't exactly lies but definitely skirt the truth. Obviously, for a power dynamic with a high need for honesty (or even transparency) and absorbing orders, this can be quite a disability. The M-type has to be very clear, and possibly resign themselves to asking more than once, or perhaps make the s-type repeat back the order. Regular check-ins with a neutral third party about miscommunications can help a great deal, as can writing everything down as soon as it is said. Where other couples may find communicating important things by email to be distancing, with this placement in the mix it may be a useful trick.

This placement is one of the indicators for both potential mental illness and potential neurological disorders. (It does not guarantee either—the individual generally needs three or more indicators for either of those.) If either of these are present, it is necessary for the M-type in this equation to research everything they can on the dysfunction, including talking to other s-types with the problem, in order to best discern how to help the communication. Enough miscommunications can make the s-type so confused that they begin the Neptunian drift away, even if the static was mostly on their end, so it's especially useful to get outside help on this one. Another risk for drifting-away behavior is when the communication gets too harsh or unpleasant.

Neptune in the 3rd House/M

Unfortunately, s-types are not the only ones who may be prone to the unclear, daydreaming mind. Some M-types also fall into this category, and can drive their s-types crazy with their vague orders, perhaps muttered as the s-types are leaving the room. Crisp, well-defined, precise commands spoken with a clear mental picture of the overall plan will never come easily or naturally to these M-types, and they will need to learn to compensate for these difficulties. Of course, their ideal fantasy s-type is one who can "automagically" interpret their mental static, perhaps without them even having to open their mouths, and they may be disappointed when that person fails to exist. They may also have problems with effective communication, especially about emotions; they may not be sure what they are feeling, and may have trouble understanding the emotions of others.

Like the s-types with the Saturnian third house, this placement can be one of a set of indicators for either mental illness or neurological problems or both. The M-type may feel a fair amount of shame around these issues if they are present, which can be exacerbated if the s-type is having trouble with the M-type's mental inconsistencies. The best option for any of these situations is for the M-type to research a number of compensatory mechanisms—behavioral, medical, and/or technological—and enlist the s-type as a tool to aid them in internalizing these processes and becoming more competent in their mental precision.

Neptune in the 3rd House in a Composite Chart

Having the planet of confusion in the composite third house of communications can make your verbal communications a lot more difficult and torturous than you think they ought to be. It's as if you speak different languages, and the translator is wonky and goes out when emotions are high. (Oddly enough, however, this placement sometimes enhances nonverbal communication, which is something to keep in mind.) Put things down in writing whenever possible; you may want to put together a written contract, if only to make sure that the two of you are on the same page about definitions and expectations. If you aren't sure how to express certain feelings, try playing each other songs or reading poems that describe them better than your words could, at least to start the discussion—Neptune is right-brain as opposed to left-brain communication. Take time to prioritize relationship check-ins and encourage each other not to sacrifice talking about problems in order to keep the peace.

This placement may also create trouble with relatives, and communication with them. The M-type may want to control the s-type's access to family members, especially if they are difficult and dysfunctional. The communication vagaries may tempt the s-type to hide family problems from the M-type. On the positive side, words (mantras, prayers, or even just single conditioned trigger words) are very useful for helping the s-type to push through the noise of life and get to a state of surrender.

s/Neptune in the 4th House

This is the house of home, family, and all the patterns you inherit from your childhood. Going cleanly into a power dynamic will be very hard for these s-types until they have worked through the issues of their childhoods. Traditionally Neptune here indicates an early life in which parents were absent (physically or emotionally) perhaps due to divorce, death, addiction, poverty, physical or mental illness, or just being very unsuited to parental life. The early home like was confusing, inconsistent, and possibly full of "dirty little secrets", and the children were expected to sacrifice themselves to take care of, or compensate for, the incapable parents. This environment can create an adult who instinctively believes that their role is to sacrifice themself for their loved ones, even if those loved ones are unworthy or even abusive.

Their image of submission is often fairly codependent — the selfless giver who has no boundaries (and, in some cases, is loved for what they have sacrificed). This is one of the astrological placements that puts individuals at risk of ending up in abusive relationships where they give until they crack. Being a "house slave" is important to them; domestic service looms large on their horizons, because at least it theoretically means a neat, ordered, and safe home. They will not tolerate a long-distance relationship for long. As this is the house of ancestry, they may idealize historical images of submission. A wise M-type will encourage them to have thoughtful boundaries, and might level a discipline of self-compassion at them, encouraging them to be kind to themselves. They need to learn that the goal is not to be the perfect selfless sacrifice, nor should they feel guilty for not being able to achieve this state. Instead, the goal is to be a balanced human being who is free of the semi-conscious patterns that drag them back toward childhood, and who can choose cleanly when to give to others and when to give to themselves to replenish the fountain. Not getting replenishment can start the Neptunian drift away.

M/Neptune in the 4th House

M-types are not immune to difficult, confusing, and sacrificial childhoods either. However, when someone with a more dominant personality grows up having to take care of and compensate for weak, crazy, addicted, distant, abusive, or entirely absent parents, they are often at risk for being a somewhat different sort of sacrificial character than the s-type version of this placement. They are at risk for becoming the Savior Master, the one who can "fix" all the s-types who just need to be properly loved and directed, who just need someone who understands them.

Except that this M-type can't really fully understand an s-type until they have cleaned out their own baggage from the sacrifice that was forced on them as children, so that they are no longer simply reliving their early situation. Once that happens, they will have a clearer idea of which s-types are beyond their skills and patience to accept. Before that, though, they are at risk of picking up broken people who will then take advantage of them. They may be unstintingly patient and caring with them, never showing their pain and distress, because they have been taught that if you're strong, then you should be able to sacrifice anything without flinching, or without thought for yourself.

Their image of the ideal submissive partner is someone who gives just as uncomplainingly as they do, if not more so. Since they tend to pick up s-types with problems, at least at first, they are usually heartbreakingly disappointed, although they will not generally show it. Having a home that is a safe haven is important to them, and they want their s-types close at hand and preferably helping to make the home a lovely place; they will not be satisfied with long-distance relationships. The fourth is the house of ancestral inheritances, and they may take inspiration from historical archetypes of hierarchy for their power dynamic structure.

Ideally, they should work on their own discipline of self-compassion, and be very clear that they are getting their own needs met. It sometimes helps for the s-type to encourage them to be more selfish. It also helps to have an s-type who is sturdy and solvent and doesn't need to be "saved", and who can perhaps give the M-type the reliable, consistent nurturing that they never got, secretly crave, and will rarely admit to needing.

Neptune in the 4th House in a Composite Chart

Having Neptune here in the house of home and family means that you both dream of the perfect home and family, where there are plenty of resources, lots of peace, and warm relationships all round ... but it may take a while until you achieve that dream, and it won't come without hard work. Since the fourth house is also the house of your pasts (and how they mesh or clash), Neptune here can create problems with idealizing the way things were done in your childhoods (and comparing your partner negatively to the perfect authority figure or servant in your head) or reacting to negative childhood patterns (and reflexively being triggered by anything your partner does which is even remotely like that, which in a power dynamic is common). Each negative reaction needs to be noted and talked through, ideally figuring out its genesis and how to make the dynamic different enough that it does not get triggered again.

If you can move past the fantasy of recreating the perfect childhood, you'll find that incorporating small bits of a parent/child dynamic, if only subtly, can help the s-type move into a space of surrender. You may also romanticize unequal relationships from the historical past; this can be a good inspiration for your power structure. At its most positive, Neptune in this house can indicate that your mutual spiritual beliefs are the foundation of your relationship, and they set the tone for your home.

Neptune in the 5th House/s

This is traditionally the sign of the hopeless romantic, wearing those rose-colored glasses and all too often falling madly in love with the wrong people. Having the planet of sacrifice in the house of romance can be problematic, especially for the s-type who is ideally looking for a relationship where they will be vulnerable and have less recourse. One of the best things they can do for themselves is to find a trusted friend — ideally an older and more experienced s-type, or a couple of them — who agree to act as perspective and check out the dominant dates before anything goes too far. The s-type will be driven to offer their heart as soon as possible in the relationship, because with the planet of surrender in the house of love-at-first-sight, it's first on the list of gifts to offer. It will be a painful struggle to hold back until the potential M-type has proven their trust, but it will pay off in fewer horrid breakups where the s-type gets used in all the wrong ways.

This is also the house of creativity, and creative work can be sacred to the individual with this placement. It is important to find the M-type who will appreciate and encourage that creative work, not put a damper on it every time that it interferes with their convenience. It is also the house of children, and the s-type may be interested in ageplay, becoming the innocent, magical child for the right "parent". Either a lack of romantic gestures or a block to creativity can begin the Neptunian drift away from the relationship.

Neptune in the 5th House/M

M-types can wear rose-colored glasses as well, and they can also fall madly in love with inappropriate people. In the M-type's case, however, the natural compassion of Neptune makes this another one of the placements that puts them at risk for a Savior Complex. Just as the world of would-be power exchange people is riddled with short-sighted and irresponsible M-types, it's also riddled with broken would-be s-types wishing for someone else to take charge of the dumpster fire that is their life. Having Neptune in this house makes the M-type a soft touch for the waif who says, "Save me!" It also inflicts some difficulty in judgment regarding what is above their pay grade to handle. It doesn't help that this is the house of gambling, and Neptune here whispers that this person isn't nearly as much of a terrible risk as people say, and anyway you have to risk a lot to get a lot! (This gambling problem may manifest in other ways in the person's life.) It might be useful to get some outside perspective on potential partners, just to screen out those tempting hard cases.

This is also the house of children and romance, and for people on both sides with this placement, the fantasy ideal submissive is playful, full of childlike innocence, and able to take on whatever role the M-type thinks of as most romantic. As the house of creativity, the M-type may want a Pygmalion role, artistically reinventing the s-type. This can be a positive thing as long as the M-type can take "No, this isn't working," for an answer, and the s-type thoughtfully considers and communicates the effects of each change.

Neptune in the 5th House in a Composite Chart

This placement indicates great idealism about love, and what it means. You need to be careful that your mutual ideal of love is not set so high that your relationship will never live up to it. (That includes an over-idealistic "We can't fall in love, because we are Master and slave and it isn't appropriate!" Expect that to go sideways.) Neptune likes to ignore all the grubby details such as who said what or is responsible for what, and Neptune here may make you both say things like, "Let's not talk about that right now—it will ruin the mood!" Just be careful that you don't sacrifice honesty for the sake of maintaining the sexy feel of power exchange.

There are two other main dangers with this placement. First, the romantic feelings may be one-sided (usually on the part of the s-type, but it could end up being the M-type), and may be hidden for the sake of peace. Second, the s-type may feel like the M-type is their savior, come into their life to save them from all the boogeymen and bad decisions, and the M-type may buy all that nonsense. This placement gives a high risk for "white knight" syndrome. Don't fall for it. The M-type might want to consult with a therapist to discern what they can actually help with, and what is above their pay grade.

On the positive side, this placement heightens the romance and sexiness of "acts of dominance and submission". The two of you may notice that when you are enacting the small (or not-so-small) gestures that reify and remind you of your power dynamic, you almost enter an altered state together. This helps the s-type enter a more profound state of surrender, and creates a bonding experience for the M-type, where they are better able to be nurturing toward the one at their feet.

s/Neptune in the 6th House

With the planet of confusion in the house of maintenance, health, and scut-work, this placement traditionally indicated someone who had trouble with the practical details of life—remembering to show up for work, organize their life, and take care of their body—and often ended up under the thumb of another person in order to outsource the life-organizing. The other side of that coin is that this is the house of service, and having Neptune here indicates that serving can be a deeply satisfying experience for this individual. Their internal ideal of what an s-type should be revolves around perfect, selfless, and likely invisible service that is always fulfilling even without any recognition or feedback. In reality, of course, Neptune's confusion can cause them to need a fair amount of course corrections.

Even if the M-type is patient and willing to allow them to make errors and learn over time, the s-type may be hard on themself for any imperfection in their service. In their mind, they should be super-competent and not need all the life-organizing that they probably want, and are ashamed of wanting. (This is especially tricky for the M-type managing their health problems; people with Neptune in the house of health are infamous for having numerous weird undiagnosed ailments.) The best bet for the M-type in this situation is to hammer home the idea that no one should expect perfection, only consistent application, and that it is the M-type, not the s-type who gets to judge whether service is rendered properly, and what will ensue if it's not. (Ideally more practice, not remonstrating. Oh, and making the s-type use lists is a good thing. Lots and lots of lists.) If they don't have meaningful service—which means they're reasonably good at the service, it seems to be useful, and it pleases the M-type—they may begin the Neptunian drift away.

M/Neptune in the 6th House

If the M-type with this placement has the "traditional" issues of trouble remembering the details of life, health, and general maintenance, it's no wonder that they might fondly imagine the perfect s-type as being the superefficient personal assistant who can handle all that for them. Being served is very important to them—and you notice how I phrased that: "being served" — not perfecting the s-type's service through constant micromanagement, but having things happen "automagically". They tend to love proactive and even anticipatory service; they don't want to train the s-type to clean a floor and inspect its standard; they want a "self-cleaning floor" that they don't have to think about.

This can be a wonderful thing with the right s-type, but it can also go badly if certain issues aren't kept in mind. First, if they aren't interested in doing the service training, it might be useful to outsource that to another M-type or s-type or even a professional company, depending on the service desired. Second, s-types do need at least some recognition; one way to handle that could be that the s-type is under orders to ask for appreciation when they feel they need it. If the M-type is going to be the one in charge, they need to be at least somewhat competent at tasks that will affect the relationship's long-term goals, and that can't be outsourced. If there are problems with the M-type taking care of their health, that can be fairly frightening for a vulnerable s-type, so it's good to use the s-type's services to help the M-type with health-maintenance.

Neptune in the 6th House in a Composite Chart

With the planet of dreams in the house of service, it follows that the perfecting of Service becomes an aspiration for both of you. Not only will your relationship have a strong service component, you will idealize the concept, and possibly also want to bring that service to the outside world. This is the house of Work, and the two of you will be the ones who Get Stuff Done. (Building the structure for a strong working partnership will be crucial for this—check the placement of your composite Saturn for where to look for aid in this.) Your relationship may have a robust component of Boss/employee to it, but the two of you should remember that all work and no hungry desire can lead to burnout. Make sure to build in plenty of deliberate time for affection, passion, and small acts of dominance and submission in order to keep the juice from getting drained dry.

Seeing the s-type as a competent, helpful servant will be very important for both of you. However, the M-type may also feel pressed to render service, to the s-type or the relationship itself or to those outside its scope. To prevent resentment, one positive compensation is for part of the s-type's service to be helping to make the M-type's service easier and more fulfilling, including the service they render to the s-type. Keep in mind also that one can serve from above; it will be good for the relationship for the M-type to learn how to do this. Since this is the house of health, part of mutual service may be caring for each other's health problems; take care that Neptune does not cause delusions of the power dynamic or the relationship being able to fix medical difficulties that require professional help.

s/Neptune in the 7th House

With the planet of sacrifice in the house of marriage, this particular placement is one of the most difficult ones of all when it comes to relationships—and for the s-type, it's particularly bad. It's very similar to having Neptune in the fifth house in this way, but with the added issue of involving marriage in the fantasy. Neptune here can make someone believe that marriage will heal everything—their problems and the problems of the lover in front of them—and end in a glorious merging, if they can just find the right person. However, they tend to end up with weak, unstable or addicted partners because Neptune pushes them to offer healing to the afflicted. This ends up in a series of difficult and painful relationships, until they realize that their judgment is not necessarily the best. If this is someone who craves a power dynamic, it can be even worse, because they will give themselves to unsafe people who cannot be trusted, and it may take a long time for them to extract themselves.

Their ideal of an M-type is bound up with their ideal fantasy of the spouse. The wedding ring and the collar are one and the same, and the fantasy ends in a magnificent monogamous Master/slave happily-ever-after (except in the rare cases where there is some Uranus involvement, in which case they may be fantasizing about the perfect polyamorous family).

They will be heartbroken if the M-type doesn't want to get married (and it will be the main reason for the Neptunian drift), but if they do marry, they may be disappointed because it doesn't live up to the imaginary dream. They will, however, be willing to sacrifice a great deal to get and keep a committed relationship, and a wise M-type will not commit unless they understand how important this is to the s-type. For themself, the s-type needs to keep a close eye on their needs and make sure they are getting met. Outside perspective from others can help. This placement sometimes indicates a desire for a spiritual marriage, where the two come together in sacred archetypal roles.

M/Neptune in the 7th House

Like the M-type with Neptune in the fifth house, this Neptune placement also puts the native at risk for a big White-Knight complex, but tops it off with a fantasy about how the perfect spouse will be smoothly subservient to them, and satisfy their every fantastic desire. When they do get married—and it's highly likely that they will—they may expect too much, as if putting a wedding ring on someone ought to turn them into a character out of a softcore porn novel.

This may be made worse by the fact that this placement tempts the M-type to rescue all sorts of human strays, believing that with a combination of enough love and a power dynamic, their erring ways can be corrected. This can get them used, over and over, by irresponsible and unstable people who learn that looking helpless, appealing, and in need of guidance can get them a sugar daddy or mommy. Being the M-type with a placement that tends to make them give more than they take can be difficult, and outside perspective from other M-types can be useful.

One way to more effectively use the tendency to idealize marital relationships is to work with the archetype of spiritual marriage. Using marriage as a spiritual discipline puts equal responsibility for success on both people, rather than one strong one who gives and one weak one who takes.

Neptune in the 7th House in a Composite Chart

Having the planet of sacrifice in the house of partnerships can mean that one person chooses to make sacrifices for the other. In a power dynamic, this isn't such a surprise; however, it's important to remember that the composite planet goes for both people, and it may be that the M-type ends up making some willing sacrifices for the s-type as well. As the planet of idealism and delusion, however, Neptune is less safe; this placement can mean that both partners have a lot of illusions about what the relationship is and can be, and they need to work on accepting the grubby reality of what it actually is in order to improve it. Illusions about the nature of marriage (and what it can and can't fix) might also be a problem. Both partners may see marriage as part of surrender, at least for the s-type; the "wedding ring" and the "collar" may be effectively the same thing.

Another Neptunian peril is the relationship becoming a dynamic with one person "saving" the other "helpless victim", which can end up in all sorts of unpleasant places. However, Neptune is also the planet of spirituality, and this can indicate a good possibility for a spiritually-based relationship, or at least one that feels very sacred to both people.

s/Neptune in the 8th House

In the house of Hidden Mysteries, Neptune creates a fantasy in the mind of this s-type of the shadowy, enigmatic M-type with the dark, romantic soul that opens only for their sacrificing love interest. This mysterious M-type can, of course, do magic—and indeed, magically make situations go right when they are going wrong, with a wave of their hand or a click of their cell phone. (Yes, the combination of dreamy Neptune and the dark eighth house actually does produce this sort of illusion.) This is completely unfair to the ordinary human M-type that they are likely to be facing, and they are likely to be vaguely disappointed when their human dominant partner responds to difficult situations like anyone else — sometimes able to rise to the challenge, and sometimes being entirely overcome. (Or, worse, expecting the s-type to help pick up the pieces.) Their vision of the perfect s-type is also magical — perhaps the faery creature trapped in the underworld who needs to be rescued, but can grant wishes once it's done. They tend to be disappointed in themselves as well, once they are "rescued" and no wish-granting appears. They may well accuse the M-type of not having "rescued" them enough from whatever it is that is keeping them in their own private underworld.

The most important magic the M-type must do is sexual. (This is the house of sex, after all.) Sex with them must move the Universe, and create a mystical bond between the two partners. If it doesn't manage this — or if the s-type imagines that it does, but the M-type doesn't act like that actually happened — the s-type will be disappointed, and may decide that this isn't the "real" magical dominant partner of their fantasies. The problem is, of course, that this kind of magic happens over time, with open and honest communication between both partners. If the s-type can find someone willing to share openness for the long haul, the magical goal can be met, at least with sex and deep bonding. (If the sex never gets to a satisfying intensity point, that can induce them to begin the Neptunian drift.) As for daily emergencies, a smoothly-functioning power dynamic can do a lot of magic there, but this also requires a long time and a lot of work to pull off.

M/Neptune in the 8th House

While the 8th house generally shows Saturn its rulership over other people's money, this is mystical, dreamy Neptune, who remembers that this is the house of sex, death, and the Hidden Mysteries. This creates an image of the mind of the M-type of a perfect s-type who has mysterious sexual powers, including the ability to sexually surrender so deeply that an occult bond is created between the two of them. While sex laced with dominance and submission can be very, very hot for people with the wiring for it, when a scene or a dramatic, romantic bed-tumble doesn't result in this magic (especially the first time) the M-type may blame the s-type on some semi-conscious level for not being "magical" enough. Of course, this is just as unfair to the s-type as it is to the M-type facing the issue in the above section, and multiple s-types may slip away in frustration when the M-type can't articulate exactly what it is that they want.

This is a rough and strange place for Neptune to be, and the only real solution is that the M-type has to be their own magician. They need to understand that the magic doesn't come without deep emotional bonding, and deep emotional bonding takes time and a commitment to openness with someone who has the same commitment to them. Opening their own heart will be the magical act, and they must do it themselves. A mutual commitment to radical honesty may help here, if only in weeding out the unsuitable partners.

Neptune in the 8th House in a Composite Chart

Traditionally, most astrologers look at Neptune in the composite house of other people's money and start talking about how there will be a lot of fuzziness around shared finances. From a power dynamic perspective, this will most likely be a problem if the s-type gives up control over their finances and personal possessions to the M-type. If this is something both people want to do, the M-type should be extra careful with that responsibility, and perhaps make and follow a clear plan to do right by it.

However, this is also the house of sex and personal transformation. For the first rulership, people with this composite placement may have beautiful illusions about sex and its power in the relationship. This placement does encourage sex that is spiritually oriented and capable of deep bonding between partners, but it will not heal all ills, and should not be expected to do so. On the other hand, it can be a force of personal transformation for both people.

All relationships change the people in them, but with this placement there may be a fair amount of confusion over who needs to change, in what way, according to whose standards, and by what means? Getting outside perspective on this matter may be the best choice if the partners come to a stalemate — or, more likely, a bewildered fog — about it.

s/Neptune in the 9th House

Putting the planet of spirituality into the house of religion and mind-expansion means that the main issue of this placement is Faith. That includes individuals who don't believe in religion. They still have boundless faith, often in their own luck or skill or ability to pull themselves out of the fire just in time, after their tenth bad idea. Optimism flows through their veins, sometimes to the point of very unrealistic expectations. Then, when situations don't go the way they hoped, they crash into depression. If it happens often enough, they may begin the Neptunian drift away from their M-type.

In their minds, the ideal s-type would be eternally optimistic, always happy about their job, or at worst philosophical about the hardest parts. They are emotionally sturdy and sunnily believe in the amazing qualities of the dominant partner. They would never want to throw up their hands and scream because the cats have pissed on the carpet, or feel hopeless because their M-type ignored them for a week straight. In real life, of course, sooner or later they will crash and run out of faith, and then they will feel as if they have failed.

The M-type who uses this s-type as a portable on-demand ray of sunshine and ever-faithful sidekick has to keep in mind that sometimes they will need to reverse roles. Sometimes the most faithful sidekick gets their nose out of joint and needs to be bucked up themselves, and this is where the M-type needs to have some faith and share it with them. In addition, these s-types tend to have Grand Schemes, many of which are not terribly realistic, and the M-type may need to act as a kind of brake on their soap-bubble castles, in a firm but gentle way.

M/Neptune in the 9th House

If unrealistic Grand Schemes are difficult with an s-type, imagine how that functions if they come from the dominant partner! These M-types have great faith in themselves, and generally they have great faith in their s-types as well. This can be a beautiful thing—I am reminded of the mantra for s-types with self-esteem issues: "I believe what my Master believes, and my Master believes in me!"—but it can also be an impossible thing. The faith of such a Master in the abilities of their s-type can inspire them to new heights or set them up for a very ugly failure, if the M-type's faith is misplaced or unrealistic.

Like the s-types listed above, their ideal s-type is one who never loses hope, whose optimism matches their own ... and in some extreme cases, who never complains about what is expected of them. This can cause an M-type to run through a lot of s-types, assuming that a "real" submissive or slave would adapt themselves readily to the role and not bother the M-type with tearful or angry scenes. In real life, of course, it is the s-type's right to bring difficulties to the M-type, and to ask for help with them, and it is the M-type's obligation to help them.

This can be a problem, and so can the Grand Plans, which can frighten the s-type when they go wrong and lose money or resources. One of two things must happen here. Either the M-type needs to allow the s-type to be their "brake" and extra perspective as a service, and actually consider their views, as a king or queen would listen to a wise minister ... or they need to find someone outside the relationship whom they trust to give sound advice, and the s-type can go to them when the M-type is having trouble listening to the s-type over the noise of their Great Dreams.

Neptune in the 9th House in a Composite Chart

This composite placement indicates that this couple have high ideals and plenty of optimism. When it comes to power exchange, they may have a lot of idealistic thoughts on how it should go, possibly including faithful adherence to rules and protocols that they have read about. (This is the house of higher education, and they may decide that books are the best way to figure all this out.) If they can keep that optimism throughout all the mistakes and disappointments that are inevitable in a relationship, then it will stand them in good stead. Having a shared world view will be very important to them, and it's possible that they come very different countries or cultures and will have to merge two different ways of looking at the world.

This is the house of travel, and these partners may get the idea that running away from problems (even if running away together) will solve everything. While it might give both partners time to breathe and figure things out, it's not going to fix broken situations, and this needs to be faced. This is also the house of religion (as opposed to unlabeled spirituality) and this placement may indicate a religious side to the power dynamic.

s/Neptune in the 10th House

Putting the planet of confusion and illusion in the house of the career path can indicate someone who never seems to figure out what they want to do, or has a lot of romantic ideas about what they'd like to do which never seem to come to fruition. Ruining one's career with alcohol or drugs is an extreme example of this placement. The more positive manifestation might be a career with a Neptunian theme, such as spirituality, art, music, or taking care of the helpless.

If the M-type in the equation ends up with the first sort, they might discover that the s-type is looking for a power dynamic to save them from having to deal with a career at all. This can work if the M-type likes the idea—that their "career" will be sacrificing their lives to serve the M-type—but forcing them to go back to work if finances pinch may disappoint them terribly. If it is the second type, their career is likely quite spiritually important to them, and it would be unwise to curtail it in any way, even if the s-type offers to sacrifice it in the first flush of enthusiasm.

This is the house of Public Status, however, and their idea of the perfect s-type may be fed from the writings and opinions of apparently respected people in various communities of power dynamic folks. If their M-type has different ideas, a power struggle may come about, but if the s-type doesn't have that status and respect, they may feel like a failure. They might attempt to gain status by showing how much they have sacrificed, exaggerating or at least calling a lot of attention to the extremities of their power dynamic. Encouraging them to give a little selfless service to others in these communities may be a healthier way for them to get their tenth-house needs met.

M/Neptune in the 10th House

Like the s-type above, it's not unusual for the M-type with this placement to be in one of the same two categories — the dreamer who doesn't know what they want to do or has beautiful career fantasies that never seem to work out, and the person with the spiritually important Neptunian career in art or spirituality or helping the helpless (which may not be all that financially lucrative, because money is less important than the deep satisfaction of doing it). Sometimes there's a third category of people who would be in the first category except that they are disciplined enough to work an unsatisfying job to make ends meet, unless there are more positive career pointers elsewhere in the chart.

None of these is exactly what the s-type seeking support is going to want. On the other hand, the s-type who is gainfully employed and doesn't need to be "kept" might be just fine with the big-dreaming M-type, and might even be willing to become a sort of patron-slave who supports both the M-type and their career experiments. This works especially well when the M-type can provide compassionate perspective on the s-type's working life — and the planet of compassion in the house of career is particularly good at doing just that. However, the M-type will do well to have an outside source of perspective who can help put the brakes on especially unwise experiments.

The M-type may have an internal vision of an s-type of whom they can be publicly proud, and not just as arm candy. They may want the s-type to be quite successful in their career, and to be someone respected by many in their community. There is, of course, a certain satisfaction in being the dominant partner of a publicly dominant person; it's like having an exquisitely behaved guard dog on a leash rather than a poodle. This can put a fair amount of pressure on the s-type (all dominant financial experiments aside), and the M-type needs to remember the compassion point when the s-type seems to be under too much strain. Encouraging success is good, but it's important to protect the s-type's well-being.

Neptune in the 10th House in a Composite Chart

In a natal chart, the tenth house is the house of career and public life; what people know about you when you leave your house and go into the public world. In a composite chart, this reflects how people perceive both partners publicly — yet Neptune is the planet of all things hidden and mysterious. This can indicate that the couple will be living, in some sense, a double life. They will have one face for the public, which will be very different from their internal selves in their relationship. For a power dynamic situation, this may mean that they are heavily closeted, and do their best never to let the outside world know what they are doing (and, if they have children or others living with them, they may hide it from those people as well).

The composite Neptune is also concerned with practical goals for the relationship, and Neptune here may mean that they don't really have any. Perhaps they just take things a day at a time and like to see how they turn out. Perhaps they haven't been able to agree on goals, they are confused about where the relationship is going, or obstacles have cropped up when they tried to set goals, so they stopped trying.

This relationship is likely to be one where the s-type has the more serious career and perhaps is the breadwinner, unless there are other aspects in the chart which contradict that. The s-type may pursue a career less for their own personal fulfillment and more as a service to support their family and household.

s/Neptune in the 11th House

With the planet of dreams in the house of friends and groups, people with this placement tend to attract a lot of weird friends — unusual and creative friends, spiritual friends, artistic friends, people who want to save the world. Friends with a lot of problems who may absorb huge amounts of time and energy for very little return. Friends who want to use the Neptune person for their own gain, because with this placement, friends are their weak point.

If this is the s-type in the picture, the M-type coming into that room needs to find a good balance between protecting the s-type from the users — even the well-meaning but hapless ones — and yet allowing them access to a wide array of interesting people with which to hang. It may be useful to work out a system of how much time and energy can be given to which people, and make that a rule. Since this is also the house of interest and political groups, the s-type is going to be a fairly social animal and want to be in the thick of these groups, especially if they are spiritual, humanitarian, artistic, or otherwise engaged in making the world better. The M-type who tries to keep this s-type isolated at home will watch them wilt, and possibly start that Neptunian drift.

Part of this s-type's secret ideal of the perfect submissive is someone who is the servant to many different and fascinating people. In their fantasies, they may be the slave who is traded around to an array of captivating Masters and Mistresses. The more possessive M-type may have a hard time with this one, and it may work out better if the s-type has additional outlets. These need not be sexual; they can be sent to give nonsexual service to other M-types for short periods of time, especially ones whose work falls into their Neptunian categories. They can also render less personal service to volunteer organizations and interest groups. It's just a matter of the M-type being willing to sometimes see them as a resource to be gifted, like royalty's largesse, to the rest of the world.

M/Neptune in the 11th House

Like the s-type mentioned in the above section, the M-type with this placement generally also has a wide variety of unusual friends who may enrich their life or bring chaos into it. They may also belong to a number of interesting groups, many of which will have meaningful goals. The s-type walking into their house will be expected to treat all their friends courteously — even the annoying ones. They will probably get dragged into the M-type's pet groups, and probably be given volunteer work to do, which they must never let on is not necessarily voluntary.

It is also possible that this M-type's ideal servant does indeed serve many people; whether the M-type fantasizes about lending them out sexually or not will depend on other parts of their chart, especially how strong possessive Pluto may be. At any rate, they will likely have no compunction about lending their s-type out to their various friends for other purposes — helping them lug boxes, cleaning their house when they are ill, driving them to the airport, translating that paper, and any number of other good deeds. The s-type may not have intended to become a general resource for improving people's lives, but if they find themself in this position, it helps if they can find some satisfaction in the positive impact they are making. It's certain that if they ask their M-type about it, they can easily get a long speech about how wonderful it is to help others and be a force of good in the rest of the world.

Neptune in the 11th House in a Composite Chart

This is the house of friends and groups, and having the composite Neptune here indicates that both partners will be a soft touch for a wide variety of Neptunian friends. These will range from artistic to psychic to spiritual to vague wanderers to those who are helpless, needy, and desperate. As a couple, they will have to guard against giving away too much of their energy and resources to the latter bunch, who will be drawn to their generosity like moths to flames.

The same problem may exist for social and community groups if they belong to any. With Neptune here, they may get sucked into groups that need help, volunteer out of good will, and then realize that they have been left holding several bags. It's all right to be generous, but they should keep good boundaries and not let themselves be persuaded to cross them. Neptune here can also indicate very idealistic ideas about community, perhaps hoping that if they look hard enough, the "perfect" community will appear. Both may be fascinated with the idea of the s-type serving more than one Master, or at least more than one person under the M-type's eye. Again, make sure that boundaries are clearly designated and firmly kept.

s/Neptune in the 12th House

This is Neptune's own house, and this placement makes the s-type very sensitive and intuitive. However, they may have problems communicating because they freeze up — one side effect of this placement can be paralysis when things get intense — and while they may want very much to express their submission, it may take a long time before they get over the fear and guilt to be able to do so.

On an unconscious level, their ideal of the perfect s-type is someone so sensitive that they know instinctively, without being told, what their M-type wants. Even less constructively, as this is the house of confinement, they may be entranced with the idea of being completely passive and bound — perhaps a prisoner, or kept in a box, or otherwise helpless and without agency to affect their life. This sort of situation can be done for a short period of time for kinky sex, but most healthy M-types want the s-type who can think and make at least some decisions, and these s-type may be rather disappointed if they are expected to work or be more than passive objects. It might be worth it to the M-type to make sure they have periodic "object time", whether in bondage or confined, to clear their heads and let them recenter. For someone with this placement, it can actually be very meditative. This is also the house of monasticism, so living like a monk or nun in some ways may be attractive to them.

Like those with Saturn in the twelfth house, they may be quite prone to guilt. However, where Saturn lays the guilt trip for not being competent enough, Neptune's is even more nebulous. They may feel guilty for not being able to be telepathic in their service, or otherwise superhuman, the perfect slave or servant. A wise M-type will remind them that the standards they must live up to are the M-type's, not their own fantasies.

M/Neptune in the 12th House

Sensitive, intuitive, secluded, compassionate, psychic, crazy, spiritual, and lethargic—these are just some of the adjectives used about people with this placement. Not all of them may be true for any given person, of course, as there's the whole rest of the chart to potentially counteract things, but you'll notice none of these adjectives resemble what most people would think of in an M-type. That doesn't mean that they can't be M-types; it just means that they need a very special s-type who appreciates their nature. If Neptune has not overwhelmed them into a state of mental illness, addiction, or complete social withdrawal, then the M-type who can look at the s-type's wounds and be compassionate can be an attractive proposition.

This is the house of confinement, and these M-types may be fascinated by the idea of keeping the s-type tightly confined—either in a strict monastic-style life where they rarely leave the house, or literally chained in some way. As long as they are realistic about it, and don't let their Neptunian fantasies take it to the point of unhealthiness, this can be very attractive to the right s-type. Like the s-type with this placement, the M-type can also be very drawn to spiritual matters, and may be very skilled at helping the s-type to altered states via BDSM, if this is something they practice. However, these M-types need to work on being able to speak their needs, feelings, and desires with authority, and not just secretly hope the s-type will telepathically figure it out.

Neptune in the 12th House in a Composite Chart

With this placement, just being with each other will increase both partners' sensitivity to the energies of other people, nature, and all the mysterious things in the world. It can also create a fair amount of confusion, and an urge for both of you to sacrifice together. It's less about the s-type sacrificing to the M-type, and more about both people as a team sacrificing to a great goal which touches both people on a deep level. This placement can create an undercurrent of guilt when either partner does their job in the relationship less than perfectly; they should be patient with themselves and each other, and perhaps take turns giving each other compassionate pep talks about how perfection isn't the point, and there's always another chance to do better tomorrow.

As a couple, they may be drawn to monastic-style discipline, or the idea of keeping the s-type very closely confined — perhaps only rarely leaving the house — even if neither party had been interested in such a thing previously. Neptunian enthusiasm can be unrealistic, though, so they should be careful not to stunt the s-type's life and personal development through such striving.

Transparency may be a struggle for them, with Neptune strangling words before they can be said. Both partners should probably push hard to be as open and honest as possible, perhaps writing journal entries and sharing them.

Neptune in the Transposed Houses

As we've already done with Pluto and Saturn, so we will also look at Neptune. Find the sign and degree of each person's Neptune, and then figure out where it would be in the other person's chart. Neptune makes the work of a house more idealized, and possibly more spiritual, if either of you go in that direction (and sometimes even if you don't intend to do so).

Neptune in the transposed house will show where you are most likely to idealize the other person, where you will feel the most drawn to sacrifice for them, and where your compassion is likely to flow forth to help them. M-types and s-types may approach this differently, but in the end people in a relationship do and should want to give help and support to each other. There are more dominant and more submissive ways to do that, to be sure, and that's something to keep in mind when you both feel like the power dynamic is slipping ... and "too many sacrifices" is high on the culprit list. Neptune is the first place to check for that, and perhaps reframe how to give gifts or services in that area which reinforce your job in the relationship instead of undermining it.

For example, a partner's Neptune transposed into your tenth house may push you to sacrifice for their career. Are you going to submissively give of yourself — perhaps adjusting your own career to move when theirs moves, or cutting back your hours to be there for them — or will you give them the support of a place where they can forget about their career and not have to make hard decisions, or perhaps even decide that their career is "…one of our goals, and I want you to work hard and make me proud of you! Now tell me how you're going to do that." Either way can be wonderful; it's all about how the act of giving is reframed. Neptune makes you want to give in that area. Problems arise when the giving goes over the line to make the M-type feel like they aren't really in charge any more, or make the s-type feel like they are shouldering too much of the responsibility for things going well.

Transposed Neptune can also be a source of healing; Neptune can make each person feel instinctively where the wounds in that house may lie, and guide them to reach out and help the other person heal. To once again pull examples from our own life, I grew up with a highly dysfunctional and abusive family where I had little control over the terrible things that happened to me. My slaveboy had a series of relationships where he constantly felt that his natural way of being wasn't ever going to be good enough for a long-term relationship, and that he would just end up inadvertently hurting and disappointing his partners, because that was his repeated experience. His Neptune falls in my fourth house of home and family, and his submission and obedience has been instrumental in healing many of my old wounds around helplessness, and provided a safe place for me to be vulnerable. My Neptune falls in his seventh house of partnerships; my acceptance of him as he is, my continued insistence that he's worthy if I say he is worthy (and I'm the Master, so my opinion counts, damn it), and my willingness to patiently train him to be a good slave for me and not expect him to "just know", has healed many of his wounds around being "good enough" as a partner. Both of these healings took place firmly ensconced inside our power dynamic, but both were the kind of heart-gifts that Neptune teaches us to give — if we can get past our illusions of the partner and see the reality of what they actually need.

s/Neptune in M/1st House

This aspect inspires the M-type to want to change their appearance in order to please the s-type, or to better suit the "ideal" of the mutual relationship. It can also cause them a fair amount of confusion around how they ought to look and present themselves. Rather than sacrificing themselves in this way, it would be better if they could actively experiment with appearances in a way that helped the s-type to better see the M-type's own authenticity shine. The s-type's adoration can heal some of the M-type's old insecurities around their body and their attractiveness.

M/Neptune in s/1st House

When the M-type's Neptune falls into the s-type's first house, especially if it is near the Ascendant, the s-type has the strong urge to change their appearance to please the M-type, and they may idealize the idea of style-shifting to be more "slavish". Care should be taken to make sure that new style changes do not force them into a mask that will feel repressive to them in the long run. On the other hand, the M-type's regard can heal some of their insecurities about being attractive or having a body worthy of desire.

s/Neptune in M/2nd House

The M-type may look at the s-type's life and feel like they can help with a generous application of money. It feels right to them to pay for the s-type's expenses, and buy them gifts, but they need to be honest and straightforward about what is expected in return, and not assume that the s-type will know. The s-type has a chance to help the M-type feel better about themself and shift their values more positively, probably just by being themselves.

M/Neptune in s/2nd House

The s-type may want to sacrifice financially for the M-type, whether that is giving them money in an ongoing arrangement or surrendering all their finances and possessions. As with all things Neptunian, use good judgment on both sides. They may also feel simultaneously strongly affected by the M-type's values, and confused about their own, and may end up taking on some of those values, sometimes without noticing that they have crept into their heads. The M-type has the opportunity to increase the s-type's self-esteem and help them to value themselves better.

s/Neptune in M/3rd House

This can be a hard one, because the M-type feels like they should censor their honest communications in order to make the s-type feel better. This kind of communication backfires, however. The s-type may sense that the M-type is not being fully honest with them, and may lose trust, or the M-type may wake up one day and realize how much they have sacrificed for the s-type's emotions. The M-type needs to remember that the s-type will not improve without accurate feedback, and robbing them of that will leave them in the dark. This interaspect can also make the M-type feel like there is less clarity in their words; it can help to give the s-type more written instructions, so that the M-type can have a few minutes to review them and make sure that they say what is intended. On the other hand, the s-type has the opportunity to heal some of the M-type's old pain around not being heard and understood.

M/Neptune in s/3rd House

This one is also rough on communications, as the s-type will be tempted to censor themselves so as to not upset the M-type. Of course, in the end this makes everything less clear and less functional, and does more harm than good, but Neptune's effects can convince the s-type that the M-type, on some level, can't handle the raw ugliness that is their negative emotions, so the s-type decides not to have any of those where the M-type can find out about it. The relationship may also make the s-type feel like their usual modes of communication aren't adequate, and they may be confused as to what to do. Bringing in a little Saturn energy and coming up with formal, or at least specific and agreed-upon, ways of communicating may help demystify the situation. The M-type has a chance to heal some of the s-type's old pain around not being listened to or taken seriously.

s/Neptune in M/4th House

This interaspect can bring up a swirl of confusing baggage from the M-type's childhood, including — oddly enough — times when the M-type felt most helpless. This can be turned into compassion or at least sympathy, helping the M-type to understand better what it is to be vulnerable. It can also, if handled unskillfully, cause the M-type to lash out at the confused s-type; some outside perspective may help the M-type to catch this behavior and remember that they are in charge and can change things. The home, how it is kept, and whether it is made welcoming, may be the hub of many arguments. The s-type has a chance, if they handle it gently, to heal some old painful scars the M-type may have about their early home life.

M/Neptune in s/4th House

The particular style of this M-type will bring up a lot of old baggage around bad power situations from the s-type's past. The s-type may project ridiculously out-of-proportion demons onto the M-type, then turn around and idealize them again, which can be very confusing. Regular rituals in which the s-type acknowledges that the M-type is not the former parent or past partner can help with mindfulness on this score. The M-type may have the urge to sacrifice their comfort and put up with being periodically demonized; they should resist this urge and calmly set boundaries to protect themselves and not undermine the power dynamic. The M-type has the chance, if they are careful and compassionate, to help the s-type heal some of their old wounds from childhood. The couple may end up interested in ageplay for this purpose.

s/Neptune in M/5th House

The M-type may have the urge to sacrifice some of their emotional needs in the face of the s-type's clear love and devotion. They may not want to disappoint them, or they may just melt when faced with those big eyes full of sincere feeling. Later, they will realize that they've given in again and may feel resentful. They need to be able to take a breath (or a moment alone) and set calm boundaries around what they will and will not do for romance, or even just for fun. On the other hand, the s-type has an opportunity to heal part of the M-type's heart—the part that needs to be wholly, unconditionally loved.

M/Neptune in s/5th House

The s-type will feel pushed to surrender to the M-type's powerful current of love and romantic gestures, even if they feel that they aren't quite ready yet. This is an interaspect that often results in "swept off their feet," and perhaps "…realize they just washed up on a very strange shore." This feeling may lead them to commit too quickly, agree too quickly to have children, and agree to "fun" activities that they aren't really into. Later, they will realize that they have sacrificed past their boundaries and will be angry at either themselves or the M-type or both. With this aspect, they should take time to think alone over any decision that gives them that funny gut feeling, and maybe get outside perspective. On the other hand, the relationship can energize their creative work in a great way, and there's a chance that its emotional intensity will heal old wounds around not feeling loved enough.

s/Neptune in M/6th House

This interaspect can sometimes indicate that the s-type has health problems that affect the power dynamic, preventing them from doing and/or being what the M-type wants, but that the M-type is prepared to sacrifice those desires for this particular s-type. At the same time, it can also make the M-type very idealistic about service and what it can be; this can be as positive as finding new and creative ways that the s-type can serve, or being disgruntled that the s-type can't live up to those fantasies. Bringing the situation back down to reality is painful but necessary in the latter case. On the positive side, the s-type has the chance to heal some of the M-type's old wounds around being competent in areas of daily work.

M/Neptune in s/6th House

This may indicate a relationship where the M-type has some sort of health problems and the s-type must give service to care for them, perhaps sacrificing some of their ideas of what the M-type should be and do. They may end up the personal care attendant, perhaps holding things together for periods of time while the M-type recovers enough to get back on their horse and make decisions. This interaspect can also make the s-type extremely idealistic about service and what it can do, and they may berate themself if they can't get it fantasy-perfect enough. A wise M-type will remind them of self-compassion, and that "protecting the property" also means not wearing themself out in attempts to be flawless. The M-type has the chance to heal some old wounds around the s-type's competence at their work.

s/Neptune in M/7th House

The M-type may be put in a situation where they cannot have the relationship structured the way they want, and must sacrifice some of their desires in order to stay in it. If it is worth it to them, they must find positive reasons to choose it of their own accord and not build up sadness or resentment over the situation. Vagueness and confusion over what can be done with the relationship structure may be rampant and frustrating. On the positive side, the s-type has a chance to be loyal in spite of these issues, and to heal something in the M-type's soul where being partnered is concerned. This aspect can also make both partners pursue the idea of a "sacred marriage", whether or not legal marriage is involved.

M/Neptune in s/7th House

The s-type may feel pushed to sacrifice their needs and desires around how the relationship will be structured, whether due to giving in to the M-type's desires or being prevented by outside circumstances. Like the above situation, the couple may be plagued with confusion and bewilderment about how the relationship should be structured and what its overall rules and social status should be. On the positive side, the relationship can have a strong spiritual aspect to it, and it has the potential to heal parts of the s-type's pain around a partner leaving when times are difficult and unclear.

s/Neptune in the M/8th House

This interaspect often indicates a relationship where the s-type is unable to offer the M-type the sexual service that they want, perhaps due to physical or psychological disabilities, and the M-type feels like they must sacrifice those needs in order to keep the relationship. I've also seen it be a situation where the s-type has significant money but cannot, for some reason, share any with the M-type. The eighth is a very deep house, and it is also the house of Power, so when the M-type makes these sacrifices it gouges deeply into their sense of being powerful. They will need to clean out any Neptunian fantasies about what power means, and instead focus on the power of coping with a difficult situation and finding other ways to get one's needs met. (Make sure to use ethical means—this placement sometimes suggests less kind power moves.) Paradoxically, the s-type has the chance to actually heal some of the M-type's sexual problems, if they are kind and ethical themself.

M/Neptune in s/8th House

This synastry placement inspires the s-type to sacrifice sexually for the M-type, perhaps giving up their sexual needs and adapting to what the M-type wants, even if that is to keep them in chastity or engage in extreme sexual practices that give the s-type no pleasure. They also may feel pushed to hand over money that does not necessarily fall within the M-type's right to manage. Discussion needs to happen around what they are comfortable with, and they need to be honest where their sacrifice makes them genuinely uncomfortable. On the other hand, the M-type has the potential to heal some of the s-type's sexual issues, if they are careful and respect limitations.

s/Neptune in M/9th House

This placement often makes the M-type choose between this relationship and their philosophical view of life; they may feel that they have to change and sacrifice in order to be the right M-type for this particular s-type. The relationship may require them to settle down if they were constantly traveling, or to shift religious beliefs, or to give up further education in trade for a responsible job. In order to keep from being trapped, they need to reframe the situation as something they are powerfully choosing for good reasons ... or they need to figure out the line where they start to feel like they aren't in charge any more, and set firm boundaries in order to keep the power dynamic from becoming unreal for them. On the positive side, the s-type has a chance to heal the M-type's old pain around not being a good enough student, or running away too often, or possibly religious or philosophical wounds inflicted by past intolerance.

M/Neptune in s/9th House

The s-type may end up sacrificing their higher education chances, or their religious beliefs and morals, or their ability to travel when they want ... or even their philosophy of life. They may feel fairly confused about what they are supposed to replace them with, or whether what the M-type is selling is actually something they are obligated to buy. It may help to get outside perspective, perhaps from someone that both partners consider to be very "learned" in some way they both value. More positively, the M-type has the potential to heal some of the s-type's wounds around education, or religion, or running away from problems, or a general world view that has been badly poisoned by negative experiences.

s/Neptune in M/10th House

The relationship, or some circumstances surrounding it, are going to change the M-type's career in some way. It might interfere—I know one M-type with this interaspect who did give up their career to go live with an independently wealthy s-type in another part of the country, and another who gave up their heart-path to take a more lucrative job to support their s-type and the s-type's three children — or it might be that the presence of the s-type inspires them to Dream Big career-wise and try for something larger than they had considered before. The s-type has the chance, through giving the right services, to heal some old pain the M-type may have around their career path and choices.

M/Neptune in s/10th House

The relationship's circumstances — or the M-type's desires — may push the s-type to feel like they need to sacrifice their career, perhaps to stay home, or perhaps to take on a different career that the M-type thinks is more appropriate. This needs to be carefully considered, and should not be a quick deal. On the other side, the M-type can sometimes push the s-type toward a "dream career" that the s-type would not have thought possible. Either way, this interaspect will change the s-type's public image in some way, perhaps making it more glamorous, perhaps making it more nebulous and shifting. On the brighter side, the M-type has the potential to help heal some of the s-type's pain around their career issues.

s/Neptune in M/11th House

The circumstances of this relationship may push the M-type to sacrifice some or all of their friends and the groups to which they belong. This can come about due to external issues, because the friends or groups will not accept the s-type, or because the M-type becomes so caught up in the power dynamic that they put aside all other social connections to concentrate on this new fascination. After a while, though, this can lead to isolation, and possibly being torn between wanting friends and feeling loyal to the relationship. This is especially problematic if it's the s-type who has struggles with the M-type's friends, and the M-type feels obligated to protect them. A balance needs to be struck, and the s-type needs to see that the M-type associating with people they don't like is not disloyalty. On the positive side, the s-type can become the M-type's best friend and heal some old pain about friendship and group belonging.

M/Neptune in s/11th House

The s-type may feel pressured to sacrifice some or all of their friends and the groups to which they belong; perhaps because the M-type does not approve of them, or wants the s-type to focus on the M-type, or because outside circumstances make the friends drift away. However, peer support can be important to an s-type, and isolation is not necessarily the best thing for one; a wise M-type will make sure that the s-type gets some satisfying social contact. Even the M-type becoming the s-type's best friend will not replace all need for outside connections, although both may believe that it will in the face of Neptune's idealistic haze. However, it has the potential to heal much of the s-type's pain around friends and group involvement.

s/Neptune in M/12th House

This is, in many ways, the hardest Neptune placements, because the twelfth is Neptune's own house and its confusion is strongest here. In the M-type's mind, the s-type becomes the ultimate, archetypal Neptunian s-type, whose most amazing quality (setting aside all the selfless service and flawless surrender) is sensitivity so strong that they can read the M-type's mind and know exactly what to do, without being verbally ordered to do it. Neptune's strength here can make the M-type unreasonably resistant to seeing and accepting the s-type's flawed humanity. It can also inspire the M-type to sacrifice themselves to the archetypal s-type they are projecting onto the flesh-and-blood screen; there may be noble sacrifices made to the projected assumptions of what the s-type wants, while the actual s-type stands there saying, "But you didn't ask me what I wanted, and this isn't it!" It may be necessary to get some outside perspective to sort out all the projections with this nebulous aspect, but if both parties are willing to be extremely mindful, it can blossom into a deep understanding and compassion, once all illusions are stripped away and the real souls are laid bare. If the two are still together at that point, the s-type has the potential to help the M-type feel seen and loved for who they are, which can be immensely healing.

M/Neptune in s/12th House

The big difficulty with this interaspect is that Neptune here sings the song that says, "This person will understand me completely!" It's a tricky aspect, because it encourages the s-type to idealize the M-type to the point of being determined to see them more as an archetype than a human being. Then, when the M-type doesn't instinctively "get" the s-type on an immediate deep level, they are demonized as much as they were idealized. The extreme resistance to seeing the M-type as the flawed human being they really are, and being all right with this, will be very surprising to both partners. They may need to get some outside perspective to bring them both past the illusions into the reality of seeing the very human soul of the partner. Once this happens, however, the M-type can give the s-type the experience of been fully seen and accepted, flaws and all, and this can be a very healing experience for them.

NEPTUNE INTERASPECTS

When one partner's Neptune aspects one of the other partner's planets, things get a little more confusing, and a lot more idealistic, sometimes to a fault. Where the M-type "Neptunifies" one of the s-type's planets, it makes them want to surrender those areas to that M-type (and possibly only to that M-type; those areas might have been activities or rights that they had no previous desire to give over) regardless of whether it is situationally appropriate. At the same time, the s-type will idealize the M-type as being a perfect archetype of the best of that contacted planet. (Whenever there is starry-eyed idealization, Neptune is often involved — and usually it ends up being smashed into disappointment.) The M-type will feel that pressure to be the perfect whatever, and may veer between desperately trying to live up to it, and being resentful that the standard seems so superhuman. Since Neptune likes avoidance, the M-type may withdraw from the s-type's questions in those areas. Both may collude on ignoring the mistakes that don't fit with the ideal stereotype, until it all falls down. If the s-type can recover and come to see the M-type as simply human — and turn the Neptune energies to compassion for their humanity rather than idealization of their perfection — then things won't be as dire, and the relationship has a chance.

In the other direction, when the s-type "Neptunifies" the M-type's planets, the M-type can project their planetary version of the perfect submissive partner onto the s-type, and then be disappointed when the s-type doesn't live up to the fantasy. The s-type may respond by exhausting themselves to live up to that standard, or by rebelling against the expectations, or by withdrawing into themselves and not talking about their issues, or all of these by turns, until it explodes. As with the opposite side, the M-type will have to be realistic and compassionate about the s-type's actual limitations, and let go of wishing for the ideal. As a friend of mine said, "You have to master the slave in front of you, flaws and all, not the one in your fantasy."

Neptune interaspects are a warning sign. Where Neptune is touching, expect that the Neptunian fog will set in and the person being contacted will have trouble seeing the other one clearly. Getting third-party perspective on these matters can help a lot (although perhaps you should check the third party's Neptune aspects against both partners first, in an ideal world).

If the interaspects are challenging, it will make it a lot harder to get through the idealistic fog, and there will be more risk of demonizing the partner just as unrealistically after the disappointment sets in. However, the harmonious aspects can still carry some of that pattern, and even the worst of the challenging ones can be dealt with, if both parties are patient, objective, and willing to work. In other words, Saturn is a good cure for Neptune issues. If there are any positive Saturn interaspects between the charts or in the composite (and with power dynamics, it's unlikely that there won't be), lean on those hard when the Neptune problems occur.

Neptune's not entirely a bad guy, though, and Neptune has its value in a power dynamic. As the planet of surrender and sacrifice, Neptune shows where the s-type has the potential to achieve a wonderfully satisfying, soul-deep submission, if they can go into it realistically. Sometimes that can only happen after the Neptunian disappointment, so one way you can see that crash—if it occurs—is as the restarting point. "Now that's out of the way, we can try again and really get this right."

My relationship with my slaveboy has so many difficult Neptune aspects that it's a wonder we made it through the first few years, with their disappointments. His Neptune squares my Saturn, Chiron, Mars, Uranus, and Pluto; mine conjuncted his Mercury, Venus and Uranus, squared his Mars, and opposed his Chiron and Vesta. What this meant was a lot of disillusion with each other a few years in, as the glitter wore off and faded. We had a few things going for us, though: strong Saturn aspects and an early commitment to radical honesty, among other things. However, our mutual opinion is that our biggest asset was our commitment to making this power dynamic into a spiritual path for both of us.

This isn't going to be everyone's cup of tea, but Neptune also rules spirituality, and traditionally one good solution for Neptune problems is to hit the spirituality button, again and again. That doesn't have to be embracing a particular religion or believing in a personified deity, although that's the route we two took. Meditation is as Neptunian as prayer; mindfulness is as Neptunian as faith. Compassion is the root and the goal of this planetary energy, and there are many roads to that goal. The s-types can get there by surrendering to a person who has earned their trust, and making the work of serving and obeying this flawed human being into an art of putting aside the ego and merging into the will of another. The M-types can get there by making every order come from a clean place of self-awareness, and of cultivating boundless compassion for the flawed human being who is their responsibility. This is the best road out of Neptune problems that we know. If it calls to you, find your own version of it and walk it together.

s/Neptune in Aspect to M/Sun

The M-type may see the s-type as their ray of sunshine, their joy and good cheer in the world. It may be difficult for them to see the s-type's human flaws clearly — perhaps initially idealizing them and then demonizing them when they turn out to have the same clay feet as anyone else. It will be important for the M-type to be as realistic as possible, perhaps getting outside perspective on the s-type and their problems. The s-type, in their turn, will feel driven to sacrifice themselves for the M-type; not for any particular purpose but just for them. Their sacrifice may have an air of "I want to heal you, Sir/Ma'am," and the wise M-type will put a brake on this and not allow them to wipe themself out over it.

M/Neptune in Aspect to s/Sun

The s-type will see the M-type as amazing, glorious, magnificent, multitalented, and all sorts of other idealistic adjectives. They will bubble over with all the wonderful things that their M-type is … until they prove to have defects just like everyone else, and then they become the Worst Master Ever. It's important for both parties to understand that this will be the s-type's tendency, and they should attempt to be gentle, compassionate, and realistic about belonging to an ordinary human being who makes mistakes. The M-type will feel driven to help the s-type to heal and be a better person; they should take care not to take on help that is beyond their skill level, or be too ready to characterize the s-type as weak, and thus not responsible for their actions.

s/Neptune in Aspect to M/Moon

The M-type may see the s-type as more emotional than they are (whether true or not). They may also cast the s-type either as a child in need of care, or a nurturing figure who ought to care for them. They may have trouble deciphering the s-type's emotions, and outside perspective may be useful for this. The s-type will be driven to sacrifice themself when the M-type is having difficult emotions, perhaps putting aside or hiding their own feelings in order to comfort the M-type. If both people know this is a tendency, it can be mindfully prevented.

M/Neptune in Aspect to s/Moon

The s-type will see the M-type as the ideal parental figure — or at least they will at first, then once the M-type makes a mistake, they will project all the mistakes their own parental figures ever made onto the M-type. They need to be aware of this tendency, breathe, and tell themselves that the M-type is not their parents and they are not a child who has few choices. At the same time, the M-type may feel as if they need to be strong and be there for the s-type when they are having emotional issues or outbursts, possibly even putting aside their own feelings in order to do this. They need to be careful of falling into the false archetype of the "rock" who always gives the care and never needs it themselves.

s/Neptune in Aspect to M/Mercury

The M-type sees the s-type as smart, capable, mentally resourceful, and likely to make the perfect secretary or personal assistant. However, Neptune distorts expectations, and the M-type may overreact when the s-type forgets to make notes or writes down the wrong phone number. Support and training may be of more use than expectations here. The s-type will be driven to attempt to be the perfect boy- or girl-Friday for the M-type, perhaps to the point of hiding their questions or difficulty with organization in order to look competent and quick. Regular check-ins, with the question of "What service was exasperating to you today?" may help them to calm down and be honest about their abilities in any given situation. The s-type may also feel like there are many things they can't say to the M-type, which can lead to dishonesty; writing a journal and letting the M-type read it can be useful here. The M-type should compliment them on any show of difficult honesty.

M/Neptune in Aspect to s/Mercury

The s-type sees the M-type as brilliant, articulate, and omnicompetent, at least until they forget something or misspeak or are disastrously disorganized one time too many, and then they are The Dumb Boss I Have To Do Everything For. It's all right for the M-type to use the s-type's service to help with their organizational problems, but the s-type should try hard to do it with a good attitude, and not expect perfection. The M-type may feel pushed to help the s-type be more competent and organized, perhaps at the expense of their own organization levels. They may also find themself censoring their words so as not to distress the s-type, which can eventually feel like evasion or even dishonesty. To assist with this, the s-type can encourage them to say the words that are hard to hear, and then take a breath and humbly thank them for doing so, showing that they are capable of hearing those words without freaking out.

s/Neptune in Aspect to M/Venus

This is an interaspect that will make the M-type fall madly in love with the s-type, even if they didn't intend to at the start. The relationship may take on a fairytale quality in their mind, and they may cast the s-type in the role opposite to their dashing, dominant hero. The problem arises when the s-type doesn't stay within the romantic part assigned to them, at which point the M-type may feel hurt and withdraw, imagining that they aren't loved enough. The s-type will feel driven to surrender to the M-type over and over again for romantic reasons, and may excuse all sorts of bad behavior in the name of love, or fail to bring up problematic actions on the M-type's part because "at least they love me." If both parties can learn to see each other realistically, then a deep affection and tolerance can grow in place of the idealization.

M/Neptune in Aspect to s/Venus

The energy of Neptune and Venus is going to make the s-type fall madly in love with the M-type, regardless of whether they intended to in the beginning. The M-type may take on a romantic archetypal — perhaps even fairytale — character in their minds. This will last until they enact the usual interpersonal clumsiness that happens sooner or later in relationships, and then it's If You Love Me, How Can You Do That To Me? The s-type needs to understand that loving a real human being means loving their flaws as well. On the other side, the M-type will not only feel pressured by the Perfect Dominant Lover role, they may end up hiding parts of themselves in order to seem more romantic, and/or take on romantic activities to please the s-type when they'd really rather just hang out in their underwear. Again, it's important to be realistic about each other, so that compassion and acceptance can grow.

s/Neptune in Aspect to M/Mars

We see this aspect a fair amount in power dynamics where the s-type has a role similar to a bodyguard or protector-servant or knight to the Queen or King. The M-type sees the s-type as strong and courageous, and is delighted to have that strength and courage laid at their feet. (Mars rules the sex drive, so there's usually a strong sexual chemistry here.) Sometimes the s-type never thought of themselves as a warrior, and they are grateful to the M-type for believing in them. Of course, no one is a brave warrior all the time, and the M-type can become disillusioned when the s-type shows their fears, perhaps being unable to support them emotionally in the face of their own disappointment. Meanwhile, the s-type feels driven to throw themselves at the M-type's feet and beg for that belief in their courage to come again. They may hide their fears in the attempt to be perfect until it all falls down. Both parties need to be realistic, and remember that courage is not fearlessness, nor lack of failure, but getting up again and trying in spite of fear.

M/Neptune in Aspect to s/Mars

The s-type will see the M-type as vigorous and courageous; someone who Gets Things Done. Since Mars is also sex, they probably also see the M-type as delectably aggressive, here to sweep them off their feet. This will last until the M-type shows fear or avoidance, or drops balls instead of leaping in and making things happen; then they will become The Cowardly Fraud in the s-type's eyes. At the same time, the M-type may feel like they have to be brave and strong all the time, and will hide any feeling of weakness from the s-type so as not to disappoint them. This can feel like—and may actually end up being—the M-type avoiding the s-type for periods of time. Both partners need to learn that part of strength is having the courage to be vulnerable, but that's not going to happen unless vulnerability gets an accepting audience. No one can be brave and strong all the time.

s/Neptune in Aspect to M/Jupiter

The M-type will see the s-type as a Giver, perhaps even the ultimate Giver. All s-types need to be givers to some extent, but the M-type may overestimate how much giving the s-type can do, and the s-type may feel pushed to keep giving and sacrificing themselves, even to exhaustion, because they want to live up to the M-type's clear pleasure in their role as the Bountiful One. At the same time, this particular aspect can make both parties encourage each other in indulgence — spend more money, have more sex, eat more, take more vacations to exotic places — possibly to the point of financial or domestic detriment. (Jupiter is also the sign of religion, and this aspect can, in some cases, create religious fanaticism.) Both partners need to be careful and honest about what is too much of anything, or it can get out of hand. The M-type also needs to work extra hard to guard the s-type's boundaries and encourage them to self-care instead of just needing more from them.

M/Neptune in Aspect to s/Jupiter

The s-type will see the M-type as a combination of Santa Claus, Daddy Warbucks, and the Fairy Godmother — a fountain of benevolent generosity who sweeps them away from their ordinary life into a place of abundance and (hopefully) wealth. If that ideal doesn't pan out, disappointment may ensue and the s-type may feel somehow betrayed. The M-type may find themselves feeling pushed to sacrifice resources for the s-type's comfort, and may feel unable to bring it up or set good boundaries without further disappointment. Like the above couple, the couple may encourage each other to excess, in money, sex, drugs, food, recreation, anything fun and enjoyable (and also in some cases a mutual encouragement to religious fanaticism). Jupiter pushes for More, and Neptune pushes for Fantasy, and it can go poorly.

Both partners need to push for honesty about what resources are actually available and reasonable to expect, from each other and from the bank account.

s/Neptune in Aspect to M/Saturn

Traditionally, this interaspect was likely to indicate a relationship thwarted by circumstances, with a round of passionate love (Neptune) followed by the cold reality (Saturn) setting in and tearing the partners apart in a tragic drama. It doesn't have to be that way, of course; both partners can figure out a way to make it work, but the key word there is work. On a power exchange level, the M-type may see the s-type as a loyal, wonderfully correct and disciplined, formal-protocol sort of slave—the perfect positive Saturn archetype—and may be disappointed when they become careless, bored, silly, or too casual—or start showing too many emotions. The s-type may feel pressured to be very formal and careful with the M-type, and hide their feelings and problems from the M-type so as not to spoil the illusion, at the same time sacrificing themself to make it a reality, even though the reality is unachievable. The M-type needs to allow them time and space to be anything but Saturnian, and encourage them to speak up. However, this may also lead to the s-type sounding critical of the M-type and bursting their romantic bubbles, so the s-type should work toward finding a good medium between censoring themself and just being honest but gentle. *(Also check the Saturn chapter for the other side of this aspect.)*

M/Neptune in Aspect to s/Saturn

First, check the point above about dangerous, thwarted relationships with drama and tragedy, and see if it applies. If not, you're lucky. The s-type will see the M-type at first as their ideal Saturnian archetype—formal, authoritarian, committed, disciplined, with unswerving honor, absolute solidity, and very little apparent emotion—the rock against which they can throw themselves, which never breaks. When the M-type turns out to have all sorts of messy human emotions, not to mention occasionally want to make jokes, blow off their exercise hour, or sit around casually in their underwear, then the s-type becomes quite disappointed. At the same time, the M-type may feel obligated to play that part for the s-type's adoring audience, suppressing or hiding parts of themselves in order to be that continual rock for the s-type. No one, however, can be the perfect authority figure all the time; Saturn is also limitations and obstacles and by its nature will drop the M-type off their pedestal in no time. If the s-type can live through the M-type's fall from perfection, and the M-type can open up and be honest, then a mutual discipline can be built from scratch from a place of realism rather than fantasy. *(Also check the Saturn chapter for the Saturnian side of this aspect.)*

s/Neptune in Aspect to M/Uranus

This can be a tricky aspect, because the M-type will see the s-type as a wild and free creature, perhaps one to be tamed and brought to hand, perhaps one that can't be tamed. The s-type may unconsciously play into this and act out when the M-type is (also probably unconsciously) disappointed when their submission seems to make them "too tame". (If this dynamic is causing problems, honest communication can usually sort it out, perhaps with the couple finding designated outlets for the s-type's wildness.) Another way this can play out is the M-type seeing the s-type as an ultra-modern progressive sort who doesn't care about what the crowd thinks, and may be surprised when the s-type shows any conservative beliefs or insecurities about social disapproval. The s-type may feel driven to go along with all the M-type's new and possibly socially unacceptable ideas, even when it costs the s-type friends, jobs, or social groups, in order to not be seen as a wet blanket or prude. The s-type needs to be able to speak up about this without getting a faceful of the M-type's scorn or attempts at persuasion, and the M-type needs to rein in extreme ideas (extreme by the s-type's definition) until the s-type is more comfortable with them, if ever. Peer support can help with this process.

M/Neptune in Aspect to s/Uranus

The s-type will see the M-type as a wild, unique, innovative genius who is ahead of their time and doesn't care about the judgment of the crowd. This can result in disappointment when the M-type shows any reservations about social opprobrium, has any conservative or unquestioned views, or perhaps isn't always as much of a genius as the s-type would like to think. The M-type may feel driven to move out of their comfort zone with regard to new activities or relationship styles; this can cause resentment and a feeling of not really being in charge. That in turn may cause the M-type to find themselves suddenly angry at the s-type for nebulous reasons; breathing and reaching for calm until it passes and they can think clearly can be useful. With this placement, it's often the s-type who is pushing subtly for running ahead into uncharted territory, and the M-type needs to lay out their personal discomfort, without justification due to beliefs or world views, and require that the s-type respects that, just as the M-type would (hopefully) respect the s-type's discomfort when the roles are reversed.

s/Neptune in Aspect to M/Neptune

With conjunct Neptunes, it just means that the two of you are age-mates, and you won't notice this aspect at all. With sextile or square Neptunes, there will be a large age gap between the two of you, and this will play out as different overarching world views. Unless both of you have strong spiritual disciplines of self-awareness, compassion, and tolerance, you'll likely just see the other partner as hopelessly deluded in some way, a "product of their time", with little appreciation for their differing views. This can be a problem with a heavily aspected Neptune, or it can be no big deal at all, depending on how much it gets in the way.

s/Neptune in Aspect to M/Pluto

The M-type will see the s-type as dark, sexy, intense, and possibly emotionally unstable. Emotional outbursts on the s-type's part may cause overreaction in the M-type, and they may need to check themselves before judging the s-type as unhinged.

The sex will probably be intense and fantasy-ridden, and the M-type may be sadly disappointed on the off days when it doesn't work due to other circumstances. At the same time, the s-type may feel driven to go along with the M-type's strongest (and possibly unsatisfied) appetites for sex, BDSM, and emotional intensity, and sacrifice themselves for those hungers even when it frays their nerves to be the fantasy-prop or even the fantasy-dispenser. When they come up against a wall with this, they may do the Neptunian withdrawal and avoidance, and the M-type may find themselves suddenly enraged as explosive Pluto is triggered. The M-type should make a space for the s-type to be able to communicate when they need a break from these sacrifices, and the s-type should find a way to communicate these issues that is calm and rational, perhaps writing it out beforehand or sharing a journal entry. *(Also check the Pluto chapter for the Plutonian side of this aspect.)*

M/Neptune in Aspect to s/Pluto

The s-type will see the M-type as the ultimate desirable Dark Lord or Dark Lady, with terrible hungers and desires, ready to control every aspect of their lives. This may both excite and terrify them by turns. They need to breathe and back up and see the actual human being with all their flaws and vulnerabilities, because sooner or later the M-type will act completely out of the fantasy character and they may be very disillusioned. Some s-types in this situation subtly push the M-type to go further across the boundaries of the s-type's physical or emotional safety, because they want those fantasies and desires met on both sides. This can go very badly when a serious error is made, for which the M-type will likely be blamed, so it is in both partners' best interests to keep a close watch on these flights of extremity. At the same time, the M-type may feel driven to pretend to be as powerful as possible, and when they can't manage it, they will tend to do the Neptunian withdrawal. This can trigger sudden anger in the s-type when explosive Pluto notices that they are left alone in the fantasy and the Dark Lord or Lady has retreated to stare at their computer. Honest conversation needs to happen around what is and is not a realistic desire, and both parties should set the goal a little more conservatively than either might dream of, to keep Neptune from pulling them into trouble. *(Also check the Pluto chapter for the other side of this aspect.)*

The Other Planets

Uranus: Conformity and Community

The planet Uranus rules freedom, nonconformity, and innovation. Uranus thinks that rules are meant to be broken and structure exists to be torn down. It's the rebel planet, defying authority and discovering new and different ways to do everything, which is why it also rules the progress of technology. Obviously, it's not a planet that seems, on the surface, to be particularly harmonious with power exchange of any sort; quite the opposite, really. Yet even the slaviest slave has Uranus somewhere in their chart. It's just a matter of the target of its aim.

While people outside of any power dynamic demographic or body of knowledge may assume that it's just rehashed "traditional" sexist marital oppression, the truth is that the modern style of consensual, negotiated power dynamics couldn't have existed before the sexual revolution. Modern practitioners have spent a long time analyzing their relationships and communicating new ways to make them work ethically and practically. Most have stripped traditional gender roles out of the theorizing, as a significant number of practitioners come from the LGBT community and find them irrelevant. The result is an ever-growing set of build-your-own-custom-unequal-relationship tools that any couple, triad, or group can use to create a unique negotiated system with built-in failsafes in case something goes wrong. Introspection, self-awareness, analysis, communication, and conflict resolution are encouraged in a way that would have been unheard-of for the average pre-sexual-revolution relationship. Complicated topics such as love, honor, parenting models, self-improvement, mental conditioning, and disability are being dissected and discussed publicly, in print and in classes. D/s, M/s, and O/p are treated as learnable alternative relationship styles, with an added postscript about how this will probably not be acceptable to the public, and that hard decisions will need to be made about closets and disclosures.

This is all very Uranian, and one can almost hear Uranus chuckling. Modern consensual "slavery" turns the old meaning entirely on its head; in fact, only in a particularly Uranian community could one hear political debates about whether using the word "slave" is disrespectful to people mired in actual chattel slavery in developing countries, or whether *not* using it is disrespectful to the "Old Guard", most of whom considered themselves rebels even when they wore chains. Where one finds Uranus in the power dynamic schema is generally on the outside of the relationship, in the communities a couple (or triad, or group) may belong to for support, or hide themselves from for safety.

Wherever someone on either side of the slash has Uranus (sign, house, or planets that it is aspecting) that's a place where they are most driven to give the finger to outside society and say, "I'll do this my own way, thank you." It's not unusual for people in these relationships to have a strongly aspected Uranus, especially if they openly identify with being part of an alternative relationship minority.

We can see how that works out for M-types; most dominants want to be in charge at least partly because they don't like to be told what to do by others. In fact, the M-type's Uranian contacts with the s-type's chart can easily be read as areas where the M-type will want to push the s-type out of their comfortable social-programming rut and on to new frontiers with them.

However, you're probably wondering what happens with a strongly Uranian s-type (or, for that matter, any s-type when they are faced with their Uranus's area of expertise). My experience is that as long as both parties are strongly committed to being on the same team—both facing outwards against the restrictive world together—the s-type is fine with obeying the M-type's rules around the subject. After all, it's their partner, not society, right? Society says that you are supposed to put what society wants above what your partner wants, especially if their wishes aren't socially acceptable. However, if the M-type refuses to listen to the s-type's values in this area, and seems to be toeing society's line without being willing to question the rule (or at least reframe it entirely as their own desire rather than what is "right" or "proper"), Uranus will cast them as one of society's repressive soldiers. Suddenly they're not on the same team, they're on the opposing teams of oppression and freedom, and Uranus will create an instinctive rebellion in the s-type's soul.

If some of the M-type's desires are suspiciously close to social norms, and those desires happen to be associated astrologically either with the sign/house area of the s-type's Uranus or with planets contacted by the s-type's Uranus (check your synastry charts!), all hope is not lost. The M-type can launch a twofold campaign to get in good with their s-type's Uranus. First, the M-type can show that they've thought about the situation, acknowledged that other options are viable for others but that this is really their preference for personal reasons, and they'd follow it even if society thought it was terrible. Second, they can find ways to reframe it as actually subversive. Even if it is a very traditional or socially conservative behavior or concept, if society says that you're supposed to accept it unthinkingly, choosing it mindfully for yourself while allowing others their own choice is subversive in its own right. That's a line of reasoning that Uranus can follow, and it has a surprisingly positive effect on these sorts of disagreements.

Mercury: Communication and Transparency

The planet Mercury rules all kinds of communication — your words, your writing, what books you read and how well you pick up information, not to mention all the rest of media, mail, and the internet. It also rules your cognitive thinking and mental processes. While it might not be the first planet you'd think of as being important in power exchange, it's actually really crucial in its own way.

Power dynamics of any kind live or die on the quality of the communication between the people involved. When communication goes down, the dynamic will likely follow. If the s-type cuts off the flow of information to the M-type, their dominant partner is trying to manage them in the dark, and will quickly plow into an iceberg of hidden fear or resentment. If the M-type cuts off the flow of information — at least around anything pertaining to the s-type, the dynamic, and their general life together — the s-type will not be able to see the plan behind the orders, and will be at higher risk of making errors. If information flows, but both are communicating so differently that they might as well not be speaking the same language, the air becomes rife with misunderstanding and frustration. A positive Mercury collection can really help with a smooth partnering, just as its lack can create utter chaos.

We don't have the room here to go over every Mercury placement and aspect, and that information is available elsewhere, but I'll list the basics for your research use. Your relationship's "Mercury collection" consists of the following points to look at and consider:

1) The M-type's Mercury sign.
2) The s-type's Mercury sign.
3) How dissimilar these signs are (same or harmonizing or clashing element; same or harmonizing or clashing modality).
4) The M-type's Mercury house.

5) The s-type's Mercury house.
6) How well the areas of life represented by these houses get along or clash, including in the lives of the individuals in the relationship.
7) Any harmonious or challenging aspects between the two Mercuries.
8) Challenging aspects to either Mercury by the other individual's planets, which can affect their understanding when talking to their partner. The biggest troublemakers are Uranus (chaos), Neptune (confusion and illusion), and Mars (aggression).
9) The composite chart's Mercury sign, and how it harmonizes (or not) with either natal Mercury.
10) The composite chart's Mercury house, and how it clashes (or not) with either natal Mercury.
11) Challenging aspects to Mercury in the composite chart.
12) Challenging aspects between the composite Mercury and either of the natal Mercuries.

If you like, you can go down this list and assign either an "easy" or "difficult" point to each comparative aspect, and to each composite aspect to the composite Mercury. If you've got more difficult points than easy ones, you're going to have to work a lot harder to communicate smoothly with each other, and you may have to set up a lot of (possibly artificial-feeling) rules to make it work. Regular sessions with a mediator who can translate each to the other, and help you both learn to speak and understand the other's language, can help a lot here.

Some useful phrases for discussion we've gleaned from our own and others' communication work include:

- ❖ "I need to talk to you about something, and I need you to listen generously."

- ❖ "The story I'm telling myself is…" *or, once you've proven you can use that first one yourself,* "What story are you telling yourself here?"
- ❖ "So what I'm hearing here is…(repeat back)?"
- ❖ "I need time to process my feelings on this so that I can give you more information on what's going on with me."
- ❖ "You're hearing me, but I think I'm not being clear enough for you to really understand what I'm trying to communicate. Let me try again. Bear with me, please?"
- ❖ Also, "I'm not communicating this well," instead of "You don't understand!"
- ❖ "Sir/Ma'am, I don't understand how the actions you're taking are going to get you the results I think you want. Can you explain it to me?"
- ❖ "You could do that, but it would change the nature of our relationship."
- ❖ "What would that look like for you?"
- ❖ "Do you want advice, or do you just need to talk it out?"
- ❖ "What did you hear me say?"
- ❖ "What would make this easier for you to handle?"
- ❖ "I'm not sure how I feel about that. Can I sleep on it and get back to you tomorrow?"
- ❖ "Tomorrow I'm going to ask you about X, so take some time to think about X before then."

While there isn't more space to discuss effective communication, both of you should understand that this can be a saving grace or a relationship disaster, and it's worth it to work hard — harder than you would for an egalitarian relationship. As we've said before, these relationships require more effort to maintain well, and keeping the lines of communication open is like keeping the garden irrigated.

Venus and Mars: Attraction and Motivation

I am combining these two planets together into their own chapter because this book isn't about sex and romance, except as it works peripherally in a power dynamic. Some power dynamic relationships are service-only, without a sexual component at all; some include sexual service but not a romantic relationship. The importance of Venus and Mars will vary depending on the intent and boundaries of what is negotiated.

Venus is the planet of love and aesthetics. Aspects between one partner's Venus and the other partner's planets will affect the flow of affection between partners; a Venus/Venus aspect can make the couple love each other in spite of themselves, although a challenging aspect may make them both a little uncomfortable with the strength of their feelings.

Harmonious aspects to the Sun and Jupiter will result in a strong flow of ardent affection even if there is no sexual component; challenging aspects can make that flow intermittent and mixed with frustration, but will not stop it entirely. Aspects to the Moon can cause either a feeling of being loved and cared for in the relationship, or conflicting emotions about whether they are (or should be) loved and cared for. Aspects to Mercury indicate affectionate conversation, or conflict over the lack of apparent affection in conversation. Harmonious aspects to Saturn indicate loyalty; challenging ones indicate blockages in expressing warmth and fondness. Aspects to Neptune increase idealization of the partner's love, for better or worse depending on the aspect. Uranus, on the other hand, has a tendency to bring up the issue of alternative relationships in these dynamics, either encouraging them or creating conflict over them, depending on the aspect. Pluto in aspect to Venus deepens the emotions around the power dynamic; it will feel "fated" and will boil up all the individuals' old baggage around feeling loved, in any way. Even if both parties agree to keep the relationship unromantic, Pluto/Venus aspects can create a psychic bond just from engaging in power exchange itself.

Finally, aspects between Venus and Mars create sexual sparks, even if the individuals start out not being interested in that aspect of relating. Venus and Mars in aspect can't help but become the point where love meets sex, and couples with one of these can be taken aback at how strong the sexual chemistry becomes. This is true for both harmonious and challenging aspects, although the challenging ones may fall into a fight-and-make-up pattern if the couple doesn't stay mindful and head off the fighting immediately. It's also useful to look at Venus in the composite chart, and see what its aspects are; compare them to the preceding list and assume that it goes for both people, although the two of you may take turns being the Venus person and the embodiment of the contacting planet.

This bring us to Mars, the planet of action, motivation, anger ... and sex. As you can imagine, a Mars/Mars aspect can create shockingly strong sexual current, if the individuals are in each other's sexual range ... and sometimes even if they aren't. Mars/Mars contacts also cause conflict, even when they are harmonious, because Mars by its nature doesn't think conflict is necessarily a bad thing. Any planet contacted by the partner's Mars in any way is going to indicate a (perhaps only slightly) higher willingness to fight each other in those areas. That isn't always negative; sometimes it takes some fire to rip the veil off of festering silences. Since Mars is also motivation, it can convince people to actually do something about it.

Interaspects between Mars and one partner's Sun or Jupiter definitely helps to give motivation for action and decision-making, for better or worse depending on the aspect. Contacting the partner's Saturn, Mars can push them past their obstacles and fears, or make them feel limited and criticized. Mars aspecting the partner's Mercury helps them to speak up, although a challenging aspect will encourage aggressive (and possibly much louder) speech. Aspects to Uranus can bring up issues around unconventional sexuality for better or worse; they can also make the partner's responses to being pushed more erratic and unusual, especially if the aspect is challenging. Mars/Pluto contacts between charts can create both immense sexual chemistry (like

Mars/Mars, but with a volcano under it) and a fair amount of anger, usually around buried issues of power that are not being discussed. Honest and perhaps painful discussion is necessary to keep this one from going sideways, particularly with a challenging aspect. It's also traditionally associated with a fair amount of jealousy, which can be tricky in a power dynamic depending on what's negotiated for what partner.

The two most difficult Mars aspects between charts are ones to the Moon and Neptune. These two planets are as unlike Mars as they can be. Mars/Moon interaspects create a physical attraction that runs deep; the Mars person wants to protect the Moon person, while the Moon person wants to spoil the Mars person. The problem is that these aspects also create an emotional roller coaster, as Mars lends fire and wrath to the Moon, and emotional reactions can get out of hand without tools to defuse the situation.

Mars/Neptune interaspects are even more difficult. Mars gives energy to Neptune's romantic idealization about the partner, which can go on for some time until things shift—because Neptune is always shifting. Suddenly the Mars qualities that the Neptune person idealized are something to be resented, or perhaps they decide that those qualities aren't there at all. These interaspects can tempt both parties to manipulate each other in order to keep the peace, which will eventually backfire. Even more so than Mars/Pluto and Mars/Moon interaspects, the only way to keep these from going sideways from blitzed romanticism to furious demonization is constant honesty, communication, and possibly plenty of third-party perspective.

Like Venus, it's useful to check the position of Mars in a composite chart, check its sign and house, and see what planets are aspecting it. Check the previous list for a quick idea of aspect effects. Remember that with a composite, it's not one person's problem, but rather it will be demonstrated by both, perhaps switching back and forth on who gets what part.

There's a lot more to say about Venus and Mars contacts in a chart, but that passes into the realm of any relationship, not just those in chosen hierarchy. For other characteristics of Venus and

Mars, whether in the single natal chart or in relationship charts, talk to an astrologer or read more specifically on those planets.

The Moon: Breaking the Mold

Every one of us is born into a power dynamic, no matter how uncomfortable that idea makes some people. Every one of us starts out as a helpless infant with no recourse, unable to communicate except in a formless wail. We are entirely dependent on parents to care for us, particularly our primary caretaker. This is usually—not always, but usually—our mother. As we grow, we also find that we are dependent on others as well—father, grandparents, older siblings, babysitters, teachers. Starting with that primary bond, these huge figures affect how we see hierarchical relationships, casting future power dynamics in the mold of what we experience whilst young and pliable. Eventually, if we come into a deliberate, consenting power dynamic as adults, we must fight that early cast-concrete pattern in order to develop our own style as leader or subordinate.

The Moon is not specifically a planet of power exchange, but it does have an effect. It describes the mold of power with which we came into adulthood, and if we are mindful and creative, we can shift that pattern and make it our own instead of a mindless repetition of childhood assumptions. The Moon's sign, house, and contacting planets indicate the qualities of our primary caretaker that we absorbed most easily, that stood out in our early experiences. In some cases, we can look at that chart information and say, "That wasn't my parents!" This may be objectively true from an adult's perspective, but it is how you saw your first "masters" when you had a small child's brain.

The Moon outlines the pattern that both M-type and s-type will carry with them. While a good experience can help either one navigate a power dynamic with a sense of what responsive, responsible mastery and devoted obedience with good self-worth looks like, more difficult or negative patterns can silently infect the relationship from both sides, seeping in and distorting thoughts, emotions, and behaviors. Sooner or later the s-type will be projecting those early disappointments onto the M-type, and the M-type will be wondering why their subordinate partner is behaving so irrationally toward them. If they are lucky enough to figure out the problem, a campaign of digging all that out and changing it will have to begin. Similarly, sooner or later the M-type will find those dysfunctional models creeping into their style of power and authority, and the distressed s-type will be wondering why the M-type does not seem to hear their pleas in the face of counter-productive orders and attitudes. If the M-type manages to see what they are doing, it will be on their shoulders to change it in themselves.

I highly recommend further study of the Moon and its many astrological afflictions, as this chapter can only barely touch on its traps and difficulties. Take up your own study of your natal Moons and their qualities, positive and negative, learn more about those early patterns. Check the Moon in your composite chart and see what patterns you will be navigating together as a couple. Of course, the Moon at its best is a wonderful planet; it's where our positive emotions as well as our negative ones gestate and are born. It's just that when the Moon acts up in a power dynamic, it's not the positive emotions that are causing problems. So in this chapter I'll go through a quick list of lunar interaspects which are the most direct routes to interpersonal conflict. (These can also be used as insight into dealing with these aspects in the composite chart.)

A Moon/Moon interaspect indicates a very emotional relationship. If it's challenging, those emotions may be uncomfortable, and it may reflect entirely opposed early experiences that are hard for each other to understand. Either way, you will not be able to be distant and cold with each other. At its best, you will have a great deal of sympathy and consideration for each other. This aspect may indicate interest in a parental/childlike role in your dynamic.

Having one partner's Moon aspecting the other partner's Sun brings up issues about whether you understand how the other person's emotional responses work. If it's a harmonious aspect, the Sun person will have a window into understanding how the Moon person's feelings work, and both parties will feel "seen". If it's challenging, it can bring up memories about parents who didn't understand their child and made it clear that this confusing creature was a problem.

Moon/Mercury interaspects indicate that talking about emotions will be very important in your relationship, even if it's painful and you have to learn to do it well over time. You may get to the point of being able to intuit each other's thoughts. This interaspect may bring up questions from childhood about whether the individual was smart enough to please their parents.

Moon/Venus aspects are usually very romantic and loving; even the challenging ones are quite tame for challenging aspects. The only hitch is a possible conflict between parentally nurturing roles and sexy, dangerous ones — the sort of thing that used to be referred to as a Madonna/whore complex, but can apply to either gender here. The parties may just have to learn that a person can be sexy and caring at the same time. Challenging interaspects here can bring up memories of possible sexual inappropriateness by caretakers, or being pressured into appearing sexually mature too soon.

Moon/Jupiter aspects are also generally positive, although a challenging angle to Jupiter always means overdoing it, so this aspect can encourage emotions to get bigger, louder, and more forceful, and perhaps have trouble calming down. This interaspect creates a great deal of generosity, and the couple may love to give each other gifts. However, the big unearthing here is of times in the past when one's parents were overly emotional, especially if it happened in a frightening way.

It's said that Moon/Mars aspects are the epitome of fertility, and make people burn to get pregnant and have babies. (I've met at least one couple with this interaspect who did have a "forced breeding" fetish.) It also creates a great deal of sexual spark, and possibly an interest in rough, primal sex. If challenging, this aspect can sometimes manifest as the Mars person chiding the Moon person for being too timid and unwilling to take risks, or the Moon person treating the Mars person like an unruly child.

Moon/Saturn interaspects are even more difficult, with the Saturn partner continually criticizing and making the Moon partner feel unworthy and depressed, possibly without meaning to do so. This is hard enough when the Saturn person is the M-type and has enough authority to be overbearing to the Moon person, but it can be just as bad if not worse for the M-type to be the Moon person in this situation and have their confidence constantly cut out from underneath them. This interaspect will bring up all the times in both people's past when they were criticized by parents for whom they were never good enough. A harmonious interaspect may come with a deep loyalty and a protective streak, but will still harbor this difficult issue.

Moon/Uranus interaspects encourage erratic emotional control, and the Moon person especially will have to watch themself for self-discipline and mood swings. This relationship may bring up issues of parental inconsistency or emotional distance — the caregiver whose thoughts were off in the future instead of paying attention to the children who were actually present.

Neptune is a particularly confusing planet, and Moon/Neptune interaspects encourage daydreaming in each other, sometimes to the point of escapism or unrealistic decisions. On the positive side, this is another point for possible psychic heart-contacts, an empathy that speaks to each other without words. This interaspect brings up a time when parents were vague, confusing, inconsistent, or absent for long periods — or, conversely, when they modeled unhealthy self-sacrificing behavior or expected their children to sacrifice themselves.

Moon/Pluto contacts are all about buried rage, and these interaspects loose those hidden pools of anger and resentment, bringing up memories of childhood fear and shame in the face of parental wrath. It needs to be handled with care and mindfulness, keeping in mind that many sudden bouts of rage are not actually about the partner in front of you, but someone gone long ago.

Moon interaspect problems often rear their heads when the s-type is going through what has been referred to as a *reactance period* — when a new benchmark of surrender has been reached and the s-type's subconscious becomes frightened for its survival. During reactance periods, rebellion breaks out, often over what seem like small, insignificant areas, which distract both people's eyes from the larger areas where the s-type is integrating the dissonance. It's best to let them have their way, at least for a time, on the small rebellions, and reiterate that this is a team process of deepening trust that can take as long as it needs to take. Keep an eye out for reactance that seems to fall into a lunar contact model. It can give valuable clues as to where the s-type can talk things through, and possibly get outside support.

Jupiter: In Santa's Lap

The planet Jupiter is bigger than all the rest, and it indicates abundance—the Gift-Giver who always has more, the birthday fairy who bestows the special talent. In a power exchange relationship, Jupiter is the place where both partners inspire each other to do better, and it actually happens. Note that I used the word *inspire*. Jupiter is a Teacher planet (along with Mercury, but a Teacher of Worldview rather than Facts or Skills) that teaches by inspiring someone to be and think differently, not just by telling them what to do. Ideally it's done almost without trying—Jupiter expresses enthusiasm and the other person catches it and follows; Jupiter expresses trust and the other person runs excitedly to keep earning that trust. Since all planetary aspects work both ways, the M-type is just as susceptible to Jupiterian grace as the s-type.

Again, I'll give a quick-and-dirty list of how Jupiter interaspects affect people between their charts, and this list can also be extrapolated into Jupiter aspects in the composite chart, remembering again that these would apply to both individuals at once or by turns.

Jupiter/Jupiter interaspects generally produce friendship, even if they aren't all that harmonious. There's a sense of being buddies, or "partners in crime"; even if challenging interaspects make the verbal exchanges into jokes at each other's expense, both will understand that it's all in fun. In fact, one of the best qualities of this interaspect is the ability to just have fun together, and to find humor in almost any situation. It's especially good for the overly serious, as it helps them to find that hidden sense of humor and builds their resilience.

One partner's Jupiter aspecting the other partner's Sun helps the Sun person to become more comfortable in their skin, and more sure of who they are at their core. It's also a wonderfully optimistic interaspect, making both partners feel like they can do anything. S-types become more buoyant in their competence, and M-types can become much more poised in their dominance. However, a challenging aspect can make either of them overly confident and apt to take risks they have not fully thought through, so be watchful of that possibility.

Moon/Jupiter interaspects are equally optimism-producing, and are particularly good for situations when someone is feeling bad and needs their spirits bolstered. They can create a strong sympathy between partners, but challenging aspects can also elicit overemotional hysteria, because Jupiter blows everything up larger than life and makes mountains out of molehills. Put structures in place to calm down and check perspective.

Mercury/Jupiter interaspects facilitate communication. In fact, they make people want to talk to each other a great deal, and in some cases it may be difficult to shut each other up long enough to listen to one another. Both partners must learn to listen as much as trying to be heard. If one partner has a career in writing, speaking, or some other Mercurial pursuit, a Jupiter aspect from their partner can help boost their career.

Venus/Jupiter interaspects are traditionally considered wonderful, inspiring ardent romance in the romantically confident and insecure alike, even when the interaspect is challenging. There will be fireworks that can be rekindled whenever they are needed. The one drawback is that it encourages both people to overdo it on luxuries, perhaps spending beyond the budget to gift each other with romantic experiences to enjoy together.

Mars/Jupiter interaspects can be good or bad, depending partly on how challenging they are and partly on what the couple decides to make of them. They can produce immense motivation with both people working as true partners, making progress like a couple of steamrollers harnessed together. Alternately they can elicit constant fighting if the overinspired Mars energy has nowhere useful to go. With this interaspect, it's best if the couple has goals that they can attack together, so that they don't attack each other. If the Mars person has trouble motivating, the Jupiter person will inspire them to move. This interaspect also tends to create immense magnetic sexual drive between both partners.

Saturn, unfortunately, is one of the few planets that can dampen Jupiter's relentless optimism, but it doesn't have to be only about discouragement. The Saturn person in the couple wants to help the Jupiter person to get more discipline and reach their potential; the Jupiter person wants the Saturn person to lighten up and enjoy themself more. It's possible to work either of these from either direction of a power dynamic, so long as the M-type remembers that it's fine to use the s-type as a tool to help themselves improve, and the s-type remembers not to assume for stereotypes but to serve the person in front of them.

When Jupiter reaches across and tweaks the partner's Uranus, the Jupiter person encourages them to release their inner weirdo. They might bring them into radical alternative lifestyle practices that the Uranus person would never have tried on their own, inspire them to craft a more unusual appearance, or introduce them to unfamiliar interest groups. With the Jupiter person around, it all seems to make sense.

Jupiter interaspecting Neptune blossoms into dreams, and a great deal of romantic fantasy. This is a somewhat dangerous combination, though, even when harmonious. Neptune is illusions and Jupiter can blow those up to the point where rose-colored glasses are practically glued to both partners' faces. If this is a strong interaspect, it's important to have some trusted people to give perspective occasionally, or they may both sail down a romantic river of denial. Another way to handle this interaspect that tends to channel it more usefully is to follow a spiritual path together.

Pluto, like Mars, can diverge into two different paths when faced with the partner's Jupiter. It can rip into rage—especially long-buried rage erupting from its hiding place—even easier than Mars, or it can be diverted into some other very intense mutual activity—passionate, forceful sex, for example, or painful but exhilarating self-improvement. It's crucial that people with this aspect have somewhere to put the energy, or it will simmer and explode. The Jupiter person can inspire the Pluto person to harness their inner intensity, and encourage them to explore their inner darknesses. In the end, it can be a gift of learning to work through their fears.

The Ascendant: Sculpting the Mask

The Ascendant, or the cusp of the first house, is not a planet. It is technically only a point, but probably the most important "only a point" of the entire chart. The Ascendant is your outward mask, the behavior behind which you hide when you face the world. It also indicates your physical body type, the way you dress and move, and how people perceive you. While you can extrapolate the effect of Pluto, Saturn, and Neptune affecting the M-type's or s-type's ascendant by reading the sections regarding the first house, and while each other's remaining planets aspecting the Ascendant are less relevant to a power dynamic, I'd like to take a quick run through what composite Ascendants look like in a power dynamic relationship.

It's not uncommon for two people to get together and assume that their relationship will have a particular "style"; that they will express a certain archetype together and that everyone will perceive them as that sort of couple. Then, once they actually become enmeshed with each other, it dawns on them that the style of their relationship is turning out to be something they didn't expect, and possibly never expected to be in with anyone … yet somehow it works. (Or sometimes it doesn't work, but we're looking at the first bunch right now.)

Many astrologers would probably look at this conundrum and mutter, "What does their composite chart look like?" Specifically, what does the Ascendant, the shared mask, of their composite chart look like? Is it in a sign that even remotely resembles or is compatible with their own Ascendants? If not, they've been thrust into an alien style that kicks in whenever they are with their partner. Sometimes one can get used to this, and even come to appreciate it. Sometimes it can be very difficult.

Power dynamic relationships, like composite charts, have many layers and variables. However, every couple tends to fall into a particular way of acting together, and especially acting in public together. The following list specifically describes how the twelve possible composite Ascendant signs can express themselves in a power dynamic relationship.

❖ **Aries:** With this fiery sign on the composite Ascendant, the two of you don't have a quiet, retiring relationship. You both react passionately to each other, and that includes anger, although it blows up quickly and then dies off just as quickly. The M-type likely doesn't mind the s-type being loud and mouthy, so long as they don't cross a line into whatever the M-type has decided is disrespect; sometimes what the M-type jovially thinks is just cute will astonish or offend other people. This composite Ascendant may make the partners more interested in takedown scenes and "funishment". Since Mars rules this sign, some Aries-Ascendant dynamics may have a military bent (or at least enjoy the uniforms) or consider themselves warrior-partners, shieldmates like the Captain and the Lieutenant, or perhaps the Captain and the Grunt.

❖ **Taurus:** Having this earthy Venus-ruled sign on the composite Ascendant indicates a love of comfort and sensuality. It's said that Taurus rising tends to two types in natal charts — the Venus type and the Earth type — and we've observed the same for composite charts. The Earth-type couple tend to be informal and low-protocol, with a comfortable, undemonstrative power dynamic that may be indistinguishable from any old-fashioned culturally mandated marriage, except when it's F/m instead of M/f, or same-sex instead of heterosexual. The Venus-type is built more around sensuality and romance, with the s-type focusing on erotic body-service of any kind — gourmet sex, gourmet food, gourmet massages, highly physical luxuries.

❖ **Gemini:** A composite rising sign in Mercury-ruled Gemini usually indicates a couple who talks a lot in public, and to each other, keeping up mutual running commentary. In power exchange, however, we've seen the focus shift to Gemini's Twin status, where the partners love the excitement of living a double life. Mild-mannered English teacher and cheerfully familiar mail carrier by day, characters from a kinky romance novel by night! Strict secrecy may be kept not so much for social approbation but for the sheer thrill of it. This placement wants to stimulate the minds even more than the bodies, so they may be attracted to elaborate erotic games and have a significant library of inspiring books.

- **Cancer:** In the sign of the Ultimate Parent, this relationship will be one of taking care of each other. It's important, however, to make a distinction between caretaker and caregiver. Caretakers know what's best for their charges; caregivers assist others to help themselves on their own track of wellness. Being a caretaker is the job of the M-type; the s-type should focus on being a caregiver. While it's quite possible to have such a relationship without any shadow of ageplay, Cancer on the composite Ascendant does make couples prone to a rather parental M-type and a more childlike s-type, or in some cases an older child/younger child dynamic. It's all about recreating the family the way they should have been for optimum growth.

- **Leo:** The couple with Leo on the composite Ascendant will be dramatic and out front. They live their relationship and their power dynamic large, whatever that means to them. This placement lends a theatrical touch to a couple's power dynamic style — they may draw their inspiration from historical or fictional roles, or be attracted to rather elaborate ceremony. If they choose to be part of a kink or power exchange community, they will be vivid and eye-catching in their approach. Privately, both will want a lot of approval and reassurance from the other partner. They should not starve each other for compliments; they will always be able to absorb more of them.

- **Virgo:** Having the modest, retiring sign of the Virgin on the composite Ascendant indicates that the relationship's outward manifestation will be one of hard-working service. The s-type will gravitate to being a helpful, competent assistant or majordomo; the M-type may also be service-oriented in a more dominant way, but equally hard-working and detail-oriented. Rules and protocols will be very important to them, as will the spit-and-polish of overseeing minutiae as perfectly as they can. In general, this placement pushes a couple to prefer working behind the scenes to being in the spotlight, and they may be much quieter and more private than others in their community. Virgo here may have a discouraging effect on physically demonstrative affectionate gestures.

- **Libra:** A Libra composite Ascendant will make this couple appear extremely entwined to outside appearances, possibly as soon as they start dating. People will quickly start thinking of them in terms of a "mated pair" who are seldom apart, and who are usually smiling and cheerful in public. In private, of course, they will argue a lot, unless the power dynamic is formal enough to forbid that. However, the Libra energies actually enjoy arguing as a sort of intellectual entertainment, so it is quite likely that the M-type will allow the s-type a certain amount of contention, so long as it is amusing, which may raise the eyebrows of those who see it. Working together, they will be able to charm people.

- **Scorpio:** Regardless of what else is going in the composite chart, a Scorpio rising will bring up issues of possessiveness, jealousy, and intense emotions—on both sides of the slash—that must be dealt with in a mature way. In a power exchange relationship, they will be at high risk for wanting to dive too deep too fast, cranking the control up too soon for the trust level to handle it, and with Scorpio's suspicious energy, trust will need extra time and effort to accumulate. This courts an eventual explosion, which—since Scorpio doesn't do things by half measures, and neither will these two—can be pretty ugly. This couple needs to grit their teeth and slow down, to discipline their passion and build trust. That's hard for anything Scorpio, but will be worth the time and effort in eventual longevity. Secrecy will be very alluring and perhaps exciting for this couple, so they may keep their power exchange very much on the downlow.

- **Sagittarius:** This Jupiter-ruled sign hates rules and details, and loves freedom and travel. As a power dynamic, it's likely that this will be a rather informal and low-protocol relationship, more likely than most to be long distance and/or not live together. The couple will come across as people who prioritize having fun and going places; the s-type could be a cheerful assistant and travel companion. They may have a number of athletic or sporty activities they share, and they will probably not be terribly interested in large amounts of control beyond their turn-ons. If they do forge something closer to an Owner/property relationship, it may well be for religious or spiritual reasons.

- **Capricorn:** This Saturn-ruled sign, on the other hand, loves the rules and the protocols, especially since Capricorn is somewhat uncomfortable with public demonstrations of affection and would much rather show regard through formal gestures and procedures. Even if both people are careless in their separate lives, this composite Ascendant will make them much more practical, responsible, and reserved with each other. The M-type's public status may be a defining factor of their identity as a couple, or they may build in a great deal of deference from the s-type to make up for the lack of such a status. They will come across as serious and somewhat reticent, and may have an old-fashioned style, perhaps drawing inspiration from classic high-status historical roles and avocations.

- **Aquarius:** This is the couple who stands out as being unique and being fine with that uniqueness. Their style may be intellectual, dorky and a little awkward; it might also be unsettlingly bizarre or radically political in some way (and if you think that people in power dynamics are all formal and staid and can't be radically political, you've never met one of these sorts), but whatever style it is, it won't be overly clingy or emotional. Like the couple with Sagittarius rising, they have a higher likelihood of being long distance or not live-in, and the M-type may allow the s-type a surprising amount of personal freedom. Technology may be a large part of how they make their structure work. Group involvement will be a big issue; they'll probably go back and forth between wanting to be part of a group and swearing off groups when they realize how hard it is for them to fit in.

- ❖ **Pisces:** Like the couple with Scorpio rising, the partners with this composite Ascendant may also prefer to keep their power dynamic secret, but in their case it's more about privacy and avoiding confrontation. They come across as very kind and forgiving to each other, and may have a situation where one partner seems like they are trying to "save" the other one. They tend to be quiet and retiring as a couple; they rarely join groups and will drift away as soon as group drama rears its ugly head. Confusing Neptune rules this sign, and one of the early complications will be a general vagueness around how their power dynamic will be structured, or what style to use as a basis. They may resort to romantic fiction as an inspiration and may be disappointed when real life turns out to require more practical solutions. Mentors can be of help during this stage. The Pisces composite Ascendant can also indicate a highly spiritual relationship.

The Asteroids: Going Deeper

As an astrologer, I do take asteroids into consideration. The problem is, there's hundreds of them. If I wrote about how even a small percentage of asteroids affect relationships in general, it would have to be a separate book. I'll discuss a scant few asteroids here, and how they can affect power dynamics. You'll have to look at your charts and make your own assumptions, but perhaps I can at least push you in the right direction.

CHIRON

Chiron is the largest of the asteroids, almost a planetoid. It's important in any relationship, because it's the planet of (mostly unhealed) internal wounds. It's also the place where you can be of most help in healing the wounds of others, once you've made some progress with your own Chiron's problems. Chiron is the raw place where you lash out when it's poked, almost instinctively. Chiron is the wounded animal within, hiding in the back of its cave. It's not the terrifying Beast. It's the one that will whimper in the dark and only cause mayhem if someone inadvertently pokes them with a stick—and all too often that someone is your partner, because you have to get close to someone to run into their Chiron.

In consensual and negotiated power dynamics, a special kind of intimacy gets formed, one that is different from egalitarian relationships. Power dynamics can poke all those issues about parents or children or bosses or older siblings or even past relationships that might have had poorly negotiated power or boundaries. We can't pretend that we aren't playing with emotional fire, because we are. (That's part of where all that heat comes from!) Checking the Chiron placements of both parties will help to figure out where the tenderest places are.

Look at the sign and house of each person's Chiron placement. (If you don't know enough astrology to figure out what that entails, ask someone who does.) This describes the nature of the wound. Next, take a deep breath and look at the interaspects between each partner's Chiron and the other partner's planets. Does the s-type have an aspect with the M-type's Pluto? Then the M-type will be driven to have power and control over that wounded area, which can be a tricky thing. Chiron problems, like Saturn problems and Pluto problems, can lash out or become worse if you clumsily get it wrong, so outside perspective may be useful. The same goes for the M-type's Saturn contacting it; they'll want authority over how the s-type goes about healing it, and may have all sorts of ideas about various disciplines that could be used, not all of them necessarily appropriate. If the M-type's Neptune contacts it, the s-type may see them as the Great Healer who can fix anyone, including themselves, or as the Wounded Hero who only needs some love to restore their broken heart. Both should be careful of those assumptions, as Chiron's triggered floundering can ruin the loveliest Neptune dream. However, a strong connection between Chiron and multiple planets in the M-type's chart may inspire the M-type to take the position of "therapist dominant", with the idea of helping the s-type to achieve their own self-healing, which can be good or bad depending on the humility with which it is pursued.

M-types often have a highly ambivalent relationship with their Chiron, because it's hard for us to open up and be seen as vulnerable, even—in some cases especially—by s-types, whom we may want to protect from having to deal with those broken parts of ourselves. But if the s-type's planets contact the M-type's Chiron, the s-type is going to end up cheerfully poking a stick into that raw spot without any intention to hurt or idea of what could be wrong there. If it's the s-type's Pluto or Saturn, it's possible that their internal image of either the Powerful Controlling Dominant or the Ideal Authority Figure shoots a dart right into the M-type's insecurities around stepping into those roles. If it's their Neptune, the s-type may see the M-type primarily as a wounded creature who needs healing, or themselves as someone whose service can heal the M-type; both need to be careful about falling into illusory perceptions about this.

In either case, mapping out that raw point is a good idea, because it means that you can both be gentle with each other's hurt places, and have a better chance of eventually becoming each other's safe space.

Finally, check the placement of Chiron in the composite chart, which will show you the biggest raw spot in the relationship. Check it for aspects to Pluto, Saturn, or Neptune, which can indicate that the power dynamic itself does a lot of poking at that wound. However, if the aspects are harmonious, it's possible that the power dynamic may eventually help to heal it. If the composite Chiron is aspecting other planets instead, it means that the worst restimulating of that wound will come from other areas of the relationship.

Pallas

Named for the brilliant, intellectual, cross-dressing goddess Pallas Athena, this asteroid indicates a mélange of qualities that include creativity, social justice, ability to recognize patterns, and propensity for androgynous behavior. Check the sign and house of each partner's Pallas (with or without external help) to see how they manifest these qualities, then check interaspects to see if either partner's Pluto, Saturn, or Neptune is aspecting the other one's Pallas.

The M-type's Pluto aspecting the s-type's Pallas means that the M-type will want power over the s-type's creative pursuits, political views, and possibly their gender expression. Obviously, these are rather sensitive areas for many people, and the M-type should tread carefully there. They may have to demonstrate their thoughtfulness and wide base of knowledge in these areas before the s-type will actually trust them. If the M-type's Saturn aspects Pallas, they will want at least some authority over these areas, and may have ideas about how the s-type could manifest them more efficiently, which may or may not go over well. If their Neptune aspects the s-type's Pallas, the s-type may see them as an Athena-like paragon of creative pursuits and/or political acumen, or even (in some cases) a gender-role-guru of some kind. As in all cases of Neptune, these should be discussed thoroughly before action is taken.

When the s-type's Pallas aspects the M-type's planets, the contact can inspire the M-type to think more strategically about their creative interests, their political views, and possibly their gender expression. If it aspects their Pluto, they may think of new ways to competently use their power; if their Saturn, they may find better personal strategies for self-discipline.

If the s-type's Neptune aspects the M-type's Pallas, the M-type may come to see the s-type as a kind of Muse-on-demand, inspiring the M-type with their stimulating conversation and scintillating presence. This can be great fun as long as the M-type isn't disappointed when the fountain of inspiration has a headache and needs to go to bed early.

Pallas in the composite chart will show an area where the two of you can be creative together and recognize the patterns in situations, the better to strategize and achieve your mutual goals. If there are multiple challenging aspects to the composite Pallas from any planets, you will have difficulty, as a couple, noticing and figuring out the patterns you both tend to fall into, and may need outside perspective to solidify.

Juno

Named for the Roman goddess of marriage, the asteroid Juno is specifically an indicator of committed long-term relationships—how you do them, what you want out of them, and what you want the role-pair to look like in public. Check the sign and house of each partner's Juno to see what they are most likely to prefer, and then check interaspects to see if either partner's Pluto, Saturn, or Neptune is aspecting the other one's Juno.

The M-type's Pluto aspecting the s-type's Juno means that the M-type will want power over the overall commitment itself and how it will be structured and look to others. This can include whether it will be monogamous or polyamorous, whether the s-type will be the primary partner or a secondary priority, whether they will be publicly acknowledged as a partner or will be a semi-secret affair, whether they will marry legally, and whether the M-type's possessiveness will be the deciding factor. The s-type may be struck with an extremely strong desire to get married (or some equivalent), and may be very upset if this can't happen.

If the M-type's Saturn aspects the s-type's Juno, they will want authority over the relationship structure, but it will probably be based more around what the M-type thinks is "proper" for the circumstances. This aspect can either prevent a legal union or force one, due to external circumstances over which neither has control.

If their Neptune is doing the aspecting, the s-type may see them as the "perfect spouse", at least at first, and feel that this relationship could be the "ideal image" of what marriage should be. Problems may occur later when the M-type fails to live up to romance-novel standards for a spouse.

If the s-type's Pluto aspects the M-type's Juno, it can inspire them to think about how the relationship — and specifically the power dynamic and their own sense of power — will interact with the social conventions of marriage and long-term commitments.

If the s-type's Saturn aspects their Juno, they may find themselves thinking about how an honorable authority figure would handle a long-term commitment, and want to do the "right thing", whatever that feels like to them. This interaspect can also indicate outside circumstances that prevent committed primary partnership for some reason.

If the s-type's Neptune is aspecting their Juno, the M-type may see them as the "perfect spouse" — the one who always wants to do what you want to do, of course — and the M-type may romanticize the idea of marriage within a power dynamic.

Juno in the composite chart will show how the two of your will choose together to handle the commitment and structure the relationship. Multiple challenging aspects to Juno often indicate a situation where a long-term arrangement, or at least a legal and socially acceptable, is not possible due to outside circumstances.

CERES

Ceres is the asteroid of nurturing — how one instinctively nurtures others, and how one would ideally like to be nurtured by them in turn. This may make many people raise their eyebrows — what does nurturing have to do with a power dynamic? — but in real life, any close sustainable relationship will have an element of actively caring for each other, even if it is sometimes done in ways that aren't romantic or parental. Check the sign and house of each partner's Ceres to see how their nurturing most easily flows forth, and then check interaspects to see if either partner's Pluto, Saturn, or Neptune is aspecting the other one's Ceres.

If the M-type's Pluto is aspecting the s-type's Ceres, the M-type is going to want control over who the s-type is allowed to throw nurturing behaviors at, and that includes if and how they are allowed to nurture the M-type. (If there are children involved, this may be problematic, and the M-type needs to check themself and to make sure they are not interfering with the s-type's parenting.) They will also likely want control over how the s-type takes care of themself, which can be helpful if the s-type has a habit of not doing it. This aspect can also push the s-type to look at how they actually do take care of themself, and want to do more about that.

If the M-type's Saturn aspects the s-type's Ceres, they will want authority over the same areas, but it will be more about setting boundaries for the s-type so that they do not use themself up too much. The s-type will probably find themselves glad about the limits, unless the aspect is challenging, and then it may feel restrictive.

If their Neptune is doing the aspecting, the s-type may see the M-type as a caring, nurturing, possibly parental dominant, at least at first, and be drawn to putting themself in a "client" or "child" role. The M-type may feel strangely driven to put a lot of time and care into the s-type, and they need to be careful not to push themself into a sacrificial mode.

If the s-type's Pluto aspects the M-type's Ceres, it can motivate the M-type to look at how they care for themself and others (including the s-type), and be more conscientious about that. They may be moved to take control of the health (physical, emotional, or both) of everyone in the house.

If the s-type's Saturn aspects the M-type's Ceres, it can have a similar effect, but the M-type may sometimes feel like the s-type disapproves of their lack of self-care, or inadequate caretaking of the s-type. The best solution for this is to use the s-type as a tool to help the M-type do better with their responsibilities.

If the s-type's Neptune aspects the M-type's Ceres, the M-type may see their partner as a wonderful nurturer "on demand" — perhaps the perfect caregiver-slave — and may idealize such a relationship. This aspect can also inspire the s-type to a level of nurturing that is either sacrificial or spiritual (or both). It can also push them to overdo the caregiving to the point of exhausting themselves, so the M-type should keep a watch on that.

Ceres in the composite chart shows how the two of you will end up nurturing each other. Multiple challenging aspects to Ceres can indicate problems — perhaps your styles of caregiving clash with each other's needs, or one of you is not comfortable giving what the other needs. If there are challenging aspects to Pluto, you may have power struggles over who is caretaking and who is caregiving at any given point. If there are challenging aspects to Saturn, the same thing may occur, but the argument may involve a clash between social roles around nurturing and the power dynamic.

Vesta

Vesta is the asteroid that symbolizes the sacred work that one is called to do in this lifetime, which is different for every person. It is a solitary and very monastic planet that describes the individual's attitude towards being alone, how much alone time is needed for them to rejuvenate, and how they should best spend that time. Look at the sign and house of each person's Vesta to figure that out — then check interaspects to see if either partner's Pluto, Saturn, or Neptune is aspecting the other one's Vesta.

If the M-type's Pluto is aspecting the s-type's Vesta, the M-type is going to want control over that sacred work, which may lead to a fair amount of power struggle. Vesta issues by definition are extremely personal, and not to be altered unless the s-type asks for help. On the other hand, the s-type may feel strongly pulled to hand over control of that work; if this is the case, the presence of the M-type and the power dynamic can put a lot of power into that work. The M-type may also feel a strong desire to control how much alone time the s-type has; be careful with this one as well.

If the M-type's Saturn is doing the aspecting, then the M-type may at least want authority over these things, but it may be more for the sake of "improving" how the s-type does this work. With this aspect, the s-type may actually go to the M-type and ask for some structure to help them succeed at this work.

If it's the M-type's Neptune that aspects the s-type's Vesta, then the s-type can view the M-type as being someone who is wise about that sacred work, or who holds some important spiritual key about it. At least, that is the way it might start. If the M-type actually doesn't know anything useful about it, the s-type may be disillusioned eventually, so it's best for the M-type to be honest up front.

When it's the s-type's Pluto that aspects the M-type's Vesta, the presence of the s-type (and possibly their service) can put the M-type's sacred work into overdrive. The s-type will likely intensely admire the M-type's sacred work, and want to help however they can. Paradoxically, this relationship aspect can cause the M-type to end up spending more time alone on their work, which can make the s-type feel neglected; design a way for them to break in and ask for attention.

If the s-type's Saturn is aspecting the M-type's Vesta, the presence (and possibly the service) of the s-type will inspire the M-type to be more disciplined about their sacred work. However, the M-type may also perceive the s-type as disapproving of the way they go about that work. They need to apply new attempts at self-discipline out of their own choice and will, and not in response to such perceptions, regardless of whether they are real or assumed.

If the s-type's Neptune is aspecting the M-type's Vesta, the M-type may see the s-type as a kind of Muse for their sacred work, somcone whose presence inspires them to persist at it. This can be fine so long as it's understood that the s-type is not to blame if the inspiration doesn't always come.

Vesta in the composite chart shows the sacred work that the two of you are to do together, as a couple. Check the sign and house to find what it is, and check its aspects to other composite planets to find out what other parts of your life together it touches. At this point, you might then discuss how that fits into your power dynamic. For example, if it is in the sixth house of service and maintenance, how can you use the power dynamic to improve that to the point of considering it sacred work to do together? If it's in the eleventh house, how can the dynamic support work that the two of you do in community? If it's aspecting Venus, can the expression of love in your dynamic be raised to a sacred art form? If it's aspecting Saturn, can your sacred work be using the dynamic to improve self-discipline in your life together? If it's right on the composite Ascendant, can you create a mutual style together that is incredibly meaningful for both of you, and visible to all? The composite Vesta can really be a touchstone for the relationship, to be looked at again and again when necessary.

The Nodes

While they are not asteroids — they're technically two mathematical points in the chart, always circling in opposition to each other — I want to mention the South Node and North Node here. In an individual chart, the North Node is the karmic goal that you're supposed to be striving for in your lifetime, defined by the sign, house, and aspecting planets. The South Node is an opposing way of being that you came into the world already understanding (those who believe in reincarnation say it's the most recent past life; those who don't say it's genetic predisposition and early childhood influences) and you revert to it in times of stress. The natal nodes aren't specifically involved in power exchange, although it's useful for the M-type to take a look at the s-type's North Node just to make sure that the power dynamic isn't preventing them from following it.

However, in a composite chart, the North Node becomes important, because it's the "karmic goal", if you will, of the relationship. In other words, it's the lesson that the two of you are meant to learn together, and the Universe will keep offering it to you over and over, so long as you remain together, so it's best to figure out what it is. (Again, check sign, house, and planetary aspects, using outside sources if necessary.) Similar to the process with Vesta, it's also best to figure out how the power dynamic can best support the Big Lesson, because you'll need all the help you can get. At the very least, the power dynamic should not be a tool to avoid it; that way lies disaster.

The composite South Node is an amalgam of the attitudes you brought into the relationship from your separate lives, and the way that the two of you behave when you're both stressed and mutually avoiding looking at hard things. For any relationship it's best to take a look at it and analyze it, so that when you're doing it, one of you can turn to the other and say, "We're doing that South Node thing again!"

Epilogue: Mastering the Relationship

The point of getting astrological information about how a relationship works—and, for that matter, how each person functions when in relationships—is not just to feel good about the parts that are easy and cry woe about the obstacles. It's to work out a plan to maximize the one and conquer the other, with the most appropriate tools.

Going through all the details of the M-type's chart, the s-type's chart, the comparison/synastry chart, and the composite chart is a matter of analyzing hundreds of points of data and figuring out the way that they affect the big picture. It's not a fast process, and it can be very intimidating, especially if neither of you are astrologers. If you're still with me by this time and not completely overwhelmed and hiring a professional to make sense of all this (and that's an acceptable option as well), I strongly suggest working this through one small step at a time, as a partnered exercise. You can take one single piece of information and study it, perhaps nightly or once a week. It can become a kind of bonding, a way to take the relationship apart and learn every tiny cog and wheel.

You can take those pieces in any order; each one makes you just a little bit more knowledgeable about yourselves, each other, and how you function together. It's a great way for the M-type to learn more about the inside of the s-type's head, and also for the M-type to find language to explain their motivations to the s-type. It's also a way to get a handle on the most difficult parts of the relationship, put words to them, and figure out how to counter them with your mutual strengths.

May the cosmic forces that turn the stars bless you both, and bless your power exchange with skill, kindness, compassion, and joy. May you never cease to learn.

Recommended Books

ASTROLOGY
- *The Inner Sky: How to Make Wiser Choices for a More Fulfilling Life* by Steven Forrest.
- *Skymates: Love, Sex and Evolutionary Astrology* by Steven & Jodie Forrest.
- *Skymates II: The Composite Chart* by Steven & Jodie Forrest.
- *The Changing Sky: Predictive Astrology* by Steven Forrest.
- *Planets in Signs* by Skye Alexander.
- *Planets in Houses: Experiencing Your Environment Planets* by Robert Pelletier.
- *Planets in Aspect: Understanding Your Inner Dynamics* by Robert Pelletier.
- *Planets in Synastry: Astrological Patterns of Relationships* by E.W. Neville.
- *Planets in Composite: Analyzing Human Relationships* by Robert Hand.
- *Planets in Transit: Life Cycles for Living* by Robert Hand.
- *Planets in Love: Exploring Your Emotional and Sexual Needs* by John Townley.
- *Planets in Youth: Patterns of Early Development* by Robert Hand.

POWER EXCHANGE RELATIONSHIPS
- *Dear Raven and Joshua: Questions and Answers about Power Exchange Relationships* by Raven Kaldera and Joshua Tenpenny.
- *The Way of the Pleasure Slave* by Andrew James.
- *Sacred Power Holy Surrender* by Raven Kaldera.
- *Real Service* by Raven Kaldera and Joshua Tenpenny.
- *Building the Team: Cooperative Power Dynamic Relationships* by Raven Kaldera and Joshua Tenpenny.
- *Unequal By Design: Counseling Power Dynamic Relationships* by Sabrina Popp, M.D. and Raven Kaldera.

About the Author

Raven Kaldera is a Northern Tradition Neo-Pagan shaman, homesteader, astrologer, herbalist, vampire, intersexual transgendered activist, and one of the founders of its current incarnation, the First Kingdom Church of Asphodel. He is the author of far too many books to list here, but a visit to his hub website at www.ravenkaldera.org will tell you more than you wanted to know. He lives with his wife, his slaveboy, and any number of friends and poly-family folks in the wilds of Massachusetts. 'Tis an ill wind that blows no minds.

www.ingramcontent.com/pod-product-compliance
Lightning Source LLC
Chambersburg PA
CBHW031642170426
43195CB00035B/293